Manuel L. Quezon High School
Senior High School

1

THE PROBABILITY OF SUCCESS IN BUSINESS OF THE STUDENTS IN

MANUEL LUIS QUEZON SENIOR HIGH SCHOOL

A research paper presented to the faculty of

practical research in Manuel L. Quezon

Senior High School

Submitted by:

John Frederick J. Avenido

Submitted to:

Dr. Mark Vincent B. Emit

March 2018

CHAPTER I

THE PROBLEM AND ITS BACKGROUND

Background of the study

Doing business is the very best thing for most of the Filipino nowadays. It has been part of Filipino culture in doing trade and it is where they practice communicating skill, decision making skill, analytical skill, and   mathematical skill almost everything are applicable in having business that's why there are Filipinos who has succeeded on this career which made their businesses grow more.

Identifying an appropriate definition and measure of business success is especially important in the study of probability of success in business (Hienerth & Kessler, 2006). The definitions of success that have previously been used in success of the business are often ambiguous, considering that each business strives to achieve a host of differing financial and nonfinancial goals (Olson et al., 2003; Stafford, Duncan, Danes, & Winter, 1999). It is important to use both objective and subjective measures in examining business success (Jones, 2003; Walker & Brown, 2004). Success in this study is defined and measured subjectively by the business owner/manager rating how successful they perceive their business is. To measure business success objectively, this study measured profitability by asking how much profit the business produced in terms of dollar amount.

Determining the probability of success in business of student is very important to those who are planning / doing an actual business for it may help them providing enough information on how to succeed with the different strategies applied by some

of the successful business owners here in the Philippines and in other country.

The aim of this study is to determine the probability of success in business of the

students of Manuel Luis Quezon senior high school by conducting a survey to those

who has succeeded in business and compare the accuracies of different prediction

models.

Conceptual Framework (CIPP)

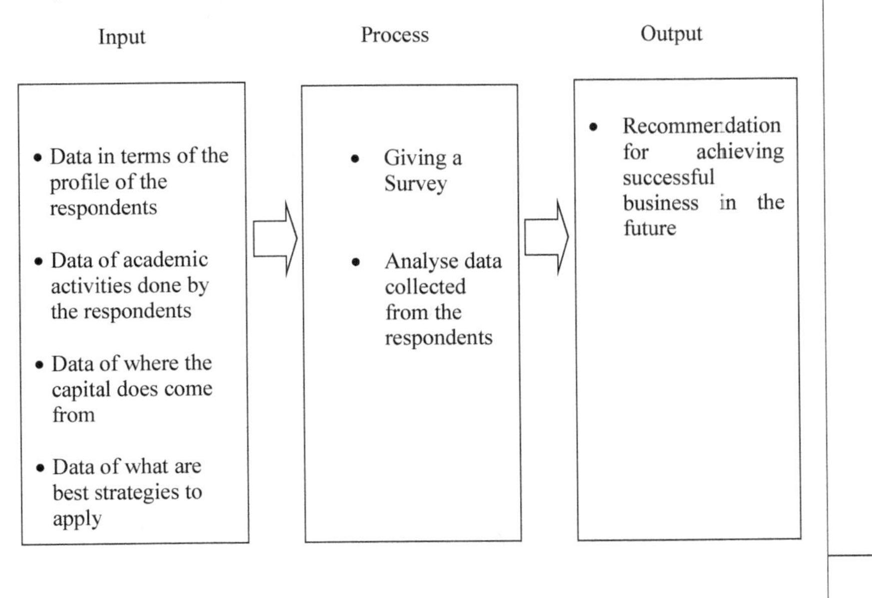

Figure 1.1 "Conceptual Framework"

Figure 1.1 shows the conceptual framework of the study wherein the input shows: Data in terms of the profile of the respondents; data of academic activities done by the respondents; data of where the capital does come from and data of what are best strategies to apply.

On the other side, the process shows the significant difference between the scores of both groups through the use of survey that will be sum up and totalled.

The researcher wants to find out the probability of success in business of the students in Manuel Luis Quezon Senior High School. The researcher will also include recommendations which may help others in analysing this study in the near future.

Statement of the Problem

1. What is the profile of the Respondents?

    1.1 Name

    1.2 Age

    1.3 Educational level Attainment

    1.4 Marital Status

    1.5 Mean of living: Employed or entrepreneur or full time students.

2. What are the academic activities done by the respondents that helped them in achieving succeed business today?

3. Where the capital of the business does came from?

4. What are the best strategies to apply in succeeding business in the future of those students?

5. What can be recommended based on the findings?

Significance of the Study

The study wants to identify the probability of success in business of the students of Manuel Luis Quezon senior high school in the future.

This study is for:

The students of Manuel Luis Quezon Senior High School, that they may read and find out the best strategies to apply in doing business. This research or study will provide them enough information on how to achieve successful business in the future. The future students of Manuel Luis Quezon Senior High School, that they may see this study and help them for creating their own.

The people who want to build their own business that they can read about the study and make it as guide and understand on how to succeed in the business

Scope and Limitation

The study will be confined the probability of success in business of the students which may help them in pursuing business career in the future.

Definition of terms

- Probability of success in business

The data gathered on the survey will be comparing to the students who are doing business inside the campus to measure its success and giving best recommendation.

- Best Strategies

These are the most often used strategies by the successful business owners which is a very good thing to follow for committing success.

CHAPTER II

RELATED STUDY AND LITERATURE

Review of Related Literature

This section begins with a summary of the research and literature presented about probability of success in businesses in general terms, including a summary of other literature reviews. The section then continues with a review of the studies on business success and profitability.

Business Success and Profitability

Bird, Sapp, and Lee (2001) conducted a study to explore how industry location and the owner's gender were related to business success among small businesses. Bird et al. measured business success by gross sales as reported by the business owner for 1994. Based on analyses of data from 423 small businesses owners in Iowa, the authors concluded that the business owner's gender had both direct and indirect effects on business success.

Women business owners had significantly less work-related experience than men owners and were less likely to have previously owned a business. Men business owners spent more hours at their businesses than did women owners, and hours spent at the business, in turn, improved small business success. Endeavoring to determine a better way to measure success in family businesses, Hienerth and Kessler (2006) suggested that many of the problems associated with measuring success was due to the ambiguity and subjectiveness of the term —success.‖ The purpose of their study was to analyze whether a success measurement using configurational fit could be used to overcome subjective biases. Configurational fit was a method used by a few researchers to attempt to reduce subjective biases from a measurement, in this case, the authors attempted to better measure business success in a manner that reduced biases.

Using a sample of 103 family-owned businesses in Austria, Hienerth and Kessler reasoned that by using the configurational fit method, the authors were able to overcome some biases when measuring business success. Walker and Brown (2004) examined success factors of small business owners, and indicated that although financial criteria have generally been considered to be the most appropriate measure of business success, finances may not be the best or only indicator of business success. They noted that business owners often have other business goals that are not necessarily financially-based, such as lifestyle, personal achievement, and pride in the business. The sample was comprised of 290 small business ownermanagers in Australia. The respondents in the study surveyed were asked to rate the importance of items relating to lifestyle and financial measures which were used to judge business success.

The results showed that a flexible lifestyle, pride in the job, and personal achievement were better indicators of business success than wealth creation or financial indicators. Thus, Walker and Brown concluded that a subjective measure of business success may be more valuable to researchers than a financial objective measure of success. Using a national survey of 673 business-owning households, Haynes, Walker, Rowe, and Hong (1999) conducted a study to evaluate factors associated with intermingling business and family finances, including the affect on family business profitability. Using a multivariate model, Haynes et al. concluded that those with legal partnerships were considerably less likely to intermingle resources than were those with sole proprietorships.

Families with businesses that were located in urban areas were less likely to intermingle resources with their businesses than families with businesses in rural areas or small towns. The findings of this study suggested that households with established family businesses seemed to have finances intertwined with the businesses to such a degree that it was often difficult to separate. The authors also noted that the intermingling may be beneficial to the family that obtains money or resources from the business, but is likely an impediment to the future profitability of the family business.

The articles in this section have all related to the success and profitability of family-owned businesses. Many of the authors have indicated a general difficulty within the field to measure a business' success due to the subjective nature of the term —success.‖ Many researchers have developed their own methods by which probability in business success could be measured. It is generally acknowledged by the authors that success and profitability of owner businesses are important to study.

Though owner business success is often ambiguous and subjective, it may be just as important to study as businesses profitability (Walker & Brown, 2004). In order to apply the information presented by previous researchers in this present research study, both subjective and objective measures will be employed.

Owning a business is very appealing to people for many reasons -- you get to be your own boss, work with amazing people, create your own schedule and turn a passion into a career. There is nothing easy about it, though.

Often, first-time entrepreneurs jump in head-first and become blindsided by the reality of running a business. So, what does it take to launch a successful business? I spoke with several business owners via a HARO query and came up with five factors that are key contributors to business success.

Related: 11 Ways Successful People Deal With People They Don't Like

1. An innovative business idea

If you want a shot at surviving, especially in a competitive industry, you need to determine what sets you apart from the other available options. Clever marketing or an exciting technology alone won't guarantee that your target customers will be wowed by what you're offering -- you have to offer real value and/or a new experience.

Richard Werbe, founder of micro-tutoring service platform Study Pool, explains his strategy for coming up with an innovative business idea, saying. "You have to pay attention to trends. Most people think they have to come up with an entirely original idea, but you can take current popular trends and build from what you're already seeing out there, creating an improved service or product."

The market will dictate whether your business will succeed -- nothing else -- and one way to stack the odds in your favor is to have an innovative product or service that will be well-received. You don't have to completely reinvent something -- just make it better.

2. The right talent

The long-term success of your business requires that you assemble the right talent to build your brand. Your team is the company's backbone, and one cancerous person can completely derail your progress. Whether you are building an on-site team or a remote workforce, one thing remains the same -- the right talent matched with the same vision will greatly improve the chances of success.

Kip Skibicki, founder of Top Notch Threads, understands the importance of assembling an all-star team. "When I started my company, I didn't have a lot of connections, but I was committed to building a team that shared my vision, along with possessing the desired experience and know-how for each role," said Skibicki.

Building a business requires a tremendous amount of work during the startup phase. Long hours and the up-and-down roller coaster ride is much more enjoyable when the entire team is willing to push hard to accomplish goals and hit milestones together.

Related: 8 Reasons a Powerful Personal Brand Will Make You Successful

3. Your network

Building a personal network of like-minded entrepreneurs has several benefits. It gives you a sounding board for when you have questions or want advice, which is a huge help, especially in the early stages of a business. As your network grows, so do your resources.

I'm a member of several professional groups and I am constantly networking. Personally, my network has been a huge part of my success, and seeing how beneficial ts has been led me to start the Mastermind House, a new virtual networkingopportunity for entrepreneurs.

"Every business, from a large law firm to a small single member startup, can benefit from having a strong network. As you become more comfortable networking, your network's size and ability to help you solve problems and make wise business decisions increases. I highly suggest you carve out time from your schedule to dedicate to networking," advises Adam Zayed, founding partner of Zayed Law Offices.

4. Hard work

If you're not willing to get your hands dirty and work in the trenches, you might as well not even start. A lot of potential entrepreneurs have a false sense of what it's really like to own a business. The media likes to glorify the startup life, but it's not all Lamborghinis and private planes. You have to be willing to put the work in if you want to be successful.

Before launching the American International English Teachers' Association, Zac Grove was helping other educational technology startups raise funds and build operations. This allowed him to learn the industry ropes, later applying this knowledge to his passion project.

"After working in ed-tech, I realized that my passion in life was launching solutions to bring about change. I would never have had the confidence to venture out on my own had I not first paid my dues and learned about building a solid business by working at another venture," says Grove. Consider developing the skills, insights and experience needed by working for another company -- it's a viable option that can pay off long-term.

Related: Habits of the World's Wealthiest People (Infographic)

5. Sales

There is one thing that will quickly prove the viability of your product or service -- sales. Not only do sales prove you have something viable, but it also injects revenue into your business, allowing you to grow and avoid

Carlo Cisco is the founder and CEO of Select, a private community that offers access to exclusive events and promotions at restaurants, hotels, nightlife venues and retailers. In order for Cisco to create a footprint for his business, he prioritized sales from the beginning.

"As an entrepreneur, you're constantly selling your vision to current and prospective employees, partners, investors and advisors," says Cisco. "Know your pitch and practice relentlessly. You need to be confident pitching one-on-one, to a room of hundreds of people or to senior executives."

Ideas are great, but without sales to accompany them they will likely fail. Mark Cubanconstantly talks about how success is based on sales. Entrepreneurs who are great at sales give their business a competitive advantage. (Opinions expressed by *Entrepreneur* contributors are their own. December 7, 2017 5 min read)

Business Success Definition

By: Brian Hill

Social

Companies also measure success by the good they accomplish for society. Some have specific social goals, such as improving the environment or providing educational opportunities for children through the products and services they offer. Others have a very high commitment to charitable giving and being good corporate citizens. Film star Paul Newman's company, Newman's Own Inc., which manufactures and markets a variety of consumer products, distributes all of its after tax profits to charitable causes. The company's charitable foundation has donated more than $300 million, according to Newman's Own website.

Longevity

With the number of businesses that fail or start out strong only to stumble in the competitive marketplace a few years later, another measure of business success is the ability to sustain success in the turbulent, ever changing business world. Book publisher John Wiley & Sons began in 1807 as a small New York City-based printing shop. Two hundred years later, in 2007, the company's revenues were more than $1 billion, according to the company's website. The company has been able to successfully adapt to changes in readers' taste but also to the technological changes in the publishing industry -- for more than two centuries.

Customer Satisfaction

Helping customers solve a problem -- that's the reason many of the products and services we use every day were created. For business owners, seeing that your products made your customers lives better in a significant way is one of the motivating factors that keeps them working tirelessly on developing even better solutions. Praise from satisfied customers provides a feeling of accomplishment that for some business owners is as important as the financial rewards they earn.

Employee Satisfaction

"Fortune" magazine publishes an annual list of what it considers the 100 best companies to work for, but thousands of business owners don't need national media recognition to know that they have made taking good care of their employees a high priority. They see it in how hard their employees work, how committed each member of their team is to the organization's goals. They measure this aspect of business success in how many employees stay with the company for five or 10 years or more -- sometimes their whole career.

Failure & Success Factors of a Small Business

by Bonnie Conrad

Starting a business can be the key to financial independence, or the road to ruin. The statistics for startup businesses are certainly grim, with some 90 percent of new businesses eventually closing up their doors forever. According to Elizabeth Wilson of Entrepreneur Magazine, while some 40 million businesses are started each year, a paltry 350,000 break out of the pack and begin growing and making money. Making sure your own company is one of the top 10 percent means avoiding some common business pitfalls.

Underestimating Startup Costs

One of the most common mistakes business owners make is underestimating how much money it will truly take to get the business up and running. Some startup costs are predictable, such as the cost of a new building or the lease on a piece of equipment. But other costs are less easy to anticipate, and companies that fail to account for those surprises can find themselves short of cash just when they need it most. Writing in "Inc. Magazine", Tim Faley points out that business owners tend to way underestimate both startup costs and the costs associated with acquiring and maintaining customers. rnrnWhen costs are underestimated, something as simple as the breakdown of a key piece of manufacturing equipment could leave a new startup unable to operate, and unable to pay its bills. To fight back against this common mistake, experts recommend budgeting more for startup costs than you think you will need.

Depending Too Much on Others

The departure of a key employee, or a disagreement with a business partner, can leave the company in dire straights unless the business owner has taken the time to learn all aspects of the firm. Relying too much on a handful of key workers can be a big mistake, and one that could even cause the business to fail. No matter what the nature of the business, it is essential for the owner to understand the variety of jobs and functions within the organization. This will allow the business owner to step in if necessary, even if that means driving a delivery route when the courier quits unexpectedly, or finding service for a server when the IT person is out sick.

Hiring Wrong People

To your customers, the people you hire are the business, and hiring the wrong people can be a costly mistake. rnrnUnlike failing to provide sufficient startup cash, the problem of hiring the wrong people can keep coming back to haunt the business again and again. Many new business owners are so eager to get the firm off the ground that the skip important background and reference checks. The same problem can occur when the business begins to grow rapidly. When the business is winning new contracts and taking on new projects, the firm might need to ramp up quickly and bring new workers on board. This can increase the chances of hiring a bad worker who could ultimately hurt, rather than help, the business succeed. Entrepreneur nagazine's 60 Second Guide to Hiring the Right Employees recommends that business owners take a minute to define the duties of the job, identify the skills necessary to perform those duties and always conduct follow-up interviews to answer additional questions and identify the best candidates.

The Methods of Analyzing Business Success

by Eric Scott

Success in business typically refers to financial success. Profits are normally the driving factor, and the reason behind many decisions. However, while profit and sales are certainly important in any business, many other non-financial factors are indicative of business success. In that sense, the old axiom is true: "Money isn't everything."

Profit

For the majority of businesses, the ultimate measurement of success is profit and growth in profit. Many companies have goals of monthly, quarterly or annual profit growth.

Sales

Company sales are another yardstick of success. These figures can help gauge the level of acceptance the product or service has achieved among consumers and the sales force's productivity. It can also validate the company's overall direction.

Market Share

Market share is another way companies measure success. Growth in profits or sales can signal the company's strategy is working. This is especially true in aggressive industries like manufacturing and technology.

Customer Satisfaction

Getting high customer service scores is a big success factor for many companies. As competition intensifies, customer satisfaction is increasingly a top priority. Many regularly survey their customers to judge their satisfaction with products, services, prices and customer relations.

Employee Satisfaction

Measuring employee satisfaction in such areas as pay structure, benefits and management shows companies where they need to improve and helps them retain the best workforce. Such companies understand that retaining happy and productive employees is the only way to succeed.

Contribution to Society

Another measure of a company's success is whether they "give back" to the community. Some donate a certain percentage of proceeds to community charities and other initiatives. Others give back in other ways, whether participating in recycling drives, environmental cleanup or encouraging employee volunteerism.

What Can You Learn by Comparing Successful & Unsuccessful Businesses?

by Rose Johnson

In many cases, few differences exist between successful and unsuccessful businesses. However, within those differences, most successful companies share similar traits and most unsuccessful companies share similar traits. As a business owner, you can learn valuable information by comparing successful companies with unsuccessful ones. Understanding the elements that lead to business success and failure can help you develop a strategy that gives you the best chance of achieving success in your business.

Management and Leadership

A company's management and leadership are two of the most important factors that determine its success or failure. Successful companies employ managers and leaders who understand the organization's vision and know how to implement it; such leaders also possess the ability to motivate employees and align them with the company's vision. According to the National Business Association, most businesses fail due to poor management and the inability to hire professionals in areas where they need help. The importance and effectiveness of leadership is one of the most important elements you'll notice when comparing successful business ventures with unsuccessful ones.

Marketing Strategies

Another critical factor to learn is the importance of proper marketing strategies. A business may possess a great product, but is likely to remain unprofitable if it fails to learn how to effectively market that product. A company's marketing strategies depend on its target market. For example, the marketing strategies of a company offering products to consumers differ from those of a company involved in business-to-business sales. Successful companies understand how to determine the needs of their target market, how to meet those needs and how to analyze its competitors. A company that fails to market its products or services effectively is most likely headed for failure.

Business Planning

Developing a good business plan is one of the first steps entrepreneurs should make when deciding to open a business. However, some business owners fail to see the importance of performing market research and developing a good business plan. According to Ron Finklestein of Entrepreneur magazine, companies do not have to develop complex business plans to achieve success, but should formulate a thorough and well-thought-out plan. Business plans not only help companies get off to a good start, but also help them navigate through uncertain economic times and prepare for market growth in good times. A company with a poor business plan lessens its chance for success.

Financial Planning

A lack of sufficient cash flow is a major reason many small businesses fail. Managers and owners of successful companies understand the importance of starting a business with sufficient working capital and hiring financial professionals who understand how to implement effective cash flow policies. Developing a financial plan allows business owners to see how to effectively spend money and measure the success or failure of their financial policies over time. Adequate financial planning takes into account the finances needed for the near future and those needed for the long term.

Top Ten Marketing Strategies

by Candace Webb

Properly marketing a business is a key to success in many fields. Marketing allows a business to reach out to potential customers. In attempting to get potential customers to leave one business and try another, marketing must invite, promise and at times give things away. A well designed marketing strategy can be developed for Internet businesses and brick-and-mortar shops.

Stand Out

Marketing must showcase why a business is different from others. Whether you offer excellent customer service, unusual products or a one-of-a-kind return policy, the difference between your business and similar companies is what needs to be marketed. A short kicky signature phrase will cement the uniqueness in the minds of potential customers.

Market Consistently

Regardless of how busy the business is, it is important to market consistently. Regular advertising, contests, giveaways and civic-minded activities keep your business name out there and remind potential customers to try your products or services.

Email Blasts

Email blasts offer a free marketing tool. Set up a system in which every new customer is asked for an email address. While some will decline, many will provide one. Arrange to have an email blast sent once a month. A blast is an email sent out at once to every customer and potential customer in the data base. Use the email to showcase sales, new products or seasonal items. Invent interesting blasts so they are not ignored. For example, tell customers that if they mention a certain thing when placing their next order, they will get a discount.

Show the Love

Maintain a list of customer birthdays. Send birthday postcards with discount coupons. Develop a monthly newsletter to send through email. Include funny stories, recipes, upcoming holidays and interweave new products and sales specials within the newsletter. On customers' birthdays send refrigerator magnets with your logo, address and phone number to keep your business on their minds.

Contests

Hold contests to promote your products. If you sell food items, for example, have an annual recipe contest in which the top three winners receive gift certificates to your store. Print and bind all entries and sell the cookbooks at the cash registers.

Internet Marketing

Design an attractive and usable. People are visual and react to what is seen. Develop the website to change on a regular basis to give potential customers a reason to come back. Tie the site for your products or services. For example, if you have a housecleaning business, offer cleaning and product tips that change each week. If you own an online clothing store, write a weekly column about fashion, tying it to your available products.

Giveaways

Spread the word about your business by giving away prizes. This marketing tool allows you to gather important information about potential customers. Choose a prize, such as a product basket, month of service or free consultation. Announce the contest and design an entry form that requires customer name, email address and mailing address. Choose a winner each month and enter the information about each entrant into a database for future newsletters and sales fliers.

Join a Networking Site

A networking site in which you place links to group member sites on your page and they place your link on theirs is a free way to reach a wide range of potential customers. Join a site with businesses that complement yours without competing.

Pump Up Site Interest

Adding an RSS news feed ability to your site will bring potential customers back often. RSS news feeds pipe breaking news onto your site for viewers to see. In addition, place links to print news stories on your page. Build ads and sales pitches around these links on your page.

Press Releases

Write press releases and place them online as well as in local newspapers. Each time your company participates in a civic event, have someone take photographs, write up what you did to help the organization and send it to publications and sites for publication. Newspapers are more likely to publish items with local flavor, so target organizations that are locally based to have a better chance of having your release published.

Most Effective Marketing Strategies

by Leigh Richards

very small business is interested in increasing marketing effectiveness. The most effective marketing strategies are those that are targeted toward a specific audience, focused on key benefits based on the audience's point of view and interests, and delivered at an appropriate time--when the audience is most likely to be attentive to and interested in the message being delivered.

Specific Targeting

Effective marketing is targeted to a specific, not a general, audience. By way of illustration, consider the different approaches that might be taken with a product as basic as rice if selling to these audiences: retirees, young mothers or athletes. By focusing on a specific audience and seeking to understand that audience's needs, interests and desires, marketers can be most effective in achieving their objectives, says Lin Grensing-Pophal, author of "Marketing With the End in Mind."

Focus on Benefits

It can be difficult for small business owners to view their business and their products from the outside in, but that's exactly what they must do if they hope to be successful in their marketing efforts, says Grensing-Pophal. "Too often we become enamored with our own products and services or we take it for granted that our target audiences will understand our products and services the way we do--they won't." Marketers need to learn about and consider audience needs and concerns, and identify potential objections that they can work to overcome in their marketing efforts. In doing so, they can identify key benefits to focus on that will be attractive to the target audience.

Good Timing

A message about female incontinence delivered through a poster on the inside of a restroom door stall is hitting an audience at just about the perfect time. The same message delivered on an overhead announcement at a mall would probably not have the same impact. Effective marketing seeks to reach audiences when they are most likely to be open and attentive to the message. Small businesses need to think carefully about their delivery mechanisms--newspaper, radio, TV, social media, and others--and consider whether messages are being conveyed in the right place, at the right time.

R.L. Adams

- Contributor

CHAPTER III

METHODOLOGY

Research Design

This section presents the research methodology of this study. It is a prediction in relation to regression analysis with field of survey. It is prediction in nature because the researcher wants to determine the Probability of success in business of students in Manuel Luis Quezon Senior High School. It is a field survey since questionnaire is administered to the respondents.

Research Instruments

The researcher uses a checklist of questionnaire in getting the relevant information for the study. It is adopted from the questionnaire used by Laureat (2006) and Tactay (2013). The questionnaire is slightly modified to suit the purpose of the study.

The Likert's five-point scale is used for the instrument for the easier comprehension on the part of the officials-respondents. The statistical range are as follows:

Data Gathering Procedure

A letter of request signed by the researcher and noted by the adviser was submitted to the respective department heads, in order to gain appropriate institutional approval to collect data and distribute questionnaires to the intended respondents.

The researcher personally distributed the questionnaires to the respondents. The respondents were specifically instructed to answer all the questions as honestly as possible or as closely as possible to their recall of their actual experience. They were given one (1) day to accomplish the questionnaires. Furthermore, the respondents were assured that their responses would be treated with strict confidentiality and would be used only for the intended purpose of the study. The researcher retrieved the accomplished questionnaires.

Data Analysis Techniques/Statistical Treatment

Regression Analysis

Regression model, basically, specifies the relation of dependent variable (Y) to a function combination of independent variables (X) and unknown parameters (β)

$$Y \approx f(X, \beta)$$

Regression equation can be used to predict the values of 'y', if the value of 'x' is given, and both 'y' and 'x' are the two sets of measures of a sample size of 'n'. The formulae for regression equation would be

$$y^* = a + bx$$

Where,

$$b = \frac{n \sum xy - (\sum x)(\sum y)}{n(\sum x^2) - (\sum x)^2}$$

$$a = \frac{\sum y - b \sum x}{n}$$

AN ANALYSIS OF FORMS OF BUSINESS IN RELATION TO THE

PROFICIENCY LEVEL OF THE STUDENTS

A research paper presented to the faculty of

practical research in Manuel L. Quezon

Senior High School

Submited by:

Rino V. Caisip

Submitted to:

Dr. Mark Vincent B. Emit

March 2018

CHAPTER I

THE PROBLEM AND ITS BACKGROUND

Background of the Study

According to the website of Entrepreneur.com (2017) The basic objective of business is to develop, produce and supply goods and services to customers. This has to be done in such a way as to allow companies to make a profit, which in turn demands far more than just skills in companies' own fields and processes. Astute entrepreneurs often demonstrate an almost intuitive understanding of the synergies that create success.

Also, the social skills of company owners, together with relationships maintained with customers, suppliers and other business people, are always vital if companies are to be run well and developed with a view to the future. Companies improve their resources by developing materials and ideas.

Hence, the goods and services produced must meet demands made by customers, other companies or public institutions if companies are to survive. Profitability results when customers are prepared to pay more for goods and services than it costs to produce them. The ability to produce this kind of added value – profit – is the basic prerequisite for business, but it is also a foundation for prosperity in society.

Moreover, only profitable companies are sustainable in the long term and capable of creating goods, services, processes, return on capital, work opportunities and a tax base. This is what business does better than any other sector. Hence, companies' basic commercial operations are the primary benefit they bring to society.

The institution of Manuel L. Quezon Senior High School it is an extension of Manuel L. Quezon High School, where in the student enter Senior High School. This building of Manuel L. Quezon Senior High School was constructed within 10 years with different contracts. The Manuel L. Quezon Senior High School building consists of five (5) floors, ground floor 2nd floor within three (3) classrooms, 3rd floor, 4th floor and 5th floor with social hall and terrace. Manuel L. Quezon Senior High School has 254 total populations including all the school authorities.

Conceptual Framework

The researcher used input process output diagram to determine the flow of the study regarding an analysis of forms of business in relation to the proficiency level of the students

According to business dictionary, which can be accessed through http://www.businessdictionary.com/definition/input-process-output-diagram.html. A graphical representation of all the factors that make up a process. An input-process-output diagram includes all of the materials and information required for the process, details of the process itself, and descriptions of all products and by-products resulting from the process.

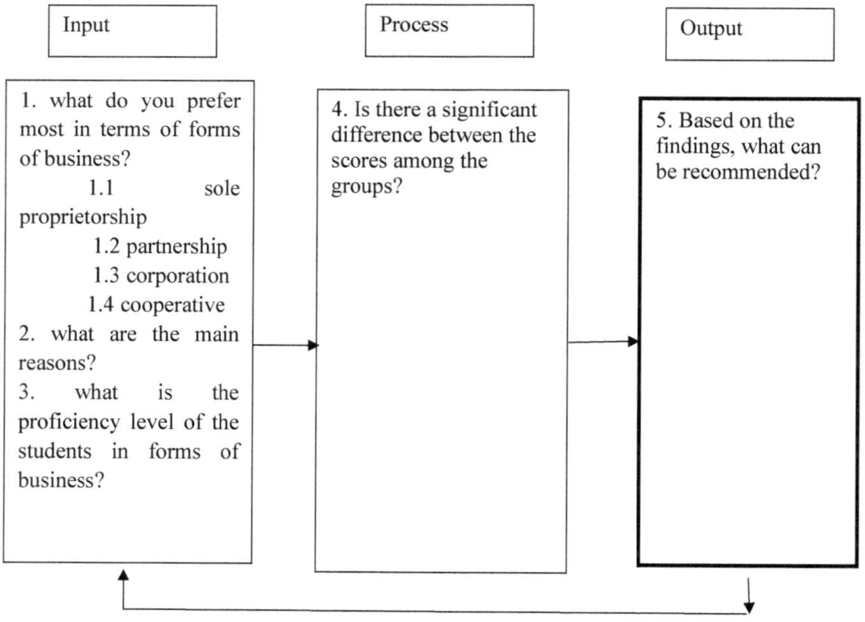

Input	Process	Output

Input	Process	Output

1. what do you prefer most in terms of forms of business?
   1.1 sole proprietorship
   1.2 partnership
   1.3 corporation
   1.4 cooperative
2. what are the main reasons?
3. what is the proficiency level of the students in forms of business?
	4. Is there a significant difference between the scores among the groups?	5. Based on the findings, what can be recommended?

The conceptual framework shows the flow of the study. It includes in the input are the forms of business that the respondents prefer most such as sole proprietorship, partnership, corporation, and cooperative. Also, the main reasons why they prefer in that forms of business. Hence, it determines the proficiency level of the students among the groups. While in the process, it partakes that if there is a significant difference between the scores among the groups. On the other hand, the output shows off the expected result from the respondents and what can be recommended.

Statement of the Problem

1. what do you prefer most in terms of forms of business?

    1.1 sole proprietorship

    1.2 partnership

    1.3 corporation

    1.4 cooperative

2. what are the main reasons?

3. what is the proficiency level of the students in forms of business?

4. Is there a significant difference between the scores among the groups?

5. Based on the findings, what can be recommended?

Hypothesis

H$_o$: There is no significant difference between the scores among the groups

Significance of the Study

The researchers are truly believed that this study has significance to the following variables:

Students. This study helps the students who wants to be a businessman to know the different forms of business to choose what is they prefer most.

Teachers. This study helps the teachers to gain some information about forms of business to teach to their students the different ideas about this.

Parents. This study will be use by the parents to influence their children to build a business and to choose what forms of business is best.

Researchers. The data that will be gather from this study will use by the researchers to conduct another research that is related to this study. The information that they gathered will be applying it to them to become a better businessman.

Scope and limitation

This study scopes the data that will be gather by the researcher regarding the forms of business. This study has a limitation because only the students and teachers of Manuel L. Quezon Senior High School are only involving.

Definition of Terms

Forms of business. It consists sole proprietorship, partnership, corporation, and cooperative.

Sole proprietorship. is the simplest business form under which one can operate a business The sole proprietorship is not a legal entity.

Partnership. is commonly formed where two or more people wish to come to together to form a business.

Corporation. exists in perpetuity, or until it is liquidated. Consequently, as a legal entity that's separate from its shareholders, directors and officers, the death of any individual who holds one of these positions

Cooperative. must operate in many ways like a regular business to be successful.

CHAPTER II

RELATED STUDY AND LITERATURE

Related Literature

According to the website of Entrepreneur (2018) A business that legally has no separate existence from its owner. Income and losses are taxed on the individual's personal income tax return.

Also, sole proprietorship is the simplest business form under which one can operate a business. The sole proprietorship is not a legal entity. It simply refers to a person who owns the business and is personally responsible for its debts. A sole proprietorship can operate under the name of its owner or it can do business under a fictitious name, such as Nancy's Nail Salon. The fictitious name is simply a trade name--it does not create a legal entity separate from the sole proprietor owner.

Hence, sole proprietorship is a popular business form due to its simplicity, ease of setup, and nominal cost. A sole proprietor need only register his or her name and secure local licenses, and the sole proprietor is ready for business. A distinct disadvantage, however, is that the owner of a sole proprietorship remains personally liable for all the business's debts. So, if a sole proprietor business runs into financial trouble, creditors can bring lawsuits against the business owner. If such suits are successful, the owner will have to pay the business debts with his or her own money.

Moreover, the owner of a sole proprietorship typically signs contracts in his or her own name, because the sole proprietorship has no separate identity under the law. The sole proprietor owner will typically have customers write checks in the owner's name, even if the business uses a fictitious name. Sole proprietor owners can, and often do, commingle personal and business property and funds, something that partnerships, LLCs and corporations cannot do. Sole proprietorships often have their bank accounts in the name of the owner. Sole proprietors need not observe formalities such as voting and meetings associated with the more complex business forms Sole proprietorships can bring lawsuits (and can be sued) using the name of the sole proprietor owner. Many businesses begin as sole proprietorships and graduate to more complex business forms as the business develops.

Furthermore, because a sole proprietorship is indistinguishable from its owner, sole proprietorship taxation is quite simple. The income earned by a sole proprietorship is income earned by its owner. A sole proprietor reports the sole proprietorship income and/or losses and expenses by filling out and filing a Schedule C, along with the standard Form 1040. Your profits and losses are first recorded on a tax form called Schedule C, which is filed along with your 1040. Then the "bottom-line amount" from Schedule C is transferred to your personal tax return. This aspect is attractive because business losses you suffer may offset income earned from other sources.

In the other hand, as a sole proprietor, you must also file a Schedule SE with Form 1040. You use Schedule SE to calculate how much self-employment tax you owe. You need not pay unemployment tax on yourself, although you must pay unemployment tax on any employees of the business. Of course, you won't enjoy unemployment benefits should the business suffer.

Consequently, Sole proprietors are personally liable for all debts of a sole proprietorship business. Let's examine this more closely because the potential liability can be alarming. Assume that a sole proprietor borrows money to operate but the business loses its major customer, goes out of business, and is unable to repay the loan. The sole proprietor is liable for the amount of the loan, which can potentially consume all her personal assets. Imagine an even worse scenario: The sole proprietor (or even one her employees) is involved in a business-related accident in which someone is injured or killed. The resulting negligence case can be brought against the sole proprietor owner and against her personal assets, such as her bank account, her retirement accounts, and even her home.

Furthermore, Consider the preceding paragraphs carefully before selecting a sole proprietorship as your business form. Accidents do happen, and businesses go out of business all the time. Any sole proprietorship that suffers such an unfortunate circumstance is likely to quickly become a nightmare for its owner.

According to Johnson R. (2018) Many small business owners starting new businesses choose to operate their companies as sole proprietorships. Sole proprietorships are the most common business structure and are owned by one person. Business owners choose to operate as a sole proprietorship because of the many advantages available. Choosing the appropriate business structure is a major decision, so knowing the advantages of operating a sole proprietorship can help you decide if it is the best structure for your business.

Also, one advantage of starting a sole proprietorship is the simplicity of formation. Very little paper work is required if you choose to file your business name. In most cases, you can visit your local courthouse and complete a "Doing Business as" or a fictitious name form to operate under your business name. A small fee is required for completing the paperwork. You are then given a certificate with the name of your business. Use the certificate to open bank accounts and apply for business credit cards. Unlike other business structures, individuals owning sole proprietorships are not required to file annual reports or legal documents required by some other business structures.

Hence, the sole owner of a sole proprietorship possesses all of the authority to make decisions on behalf of the company. Full ownership and management control is another advantage of owning a sole proprietorship. Owners are not required to attend formal meetings required of owners and members of other business structures. With a sole proprietorship, the owner can decide to sale or transfer the company to another individual and make important business decisions at his discretion.

Moreover, another advantage of forming a sole proprietorship is the taxation rules established by the Internal Revenue Service. Sole proprietors are not required to file separate tax returns for their business. Income made from the business is counted as personal income and owners pay taxes according to their individual tax rates. Sole proprietors must pay Social Security and Medicare taxes as well. The tax rules regarding sole proprietorships allow owners to avoid the double taxation of corporations. The IRS allows sole proprietors to take deductions on business expenses, which lowers owners' taxable income amount.

Consequently, if your business grows to a place that the business structure of a sole proprietorship no longer works to your advantage, you can easily change your business structure to a more complex model. The only requirement for going from a sole proprietorship to another business structure is filling out the paperwork for your new business structure. You are not required to fill out paperwork with a regulatory body because sole proprietorships are not governed by regulatory bodies.

According to All Business (2005) The most common and simplest form of business is a sole proprietorship. Many small businesses operating in the United States are sole proprietorships. An individual proprietor owns and manages the business and is responsible for all business transactions. The owner is also personally responsible for all debts and liabilities incurred by the business. A sole proprietor can own the business for any duration of time and sell it when he or she sees fit. As owner, a sole proprietor can even pass a business down to his or her heirs. In this type of business, there are no specific business taxes paid by the company. The owner pays taxes on income from the business as part of his or her personal income tax payments.

Also, Sole proprietors need to comply with licensing requirements in the states in which they're doing business, as well as local regulations and zoning ordinances. The paperwork and formalities, however, are substantially less than those of corporations, allowing sole proprietors to open a business quickly and with relative ease - from a bureaucratic standpoint. It can also be less costly to start a business as a sole proprietor, which is attractive to many new business owners who often find it difficult to attract investors.

Advantages of a Sole Proprietorship

- A sole proprietor has complete control and decision-making power over the business.
- Sale or transfer can take place at the discretion of the sole proprietor.
- No corporate tax payments
- Minimal legal costs to forming a sole proprietorship
- Few formal business requirements

Disadvantages of a Sole Proprietorship

- The sole proprietor of the business can be held personally liable for the debts and obligations of the business. Additionally, this risk extends to any liabilities incurred as a result of acts committed by employees of the company.
- All responsibilities and business decisions fall on the shoulders of the sole proprietor.
- Investors won't usually invest in sole proprietorships.

Hence, If the business is conducted under a fictitious name, it's up to the sole proprietor to file all applicable forms under the fictitious name or under doing business as (DBA). This, however, does not mean that the business is a separate entity from a legal standpoint. The sole proprietor remains liable even if he or she is doing business under a fictitious name. Most sole proprietors rely on loans and personal assets to initially finance their business. Some will elect to incorporate once the business has started to grow, while other business owners maintain their sole proprietorship for many years.

According to Griffin D. (2018) When two or more parties work together to carry on a business for profit, you form a general partnership. Although you often operate under a partnership agreement, you are not required to file one with the state and no laws require one in writing. All partners are responsible for the business, and they share all assets, liabilities and profits within the partnership as a separate entity.

If anyone can show that you in are in business with someone else, you are in a partnership. "The intention or lack thereof of having a formal partnership is not important," reports Quick MBA.

Also, General partnerships require very little paperwork. Unlike corporations, partnerships can operate in multiple states without getting a new permit for each state. Usually, general partnerships must abide by fewer regulations and are under less government supervision than corporations. Due diligence requires all partners to work together on a partnership agreement that all will follow, even though you don't need to file one with the state. Under Texas law, for example, a partnership may be formed through an oral agreement, although a written agreement is easier to prove in court.

Hence, General partnerships thrive when each partner brings a specific strength to the business," reports All Business website. Each partner should have a clearly defined role and business decisions should be handled accordingly. Offering a partner position to an important employee can be a useful bargaining chip. Unless the agreement states otherwise, all partners have equal voting rights within the group regardless of how much capital they contributed to the venture. Partners have a financial duty to one another, and are expected to act in the best interests of the partnership as a whole rather than just for their personal benefit

Moreover, because individuals form partnerships, they are taxed just like a sole proprietorship. Each partner must include her business income on her personal tax return and she can deduct business losses on her individual tax return as well. This is called a "pass through" entity because the profits and tax obligations pass through the company to the partners where income is divided according to their agreement.

Furthermore, a partnership can be dissolved at any time and partners have full liability for their business. In many states, upon the death or withdrawal of one partner, the entire partnership is dissolves, but the 1994 Texas Revised Partnership Act, for example, provides for a partnership to continue if its continuation is provided for in the partnership agreement. This provides protection to creditors so that the legal entity remains liable for the debts upon the addition or withdrawal of partners.

Consequently, while general partnerships are easy and inexpensive to form, there are some distinct business disadvantages. By nature, partnerships are limited to a small number of owners, so it is an impractical way to handle a company with hundreds of owners. If some partners do not want to retain that responsibility, or your business grows too large for personal liability to be practical, you should consider a limited liability partnership.

According to Adrian (2010) A partnership is commonly formed where two or more people wish to come to together to form a business. Perhaps they have a common business idea that they wish to put to the test or have realised that their skills and talents complement each other's in such a way that they might make a good business team. Forming a partnership seems like the most logical option and, in some cases, it is. Running a small business with a reasonably low turnover, a partnership is quite often a good choice of legal structure for a new business. The way a partnership is set up and run as well as the way it is governed and taxed often make it the most appealing form of business. However, there are circumstances where this isn't the case.

Also, Being a partnership, the business owners necessarily share the profits, the liabilities and the decision making. This is one of the advantages of partnership, especially where the partners have different skills and can work well together. However, it can obviously present some problems. Over the years, many partnerships have turned sour. Family and friends go into business together and end up falling out on a personal or business level and it all ends badly. This is one of the major disadvantages of partnerships over other business models, but it's important to be able to balance the advantages and disadvantages.

Advantages of Partnership Capital – Due to the nature of the business, the partners will fund the business with start-up capital. This means that the more partners there are, the more money they can put into the business, which will allow better flexibility and more potential for growth. It also means more potential profit, which will be equally shared between the partners.

Flexibility – A partnership is generally easier to form, manage and run. They are less strictly regulated than companies, in terms of the laws governing the formation and because the partners have the only say in the way the business is run (without interference by shareholders) they are far more flexible in terms of management, as long as all the partners can agree.

Shared Responsibility – Partners can share the responsibility of the running of the business. This will allow them to make the most of their abilities. Rather than splitting the management and taking an equal share of each business task, they might well split the work according to their skills. So if one partner is good with figures, they might deal with the book keeping and accounts, while the other partner might have a flare for sales and therefore be the main sales person for the business.

Decision Making – Partners share the decision making and can help each other out when they need to. More partners means more brains that can be picked for business ideas and for the solving of problems that the business encounters.

Disadvantages of Partnership Disagreements – One of the most obvious disadvantages of partnership is the danger of disagreements between the partners. Obviously people are likely to have different ideas on how the business should be run, who should be doing what and what the best interests of the business are. This can lead to disagreements and disputes which might not only harm the business, but also the relationship of those involved. This is why it is always advisable to draft a deed of partnership during the formation period to ensure that everyone is aware of what procedures will be in place in case of disagreement and what will happen if the partnership is dissolved.

Agreement – Because the partnership is jointly run, it is necessary that all the partners agree with things that are being done. This means that in some circumstances there are less freedoms with regards to the management of the business. Especially compared to sole traders. However, there is still more flexibility than with limited companies where the directors must bow to the will of the members (shareholders).

Liability – Ordinary Partnerships are subject to unlimited liability, which means that each of the partners shares the liability and financial risks of the business. Which can be off putting for some people. This can be countered by the formation of a limited liability partnership, which benefits from the advantages of limited liability granted to limited companies, while still taking advantage of the flexibility of the partnership model.

Taxation – One of the major disadvantages of partnership, taxation laws mean that partners must pay tax in the same way as sole traders, each submitting a *Self Assessment* tax return each year. They are also required to register as self-employed with HM Revenue & Customs. The current laws mean that if the partnership (and the partners) bring in more than a certain level, then they are subject to greater levels of personal taxation than they would be in a limited company. This means that in most cases setting up a limited company would be more beneficial as the taxation laws are more favourable (see our article on the <u>Advantages and Disadvantages of a Limited Company</u>).

Profit Sharing – Partners share the profits equally. This can lead to inconsistency where one or more partners aren't putting a fair share of effort into the running or management of the business, but still reaping the rewards.

Furthermore, there are several advantages and disadvantages of partnership in terms of a business undertaking. The two main disadvantages are the levels of taxation and the liability. The latter being negated by the ability to form a Limited Liability Partnership (a type of body only available since 2000). The Company Warehouse has a <u>Limited Liability Partnership</u> formation service that we have been running for a number of years, helping people set up their new partnerships. Our specialist team have a good working knowledge of the law and the current advantages of partnership over the other legal forms of business. So they can advise you on the best choice for your new enterprise.

According to Lorette K. (2018) If you're trying to decide whether to incorporate your business, you may be weighing the pros and cons of running a corporation. Similar to other forms of business, a corporation has its advantages and disadvantages. Evaluate the elements of a corporate form of business to determine if it is the right choice for your company.

Also, the primary advantage of a corporate form of business is that a corporation is a stand-alone entity, which means you are not personally liable for the assets and debts of the business. Incorporating protects your personal assets from lawsuits, debt collection and other business issues that can arise.

Hence, the stand-alone entity also separates tax liabilities, which is another advantage. This means that the corporation's taxes are separate from your personal tax liabilities. As a business owner, you are responsible for paying taxes only on the money the corporation pays you in the form of a salary, commission or dividends-- this is on your personal tax return. The corporation is responsible for paying corporate taxes (at the corporate tax rate) on any profit the company makes.

Moreover, another advantage of a corporate form of business is it does not die when its owners do. Because a corporation is its own entity, it lives on, even after shareholders (owners) decide to move on or dissolve the corporation or if the corporation merges with another company. It is easier to sell or merge a corporation because it is a matter of changing shareholders rather than having to establish an entirely new business.

Furthermore, one of the primary disadvantages of a corporation is the costs for running a corporate form of business. It costs money to incorporate with the state where the business operates. You can choose to hire an attorney or accountant to help you complete the incorporation paperwork, but it is not a requirement. If you incorporate directly with the Secretary of State, as of 2010, the fee ranges from $99 to $150. Beyond the initial incorporation fees, the corporate form of business also has ongoing fees associated with it. An annual report fee can range up to $150 a year for each year the corporation exists after the initial incorporation filing.

In the other hand, for corporations, the corporation ends up paying taxes twice. First, when the C corporation turns a profit, it pays a corporate tax rate on the profit amount. The second time the C corporation pays taxes is when it pays dividends to shareholders. Many businesses that incorporate choose to incorporate as an S corporation instead in order to avoid paying taxes twice. The only difference between a C corporation and an S corporation is a tax designation filed with the IRS using Form 2553. According to the IRS, an S corporation can choose to pass the income, losses, deductions and credit for the corporation through to the shareholders of the corporation for federal tax purposes. This avoids the double taxation possibility a C corporation is subject to.

Consequently. Corporations need to maintain more records than other business entities. Corporations must file annual reports and tax returns and maintain business bank accounts and records that are separate from personal accounts.

Shareholder meeting records, board of director meeting records, licenses and other corporate records also are necessary.

According to Nordmeyer B. (2017) If a small business incorporates, it's typically referred to as a C corporation, and in some cases, an S corporation. A corporation, unlike a sole proprietorship, is a separate entity from the business owner, which offers advantages in terms of protecting the owner's personal assets. But a corporation is also distinctive in its formation, taxation and its owners' liabilities.

Also, To form or dissolve either a C-or S corporation, a person must meet very specific legal requirements set by the state, which can be time-consuming and costly. For instance, to form the corporation, an owner must file Articles of Incorporation with the appropriate state agency -- often the Secretary of State; name the corporation's directors and officers, and state the number of shares the corporation will issue. State law also governs certain operational issues, such as the number of shareholder meetings that must be held.

Consequently, Double taxation is another disadvantage of some corporations. C corporation profits are taxed as income for both the corporation and its shareholders. Consequently, the corporation reports and pays taxes on corporate profits, shareholders are taxed on the profits they receive from the corporation as personal income, and the corporation's management pays taxes on the salaries, bonuses and dividends they receive. If the corporation's leaders are also shareholders, they pay taxes on their share of the distributed profits, as well as their compensation. Many smaller and some mid-size companies choose an S corporation structure; while very similar to a C corporation in certain ways, the S corporation operates as a pass-through entity for tax purposes, meaning earnings are only taxed once. An S corp passes income to its shareholders, and they pay personal income tax on their earnings.

Moreover, in terms of financial costs, a corporation must pay fees to file articles of incorporation, bylaws and the terms of stock certificates. These costs are in addition to the costs that most other businesses incur, such as technology costs, borrowing costs and the costs of equipment and supplies. In addition, a corporation is costly in terms of the time a corporation's leaders must commit not to running the business, but to shareholder meetings and other corporate requirements. Also, a corporation must comply with the regulations and requirements of federal, state and local agencies. This means that not only must business functions be performed to earn a profit, some functions must be performed in a very specific way, related records must be kept and reports must be filed to comply with government mandates.

Hence, a primary advantage of choosing to operate a business as a corporation is that neither its owners nor shareholders are ordinarily liable for a corporation's debts and risks. In the event a business is sued, the assets of the corporation are at risk, but not the assets of the shareholders. Instead, the shareholders' liability is limited to the financial investment they made when they purchased company shares. As an entity that is separate from its owners, the corporation incurs debts, not the corporation's shareholders.

In the other hand, a corporation exists in perpetuity, or until it is liquidated. Consequently, as a legal entity that's separate from its shareholders, directors and officers, the death of any individual who holds one of these positions or a change in those who hold these positions does not affect the status of the corporation. The perpetual status of a corporation enables its leaders to plan for long-term profit growth, which is one means to convince investors of potential gains.

Besides,A C corporation structure allows for unlimited shareholders and various types of stock, including common and preferred shares. S corporations, while also able to issue stock, can only issue one class of stock. Additionally, they are limited to a maximum of 100 shareholders, all of whom must be US residents and citizens. C corporations can be owned by trusts, LLCs or even other corporations, although S corporations do not allow this type of ownership structure. Given the different types of allowable shareholder levels and voting privileges in a C-corporation structure, owners and founders also typically have more voting power and control over the direction of the company than subsequent shareholders.

According to Abrugar V. (2011) Owners have limited Liability. A corporation is considered by law as a separate and distinct legal entity. Thus, owners of corporation or shareholders are only indebted to the extent of their interest in the corporation. Corporations have limited liability. This means that their creditors can only run after the assets of the corporation and not the on the personal assets of the stockholders in the settlement of the corporation's debts or liabilities.

Also, it can exist with continuity. The power of succession gives a corporation continuous existence. Unlike a sole proprietorship, where the death of the owner proprietor ceases its existence, the death of a shareholder will not terminate the corporation. The shares of ownership or interest of a corporation can be transferred from one owner to another owner. A corporation continues to exist until the shareholders decide to dissolve it or merge with another business.

Hence, Shares of ownership are transferable. The shares of stock or interest of a publicly traded corporation can be traded easily though a stockbroker. Shares of corporations are freely transferable except when shareholders have "buy-sell" agreements restricting when and to whom share may be sold or transferred. Securities laws and regulations may also limit the transferability of certain shares. For non-publicly traded corporations, the stock certificate can be transferred or assigned to another owner by executing a deed of assignment of shares of stock.

Moreover, it attracts more investors. Corporations attract investors because of its stock structure, perpetual existence, ownership transferability, and limited liability. Attracting more investors allows a corporation to raise more capital or equity to manage and expand their operations. Furthermore, because of a more regulated form of corporation and the fiduciary duties of its board of directors, it earns more trust and confidence not only from investors, but also from its employees, creditors, suppliers, customers and other outside stakeholders.

Consequently, you can be an employee of your own corporation. Since the corporation is a distinct entity from its owners or shareholders, they can become the corporation's employees or officers. Thus, they can receive salaries or compensation income aside from the dividends they may receive from the corporation. They can also be eligible for reimbursement or deduction of expenses they incurred related to their employment with the corporation.

Furthermore, the corporation pays its own tax. As a separate legal entity, a corporation is also a separate taxpayer from it owners. It has its own Taxpayer Identification Number, and it pays its own taxes, such as corporate income tax, business taxes and withholding taxes. The owners or stockholders pay their own taxes on the compensation and or dividend income they receive from the corporation.

On the other hand, Disadvantages of forming a corporation. Incorporation is costly. Incorporating a business needs to file with the Securities and Exchange Commission (SEC) and may involve a lot of formal and legal papers, such as by laws, articles of incorporation, affidavit and board resolutions. This is sometimes done by getting the service of a corporate attorney or firms which are specialized in incorporating a business. It may also require higher amount of initial or paid-up capital for other types of corporation like financing and lending corporations. Furthermore, the amount of subscribed capital is taxed with documentary stamp tax, which may result to additional expenses to be incurred by the incorporators.

Also, Corporations are highly regulated. Ordinary corporations are regulated by the SEC. Special corporations may be required with secondary licenses and are further regulated by other government agencies, such as Bangko Sentral ng Pilipinas (BSP) for financing and lending companies, Commission on Higher Education (CHED) for companies operating secondary schools and Insurance Commission (IC) for insurance companies. Moreover, corporations also need to comply with the quarterly or annual reportorial requirements with the SEC and other agencies requiring those reports for certain types of corporations. This also means that the more compliance it requires, the more paper works and cost it involves. And when there are more to comply, bigger penalties are awaiting to be paid if they are not complied.

In the other hand, Limited liability may discourage creditors. The limited liability feature of the corporation can be an advantage for stockholders. However, it can also be a disadvantage when a corporation doesn't have a good financial condition and performance. Because of the limited liability, a corporation with a low credit score may discourage creditors to lend their money to the corporation.

Besides, it may result to double taxation. Since the corporation is already taxed on its income, distributing this income to shareholders in the form of dividends may result to double taxation. This is because the dividend income received by the shareholders (natural persons) is also taxed on their personal income tax returns.

Hence, it is not easy to dissolve. Corporations are difficult to dissolve as it is also difficult to form. Everything is regulated from formation, to operation, and to dissolution. An application for dissolution must be filed with the S.E.C with complete requirements, including tax clearance with the Bureau of Internal Revenue. The liquidation process is also regulated to ensure that the rights of any creditor having a claim against it are not prejudiced.

Furthermore, Choosing the type and form of your business needs a lot of prudent considerations. It may involve assessing your financial resources, taking inherent risks and considering your preparedness. This article only aims to guide you on your way to the right formation of you company or organization. However, the final choice still lies in you. Whatever your decision is and whatever type of business you will form, always remember to do business at your best. To your success!

According to Adams G. (2017) One of the key decisions in launching any business is its legal structure. Forming a cooperative makes for a business responsive to the needs of its owner-members. While this structure has some limitations, most notably in raising capital, its advantages may outweigh them. Creating a detailed business plan and seeking expert advice -- including the services of a lawyer -- may help to avoid costly problems down the line.

Also, All the members of a cooperative are its owners. They're also called user-owners. The business operates to the members' benefit because they use the services or products produced. Cooperatives range in size from small local food co-ops to credit unions and large retail companies. Members may have multiple shares in a co-op, yet each individual has only one vote. Cooperatives can also be made up of businesses as in the case of The Associated Press or certain agricultural co-ops.

Hence, a cooperative benefit from a broad knowledge base and the ability to tap into its built-in and accessible network of members who have a personal stake in the business' health and growth. Cooperatives also benefit from increased buying power that allows them to obtain goods and services at substantial discounts. Cooperatives get a significant break from Uncle Sam, in that they aren't taxed the way corporations are, although each shareholder has the responsibility to pay taxes on income from the business. Another significant advantage is that surplus dividends paid out to members aren't taxed by the IRS. Cooperatives may be eligible for grants specifically intended to help this kind of business.

Moreover, it's crucial to consider a cooperative's financial health at the outset and strategize how to manage its capital and cash flow. While this is a key step for any business, cooperatives can be at a serious disadvantage when it comes to seeking outside financing. Large investors have little incentive for dealing with so many owners and having so little power, because the potential investor is limited to only one vote, no matter how large the investment. Another potential problem lies in the possibility of diminishing involvement by members. If active engagement drops off, it weakens the cooperative. Many cooperatives weather these challenges. Agricultural cooperatives have shown overall growth in assets, revenue and market share gains

since 1950, according to the Agricultural & Applied Economics Association's Choices Magazine.

Consequently, Meeting with potential cooperative members and discussing the pros and cons of forming a cooperative is a valuable step in assessing the feasibility of this structure. Draft a preliminary business plan to address in detail the mission statement, financing, practices, methods of conflict resolution, rights and responsibilities of members, competition and potential pitfalls. Develop contingency plans for problems with supply, sales, cash flow or unanticipated difficulties. Discuss the advantages and disadvantages of the cooperative structure in detail to check the mettle of the membership. A group that focuses on solutions and moves forward through disagreements demonstrates a better chance of success than one that becomes derailed in disagreements without making decisions.

According to Sessoms G. (2018)The cooperative business is formed and operated to meet the needs of its members. Cooperatives leverage the buying power of membership to purchase products or services. A cooperative business might focus on electricity, food, fuel or other products and services. Cooperatives must operate in many ways like a regular business to be successful. The advantages of a cooperative business derive from its structure and democratic model of governance.

Also, Cooperative businesses are as small as a community buying club and as large as Fortune 500 businesses, according to North Dakota State University. Groups create cooperatives to provide competition, reduce costs and provide services that profit-driven companies might reject as unprofitable. Farmers and small businesses own producer-owned cooperatives to sell their goods and provide resources to members for credit and financing. Consumer-owned cooperatives allow members to purchase a wide range of goods and services, such as child care, health care and utility providers. Worker-owned cooperatives might be taxi cab companies, timber processors, employee-owned grocery stores and restaurants. People join cooperative business to enjoy the benefits of group purchasing, pooled risk and the empowerment of owning and controlling the company.

Hence, Cooperative businesses are owned and controlled by members, not by absentee investors. The board of directors is elected from the cooperative's membership to represent the interests of the members. The members are the users or consumers of the cooperative's products or services. Unlike business ownership, which is based on the percentage of the business a person owns, cooperative ownership is based on how much of the products or services the member purchases. Members vote on all activities of the cooperative business. Cooperatives allot one vote to each member. A corporation allots one vote for each share, which means an investor may purchase many shares to gain many votes. Cooperative members may purchase one share of voting stock. Membership requires the voting stock and engaging in business with the cooperative.

Moreover, Members of cooperative businesses pay lower or stabilized prices for products and services because of the buying power of the cooperative. Businesses that sell to cooperatives may receive higher or stabilized prices for their products or services. Benefits are distributed to members based on usage of the cooperative's products or services. A member who purchases 10 percent of the products or services receives a return of 10 percent in benefits. Cooperative business members also benefit from shared ownership, which results in shared risk, both liability and financial, and reduced expenses for operational costs.

Synthesis

The forms of business are sole proprietorship, partnership, corporation, and cooperative. The sole proprietorship is the simplest business form under which one can operate a business. The sole proprietorship is not a legal entity. It simply refers to a person who owns the business and is personally responsible for its debts. While, partnership, is commonly formed where two or more people wish to come to together to form a business. Perhaps they have a common business idea that they wish to put to the test or have realised that their skills and talents complement each other's in such a way that they might make a good business team. Forming a partnership seems like the most logical option and, in some cases, it is. Running a small business with a reasonably low turnover, a partnership is quite often a good choice of legal structure for a new business. corporation exists in perpetuity, or until it is liquidated. Consequently, as a legal entity that's separate from its shareholders, directors and officers, the death of any individual who holds one of these positions or a change in those who hold these positions does not affect the status of the corporation. is formed and operated to meet the needs of its members. Cooperatives leverage the buying power of membership to purchase products or services. A cooperative business might focus on electricity, food, fuel or other products and services. Cooperatives must operate in many ways like a regular business to be successful.

CHAPTER III

RESEARCH METHODOLOGY

Research Design

This study conducted according to the design of mix experimental and non-experimental design of Quantitative research. In the Experimental design, it tries to emphasize objective measurements and the statistical analysis of data collected through questionnaires. While in the non-experimental design, it is a descriptive type studies that used to observe, document, and describe regarding an analysis of forms of business in relation to the proficiency level of the students.

Sampling procedure

Slovin's Formula is used to calculate the sample size (n) given the population size (N) and a margin of error (e).It's a random sampling technique formula to estimate sampling size this method will be used to get the number of respondents in this study to gather a data regarding an analysis of dorms of business in relation to proficiency level of the students.

-It is computed as $n = N / (1+Ne^2)$.

Whereas:

n = no. of samples

N = total population

e = Margin of error

Instrument of the study

The researchers used survey questionnaire for their instrument to gather a data that was used for this study. The survey questionnaire was divided into two parts which are the profile of the students and the survey regarding to an analysis of dorms of business in relation to proficiency level of the students.

According to Dave Vannette 2015 a survey is a method of gathering information from a sample of people, traditionally with the intention of generalizing the results to a larger population. Surveys provide a critical source of data and insights for nearly everyone engaged in the information economy, from businesses and the media to government and academics. The survey is the collection of information regards to the kind, action or opinion of large group of people that define as one population or wide part of research that made of variety of styles under the questions for respondents.

Data Gathering

Data gathering procedure is a process of collecting information from the respondents surveying actually involves gathering responses from the topic of the study through a written medium. The researchers will distribute the survey questionnaires to their selected respondents for the needed answer regarding an analysis of dorms of business in relation to proficiency level of the students.

The researchers used Stratified random sampling is a method of sampling that involves the division of a population into smaller groups known as strata. In stratified random sampling, the strata are formed based on members' shared attributes or characteristics. A random sample from each stratum is taken in a number proportional to the stratum's size when compared to the population. These subsets of the strata are then pooled to form a random sample.

Data Analysis Techniques/ Statistical Treatment

According to statistics. laerd.com (2015) The one-way analysis of variance (ANOVA) is used to determine whether there are any statistically significant differences between the means of three or more independent (unrelated) groups.

The researchers will be use one-way analysis of variance test to determine the result independent variables have on the dependent variable into the middle regression study.

MSFactor= $(SS\ FACTOR)/(DF\ FACTOR)$

MS Error= $(SS\ ERROR)/(DF\ ERROR)$

Notation:

MS= Mean Square

SS= Sum of Squares

DF= Degree of Freedom

LEVEL OF SOCIAL MEDIA ADDICTION AMONG GRADE 12

STUDENTS INMANUEL L. QUEZON

SENIOR HIGH SCHOOL

A research paper presented to the faculty of

practical research in Manuel L. Quezon

Senior High School

Submitted by:

Manuel V. Caliguia

Submitted to:

Dr. Mark Vincent B. Emit

March 2018

CHAPTER I

THE PROBLEM AND ITS BACKGROUND

Background of the study

Social media is currently taking over the world. In today's day and age, it is a struggle to find someone that is not a registered user of some type of social media website, be it Facebook, Twitter, Pinterest, or something else. In fact, in the past 10 years, Facebook members have increased from one million in 2004 to 1.15 billion today (Growth).The average American spends 16 minutes of every hour on a social media network (Growth).So what exactly is social media? Social media is an interaction among users where they create, share, or exchange information and ideas in virtual communities and networks.

According to Boyd (2014), "social media refers to the sites and services that emerged during the early 2000s, including social networking sites, video sharing sites, blogging and micro blogging platforms, and related tools that allow participants to create and share their own content" (p. 6). Additionally, social media enables people to interact in online communities (Boyd, 2014). It bridges the gap between not being able to physically be around people and wanting to connect with them.

Users typically access social media services via web-based technologies on desktop, computers, and laptops, or download services that offer social media functionality to their mobile devices (e.g., smartphones and tablet computers). When engaging with these services, users can create highly interactive platforms through which individuals, communities and organizations can share, co-create, discuss, and modify user-generated content or pre-made content posted online. They introduce substantial and pervasive changes to communication between businesses, organizations, communities and individuals. Social media changes the way individuals and large organizations communicate. These changes are the focus of the emerging fields of techno self studies. Social media differ from paper-based media (e.g., magazines and newspapers) or traditional electronic media such as TV broadcasting in many ways, including quality, reach, frequency, interactivity, usability, immediacy, and permanence. Social media outlets operate in a dialogic transmission system (many sources to many receivers). This is in contrast to traditional media which operates under a monologic transmission model (one source to many receivers), such as a paper newspaper which is delivered to many subscribers, or a radio station which broadcasts the same programs to an entire city. Some of the most popular social media websites are Baidu Tieba, Facebook (and its associated Facebook, Messenger), Gab, Google+, MySpace, Instagram, LinkedIn, Pinterest, Tumblr, Twitter, Viber, VK, WeChat, Wei bo, WhatsApp, Wikia, Snapchat and YouTube. These social media websites have more than 100,000,000 registered users.

Billions of people around the world use social media to share information and make connections. On a personal level, social media allows you to communicate with friends and family, learn new things, develop your interests, and be entertained. On a professional level, you can use social media to broaden your knowledge in a particular field and build your professional network by connecting with other professionals in your industry. At the company level, social media allows you to have a conversation with your audience, gain customer feedback, and elevate your brand.

There's no denying the fact that social media has changed the way we communicate with one another. For instance, when was the last time you brought a tangible photo album over to a friend's house to show off some new pictures? It's probably been quite a while ago if ever, right? This once commonplace activity has been replaced by virtual sharing via social media platforms. Photos aren't the only things we're sharing online, though. Status updates, videos, articles we've read— these are all things that we can now broadcast to the world with the click of a button. Does this ease of use make for better interpersonal communication, or is social media ruining the natural way we humans have communicated with each other for centuries? Big questions deserve big answers. Let's dig in.

In America, a survey reported that 84 percent of adolescents in America have a Facebook account. Over 60% of 13 to 17-year-olds have at least one profile on social media, with many spending more than two hours a day on social networking sites. According to Nielsen, Internet users continue to spend more time on social media sites than on any other type of site. At the same time, the total time spent on social media sites in the U.S. across PCs as well as on mobile devices increased by 99 percent to 121 billion minutes in July 2012 compared to 66 billion minutes in July 2011. For content contributors, the benefits of participating in social media have gone beyond simply social sharing to building a reputation and bringing in career opportunities and monetary income.

Some use these sites in order to communicate to their loved ones across the globe, in different countries as possible. Companies and business people use it for selling and advertising products and for gaining customers. Some also use it as a media for gaining friends and for engaging in relationships and others use these internet sites for gaming purposes. But what is bothersome today is the way students use these networking sites.

Conceptual Framework

Manuel L. Quezon High School
Senior High School

According to Wikipedia the input–process–output (IPO) model, or input-process-output pattern, is a widely used approach in systems analysis for describing the structure of information processing program or other process.

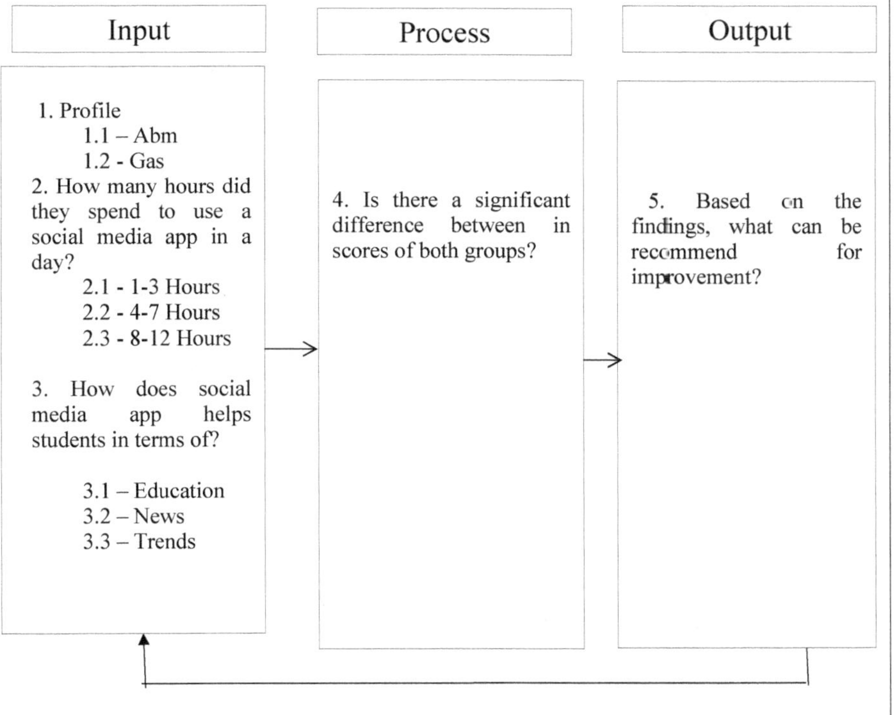

Conceptual framework presents the paradigm of the study illustrating a conceptual frame of the study. The components are INPUT, PROCESS AND

OUTPUT. The input shows profile of the Abm and Gas respondents in terms of number of students who spend time using social media app and how many hours did they use a social media app in a day. What social media app helps them in terms of: Education, News and Trends. The Process shows if there is a significant difference between in scores of both groups. The survey questionnaire will validated by the students' adviser and professor. The researcher spread the survey questionnaire to their selected respondents in Manuel L. Quezon Senior High School. The output shows off the expected result from the respondents and what can be recommend for improvement.

Statement of the Problem

This study will determine the Level of Social Media Addiction among Grade 12 Students in Manuel L. Quezon Senior high School

1. Profile

1.1 - Abm

1.2 - Gas

2. How many times did they use a social media app in a day?

2.1 - 1-3 Hours

2.2 - 4-7 Hours

2.3 - 8-12 Hours

3. How does social media app helps students?

3.1 – Education

3.2 – News

3.3 – Trends

Hypothesis

H_o: There is no significant difference between in scores of both groups

Significance of the Study

The researcher is truly believed that this study has significance to the following variables:

1. Students- The students should have some knowledge regarding social media app. To apply it in their life and to know what is the trend now and the future.

2. Teachers- This study should use by the teachers to have knowledge on social media apps. This will give information about what's happening in the world using social media.

3. Parents- This study will help to the parents to inform and to share the information about parent's relatives using social media.

4. Researcher- The data that gathered from this study will use by the researcher to conduct another research that is related to this study. The information that the researcher gathered will be applying it to himself to update what's happening about our country and to be aware of using too much social media app.

Scope and limitation

This study scoped the information that gathered by the researcher that may add some knowledge to the readers regarding hours that did they spend in social media apps and how does social media app helps students in terms of: Education, News and Trends. The researcher was interview their selected respondents inside Manuel L. Quezon Senior High School. This study has a limitation because the students and teachers only in Manuel L. Quezon Senior High School are involved. The researcher believes that this research will know and focus on Level of Social Media Addiction between Gas and Abm Grade 12 Students in Manuel L. Quezon Senior high School.

Definition of Terminologies

The following terms were defined according to be used.

Social Media - Websites and applications that enable users to create and share content or to participate in social networking.

Technology - The application of scientific knowledge for practical purposes, especially in industry.

Online Community - An online community is a group of people with common interests who use the Internet (web sites, email, instant messaging, etc) to communicate, work together and pursue their interests over time.

Application - an application, especially as downloaded by a user to a mobile device.

Addiction - the fact or condition of being addicted to a particular substance, thing, or activity.

Facebook - is a social networking site that allows people from around the world to network with friends, companies and organizations. Departments looking to build overall brand awareness should consider using Facebook.

Instagram - is a social networking site that allows users to share pictures and short videos using their mobile device.

Twitter - is a micro-blogging site that allows people to post updates in 140 characters or less. Departments looking to engage their audience at a high frequency and have the resources to respond promptly should consider using Twitter.

LinkedIn - is a business-related social networking site used mainly for professional networking. Departments looking to connect with their current employees or alumni should consider creating a LinkedIn group.

Pinterest - is a social networking site that allows users to organize and share content using virtual pinboards. With a large female audience, the website offers inspirational and creative content such as recipes, craft projects, fashion, and event planning.

CHAPTER II

RELATED STUDY AND LITERATURE

Related Study

According to Pop Culture Universe, "Social media is an umbrella term that refers to all online communities or publications that foster and encourage conversation between users and allow them to develop critique, publish, and interact with a vast array of online content." Use the following sources to learn more about social networking and social media and the social, business, and communications issues surrounding it

Social media have added entirely new meanings to interpersonal interaction and community. It is the interplay between internet and real life communication and its subsequent effect on interpersonal relationships. Social Media have bundled many of the internet communication standards such as e-mail forums, and instant messaging into one resource. However, its usage has become a staple activity in a young adult's life. While it varies slightly among gender and race groups, overall, college students who have internet access use SNS regularly for some type of social contact. With this mass assimilation into daily life, it has already begun to change the way in which interpersonal relationships are defined. It is one of the, if not the top medium for young adults to "scope out" and "research" potential partners. With SNS playing a large role in many relationships, it's important to see how this will continue to shape interpersonal communication in the future.

Recent trends show that social media usage has increased. As of October 2011, one of the most well-known social media sites is Facebook (Facebook, 2011).

This site currently boasts 800 million active users, and over 50% of active users log on to the site every day (Facebook, 2011). Members are able to connect with friends on the site, and the average user maintains approximately 130 friends (Facebook, 2011). Further, more than 350 million of these users access the site through a mobile device (Facebook, 2011). According to Eldon (2011), 51.2% of users are male, whereas 48.8% are female. In terms of age, 20.6% of users are between the ages of 13 and 17; 25.8% are between the ages of 18 and 25; 26.1% are between the ages of 26-34; and 27.5% are over the age of 35 (Eldon, 2011).

According to Vitak (2008) there are various reasons as to why individuals use a social media app. The first reason is for them to meet strangers and become friends. The majority of respondents of her research paper (57%) said that they were initially introduced to those "friends" through mutual friends, which increased the likelihood of such relationships developing into strong ties. While a significant portion of respondents stated that they have at least a few online friends, 85% said that they do not communicate with most of their online friends, and the majority of respondents said that they considered those friendships as strong ties. Through social media users tend to maintain their interpersonal relationship with their online friends because of easy communication. Therefore they can use private messaging, chat rooms, and other methods of communication provided by the website.

Social Media are influencing every realm of society, including interpersonal relationships of the members. An interpersonal relationship is a relatively long-term association between two or more people. This association may be based on emotions, regular business interactions, or some other type of social commitments. Interpersonal relationships take place in a great variety of contexts, such as family, friends, marriage, acquaintances, work, clubs, neighbours, etc. They may be regulated by law, custom, or mutual agreement, and are the basis of social groups and society as a whole. Social media app influences the interpersonal relationship of students in many ways. Through social media app, users have the opportunity to be acquainted with people worldwide. These people consequently can affect the user's interpersonal relationships with other people close to them.

Enabled by ICT, social media are instrumental in and shaping and catalyzing social change for they allow for wide participation, continued flow of communication, and speed in public mobilization. In other words, their development has created opportunities to fuel social change through building awareness, triggering public will mobilization, encouraging civic engagement, sharing knowledge, etc. Hence, their role is indeed changing in social and political processes and their significance is increasing in society. While the mobilization of social media has become an instrumental approach for social change, their embrace and strategic use may further transform them into a driving force for major political changes, if their implementation is based on a constant adjustment of strategies to political and social context specific requirements. However, a theoretical framework is needed to advance a shared pursuit toward understanding the role of social media technologies for social change, as assessing their real impact on social change is still compounded by the lack of clear empirical evidence.

Furthermore, for they are decentralized and less hierarchical and based on democratic structures, social media offer new and appealing possibilities to people in terms of expression, collaboration and participation in powerful new ways. This is due to the advent of Web 2.0 technologies that has enabled users to create and exchange user-generated content. In relation to this, the so-called citizen media could be said to meet the Web 2.0 social media revolution, with some of related applications being in part an essential constituent to social media and others losing their dominance due to no adherence to the relevant principles and practices. As a key feature, social media provide scale and are capable of reaching a massive, global audience and are accessible to as well individual as media actors to produce or consume information in equal terms, as the means of social media production are available to the public. Thus, individuals are no longer stochastically at the outer borders of media production and distribution.

According to Web Credible social media provide encouragement and support; establish identity with others and fulfill the need to feel included; provide the outlet for some people to establish their need for recognition, social status, control or leadership and provide the necessary control over aspects of lives for those who don't want to be leaders; help establish friends, relationships and the opportunity to interact with others.

The study of Kevin P. Brady, Lori B. Holcomb and Bethany V. Smith (2010), titled as "The Use of Alternative Use of Social Media in Higher Education Settings: A Case Study of E-learning Benefits of Ning in Education", was based on the educational benefits associated with the use of Social media. The study focused the graduate students enrolled in distance education courses using Ning in Education, a non-commercial, educational-based SNS. The study emphasized on the students' attitudes towards the sites as productive online tools for teaching and learning. The researchers found out that education based upon social media can be used effectively in distance education courses. They are an excellent technological tool for improved online communications among students in higher distance education courses.

However, a study conducted by Bowers-Campbell (2008) stated that Social media were used as a tool for improving academic motivation among university students enrolled in a developmental reading course. Specifically, Bowers-Campbell put forth the argument that using Social media may help students to better connect "with college reading expectations since it offers potential for battling low self-efficacy and poor self-regulation behaviours plaguing many developmental learning students". In order to address self-efficacy among students, "superlatives" or "virtual gifts" were suggested as a type of reward system to recognize the achievements of students in the course. It was also recommended that Social media can be used as a means to foster a sense of "connectedness" between the instructor and students in order to further increase self-efficacy even before the course started by having the students review the instructor's profile in an effort to familiarize themselves with the instructor.

Consequently Social media not only help to facilitate a connection between the instructor and students, but it also offers means for building peer support among students. This provides the student with an increased level of control and has the potential to create a "classroom of students who accept and support each other". Creating groups, "poking" class members, and providing photos and profiles are all under the control of the students, providing a sense of ownership and control over their learning environment. As suggested by Bowers-Campbell, "virtual class rosters and group meetings via Social media might soothe anxieties by providing an online support group of learners who care about the students' success" In terms of self-regulation, it was argued that SNS technology provides a large measure of autonomy and may "reinforce self-regulated learning strategies". Specifically mentioned was the group feature of Social media, which lends a great deal of control to the students in terms of defining their own learning goals.

A similar study conducted by Hyllegard, Ogle, Yan, and Reitz (2011) sought to understand students' motivation in using Facebook and fanning, or liking, particular brands on the social networking site. The researchers found students use the site to establish personal connections with others and use the site to create affiliations with brands that define who they are and help them establish a sense of self (Hyllegard et al., 2011). Thus, these motives are similar to the "social benefits" motive discovered by Hennig-Thurau et al. (2004), the desire to display their personality discussed by Casteleyn et al. (2009), and the desire for self-expression cited by Pempek, Yermolayeva, and Calvert (2009). In addition, Hyllegard et al. (2011) found that students "fanned" companies and brands to become market mavens who could receive and disseminate information about brands. This motivation discovered by Hyllegard et al. (2004) is consistent with the "concern for others" motive and "self-enhancement" motives discovered by Hennig-Thurau et al. (2004), as students could improve their knowledge about a product (self-enhancement), and then share this information with friends (concern for others).

In 2011, Smock, Ellison, Lampe, and Wohn applied the uses and gratification approach to analyze why individuals use Facebook in general, as well as why they use certain functions on the website. The researchers found that users who update their status are motivated chiefly by a desire for expressive information sharing, whereas individuals who post comments do so for relaxing entertainment, companionship, and social interaction. However, individuals who posted on friends' walls did so for professional 6 advancement, social interaction, and habitual pass time. Two motives, professional advancement and social interaction, were discovered as underlying reasons why users sent private messages. Smock et al. also found social interaction was the only significant motive discovered in the usage of Facebook's chat feature. Finally, the usage of groups on the site was positively influenced by expressive information sharing, and negatively by social interaction.

Consumption Patterns

In addition, companies have also begun using social media sites as a way to better communicate with customers. According to Hyllegard, Ogle, Yan, and Reitz (2011), "between 66%-96% of consumer goods companies have adopted social media, including Facebook" (p. 601). One feature of this site is the ability of users to "fan" particular products or brands so that they receive information about these products. In addition, this feature allows customers to express satisfaction or dissatisfaction toward a company or brand. Facebook reports the average user can express interest in over 900 million objects, and the average user follows 80 such pages (Facebook, 2011).

According to LaDuque (2010), companies can also utilize social media platforms to create personalized experiences, to increase brand loyalty, to generate sales leads, and to increase exposure. For example, companies which provide entertaining videos or valuable incentives may have their offerings shared between social media users through electronic word-of-mouth communication. In addition, social networking sites may also allow companies to communicate directly with customers to improve products or address issues. Facebook allows individuals to "like" pages, meaning they will receive updates 7 regarding the product or brand they have "liked." Even mutual fund firms have begun using this medium to communicate with customers, create interactive scavenger hunts, and organize contests among fans (Glazer, 2011).

Social media can also be used by both companies and customers for marketing research. In 2007, Casteleyn, Mottart, and Rutten (2009) sought to understand the behaviors of individuals who joined groups on this social networking site. These groups could be devoted toward supporting or criticizing specific products or brands and represented an early form of Facebook's "like" function (Casteleyn et al.). According to Casteleyn et al., market researchers could gain insight into individuals' feelings about a brand from reading wall posts. These wall posts could potentially include comments about the brand or photographs involving the brand. These researchers hypothesized researchers could better understand this consumer behavior by considering the agent (the individual posting the information), the act (what he or she posted), agency (the method used to post the information), the scene (the context of the post), and the purpose (why the information was posted). These findings are of significant importance, as Pempek et al. (2009) found that the average student belonged to 24.58 groups; however, Pempek et al. also found that active participation within these groups was rare.

Despite these potential benefits, companies must also be cautious when using Social media. First, culture has developed on the website, and companies must be careful to adhere to the cultural norms preset on the site (Vorvoreanu, 2009). To understand how companies could effectively engage in public relations on social media, Vorvoreanu (2009) conducted six focus groups with 35 college students. Vorvoreanu discovered some users feel as though corporations do not belong on the site, as it was meant for friends to interact. Consistent with other research studies, many users view their profiles as a means of self-expression, and becoming fans of a company allows them to express their interests (Vorvoreanu). Respondents were also accepting of small businesses which maintained a presence on the site, though this was because they often knew the owners personally (Vorvoreanu). Although respondents were unhappy that corporations had begun maintaining a presence on Facebook, they also reported that they would be interested in receiving discounts and gifts from these organizations through the social networking site (Vorvoreanu).

In addition, social media traffic also exhibits a higher bounce-rate (85%) than search engine traffic (50%), meaning people who access sites through social media are less likely to become customers (LaDuque, 2010).

CHAPTER III

RESEARCH METHODOLOGY

This chapter presents a description of the research design selection, research instruments, data collection procedure and statistical treatments used.

Research Design

It is systematically interpreted the data gathered by the researcher through it used the survey questionnaire and experimental test. Experimental design is the process of planning a study to meet specified objectives. Planning an experiment properly is very important in order to ensure that the right type of data and a sufficient sample size and power are available to answer the research questions of interest as clearly and efficiently as possible.

Sampling procedure

Slovin's Formula is used to calculate the sample size (n) given the population size (N) and a margin of error (e).It's a random sampling technique formula to estimate sampling size this method will be used to get the number of respondents in this study to gather a data regarding Level of Social Media Addiction Between Gas and Abm Grade 12 Students in Manuel L. Quezon Senior high School..

-It is computed as $n = N / (1+Ne^2)$.

Whereas:

n = no. of samples

N = total population

e = Margin of error

Respondents of the Study

The respondents of the study from the number of enrollees will be the 15 Grade twelve students.

Instrument of the study

The researcher used survey questionnaire for their instrument to gather a data that was used for this study. The survey questionnaire was divided into two parts which are the profile of the students and the survey regarding to Level of Social Media Addiction between Gas and Abm Grade 12 Students in Manuel L. Quezon Senior high School. According to Dave Vannette 2015 a survey is a method of gathering information from a sample of people, traditionally with the intention of generalizing the results to a larger population. Surveys provide a critical source of data and insights for nearly everyone engaged in the information economy, from businesses and the media to government and academics. The survey is the collection of information regards to the kind, action or opinion of large group of people that define as one population or wide part of research that made of variety of styles under the questions for respondents.

Data Gathering

Data gathering procedure is a process of collecting information from the respondents surveying actually involves gathering responses from the topic of the study through a written medium. The researcher will distribute the survey questionnaires to their selected respondents for the needed answer regarding Level of Social Media Addiction between Gas and Abm Grade 12 Students in Manuel L. Quezon Senior high School. The researcher used Stratified random sampling is a method of sampling that involves the division of a population into smaller groups known as strata. In stratified random sampling, the strata are formed based on members' shared attributes or characteristics. A random sample from each stratum is taken in a number proportional to the stratum's size when compared to the population. These subsets of the strata are then pooled to form a random sample.

Data Analysis Techniques/ Statistical Treatment

According to Ronald Fisher 2012 Analysis of variance or also known as ANOVA is a collection of statistical model used to analyze the differences among group means and their associated procedures.

The researcher will be use analysis of variance test to determine the result independent variables have on the dependent variable into the middle regression study. The researcher utilizes ANOVA test results in an F-Test to generate additional data that aligns with the proposed regression model.

Formula:

$$\bar{x} = \frac{\Sigma xi}{n}$$

Notations:

$\bar{x}$ just stands for the "sample mean"

Σ means "add up"

xi "all of the x-values"

n means "the number of items in the sample"

THE EFFECT OF TECHNOLOGY IN THE CLASSROOM

A research paper presented to the faculty of

practical research in Manuel L. Quezon

Senior High School

Submitted by:

Duanne. R. Cortes

Submitted to:

Dr. Mark Vincent B. Emit

March 2018

CHAPTER 1

THE PROBLEM AND ITS BACKGROUND

Background of the Study

Technology has increasingly become an integrated part of our lives—so much so that it seems preposterous to even think of doing the most simple, routine tasks without the use of a cellular phone, laptop computer, or personal global positioning system, more commonly known as GPS. While people of all ages increasingly use technology for routine tasks, children are among the most frequent users of technology (Kaiser Family Foundation, 2010). Just as technology has changed aspects of our daily lives, it is undoubtedly changing education. Technological advances provide easier facilitation of and access to information, but technology does not change the message received by students, or the students" ability to grasp and retain information (Thurlow, Lengel, & Tomic, 2004, p. 42). Technology that is incorporated into the classroom for the purpose of enhancing the learning process is referred to as technology enhanced learning (TEL) (Dror, 2008). Despite high expectations of the ability of school administrators and teachers to enhance student learning through the incorporation of technology in the classroom, TEL programs have produced lackluster results (Sinclair, 2009, p. 46). "The history of technology in the classroom is one of cycles of exaggerated promises, highly publicized installations with committed teachers, and masterful and inventive excuses for why the promises went unfulfilled" (Venezky, 2004, p. 3). Problems implementing TEL programs have risen due to lack of understanding of the most effective approaches of selecting which technologies to use, the most effective ways to integrate technology, and a lack of understanding of what factors may impact the effectiveness of TEL programs (Bordbar, 2010; Communication Without Barriers, 2007; Sinclair, 2009; Venezky, 2004). Additionally, during the technology integration process, a common problem is that teachers often rely on the technology to teach students, rather than using the technology as an educational tool, or the technology is used in situations that do not warrant its use (Dror, 2008; Honan, 2010). When implementing technology into curriculum, it is critical to assess what tasks can be completed without the use of various technologies, and to "remind ourselves of what may be lost when we do use them" (Beniger, 1989, p. 120).

Theoretical Framework

Philosophical Assumptions and Theoretical Framework

Although the way in which information is distributed does not necessarily change the message (Thurlow, Lengel, & Tomic, 2004, p. 42), the method of delivery and incorporation of technology can change the way the information is absorbed and how much of the information is retained (Gitlin, 2002, p. 31). The combination of technological tools, progressive pedagogy and creativity allows teachers to humanize the world and its inhabitants for students (Klein, 2010, p. 86). However, too much emphasis on the technology, rather than on the actual information, can be detrimental to a child"s development. The schools teach their children to operate computerized systems instead of teaching things that are more valuable to children. In a word, almost nothing that they need happens to the losers. Which is why they are losers... Eventually, the losers succumb, in part because they believe, as Thamus prophesied, that the specialized knowledge of the masters of a new technology is a form of wisdom... The result is that certain questions do not arise. For example, to whom will the technology give greater power and freedom? And whose power and freedom will be reduced by it? (Postman, 1992, pp. 10-11) The incorporation of technology in the classroom can be quite useful, as "the use of virtual environments for collaboration and learning can result in unprecedented flow of ideas, leading to higher levels of productivity" (Chandra, Theng, Lwin, & Foo, 2009, p. 2). However, there is an appropriate time and place for the use of various technologies. According to Draft and Lengel"s media richness theory (MRT), which is largely based on the contingency and information processing theories, certain technologies may be more desirable than others due to the fact that a particular technology has a greater ability to reproduce the information that the user intended and "change understanding within a time interval" (Daft & Lengel, 1986). Institutions must be aware of what students and teachers may be losing during the informationexchange process when new technology is introduced—balance is essential, as some classroom situations do not warrant the use of technology (Gitlin, 2002, p. 31). MRT was originally designed by Daft and Lengel as a guide to achieve effective managerial communication (Sheer, 2010, p. 224). In this concept, various communication channels or media, have different levels of "richness," which is based on the following characteristics: The availability of instant feedback, which allows questions to be asked and corrections to be made

- The use of multiple cues, such as physical presence, voice inflection, body gestures, words, numbers, and graphic symbols

- The use of natural language, which can be used to convey an understanding of a broad set of concepts and ideas The personal focus of the medium (Sheer, 2010, p. 224)

- The more characteristics and to what extent a medium possesses each characteristic determines its richness.

Although TEL has changed drastically since Daft and Lengel"s development of MRT in the mid 1980s, the theory remains relevant, because new technology can provide similar characteristics on comparable levels in different ways (Daft and Lengel, 1986). In addition to changes in the situations that MRT is applicable, the understanding of the ways in which MRT can be applied has also changed since the theory was developed. In early studies, it was viewed exclusively as a characteristic of a medium, unchanging across users and situations. The ambiguity or equivocality of a situation determined the requirements for which a medium would be selected. This research, focused largely in the organizational context and primarily on managers, was essentially normative to the population. Later approaches proposed that media richness was more of a perception of characteristics and capacities as opposed to a stable feature. (Feaster, Dimmick, &

Ramirez, 2007, p. 2) Therefore, MRT can be used not only to explain which TEL programs may be more desirable in specific situations or environments, but also to reveal the most desirable TEL programs for individual users—students and teachers. The concept of media richness has been used by researchers in various disciplines, including communication, sociology, and psychology, to explain behavior—the decision to use one medium over another. Timmerman used MRT as a basis for understanding the difference between mindless and mindful use of technology within organizations (Timmerman, 2002). It was found that "the relationships between variables from [media richness theory] and media use were significantly greater when participants were in the mindful condition," as opposed to mindless use (Timmerman, 2002, p. 111). These findings can be applied to the recommended use of TEL programs in the classroom, meaning that TEL is more likely to be effective when users are mindful of the technology"s intended use throughout the duration of the program. Nowak and Rauh"s study of technology use to enhance communication also offers invaluable insight into understanding TEL. They found that while media features or characteristics must be considered when selecting technology, "social norms and rules influence how media are, and should be used" (Nowak & Rauh, 2004, p. 3). Sheer used the media richness theory to explain why adolescents in Hong Kong preferred using MSN instant messenger over ICQ instant messenger to develop friendships online (Sheer, 2010). Respondents using both MSN and ICQ perceived MSN as a richer IM that offered greater control than ICQ. MSN"s greater richness and control relative to

ICQ"s resulted in teenage users" spending more time and discussing various topics more frequently on MSN than on ICQ. Relative factors such as richness and control have led to better friendship quality on MSN than ICQ, but have not introduced differences in the number of friendships. (Sheer, 2010, p. 223) It is important to note that media richness does not necessarily mean that quantities will increase. In Sheer"s study, students did not form more friendships online with the richer technology, but the overall experience was enhanced (Sheer, 2010). The same applies for TEL programs. When TEL programs are selected based on qualities that may enhance learning processes or make them easier to integrate into existing curriculum, the result will not necessarily be an entire student body with above-average grades, but rather a richer, more enhanced learning experience—which is to say, overall academic performance.

Conceptual Framework

Input	Process	Output

1. What is the profile of the respondents in terms of?
 	
   1. Age
   2. Gender
   3. Educational Level
 	
2. How can technology be successfully integrated into the classroom of MLQSHS?
 	
3. What should MLQSHS avoid during the integration process to realize the potential effectiveness of the technology?
	4. How does the way in which information is presented affect students" ability to grasp and retain information?	5. What factors increase the likelihood of successful implementation of technology in the classroom and improved academic performance?

Statement of the Problem

Due to the recent surge of use of TEL systems in the classroom, research including long term observations and results of incorporating technology in the classroom are not available. Current research is limited to the almost immediate impact of the incorporation of technology in the classroom. The following research questions were designed to expand existing research concerning the subject matter of technology use in the classroom to increase learning:

1. What is the profile of the respondents in terms of?

    1. Age

    2. Gender

    3. Educational Level

2. How can technology be successfully integrated into the classroom of MLQSHS?

3. What should MLQSHS avoid during the integration process to realize the potential effectiveness of the technology?

4. How does the way in which information is presented affect students" ability to grasp and retain information?

5. What factors increase the likelihood of successful implementation of technology in the classroom and improved academic performance?

Significance of the Study

As technology is increasingly incorporated into curriculum in K-12 classrooms around the globe, understanding the implications of using TEL to achieve educational objectives becomes increasingly important. The last two decades have witnessed a worldwide proliferation of information and communication technologies (ICT) into the field of education. The global adoption of ICT into education has often been premised on the potential of the new technological tools to revolutionize an outmoded educational system, better prepare students for the information saga, and accelerate national development efforts. (Bordar, 2010, pp. 179-180) The cost of technology and educational platforms has also become increasingly inexpensive, which has made technology more universally accessible (Klein, 2010). The increased accessibility of technology means that schools around the world, with students from various socio-economic backgrounds, are increasingly exposed to TEL. Therefore, understanding the impact of TEL programs, and the best ways to integrate technology into the classroom, is critical. Previous research indicates that when used properly, technology can enhance the learning experience and increase academic performance. Whether technology in the classroom is beneficial is dependent upon the way in which the technology is used by teachers implementing the technology, teacher competency levels with the given technology, the degree to which the technology is utilized in the classroom, and the type of technology used (Sinclair, 2009). A meta analysis of more research on the topic can provide insight into the integration of TEL to ensure that learning is enhanced, and external factors that could impact TEL programs.

Scope and Limitation

There is a plethora of research available concerning the effect of technology in the classroom. As technological advances became more accessible to the common public in the second half of the 20th century, the availability of research on the topic has seemingly also increased exponentially. Although there is a wide array of material available, it appears as though the majority of studies analyze the immediate, rather than long-term, affect of technology in the classroom. What began as the analysis of the incorporation of simple technologies, such as digital cameras (Abbott & Shaikh, 2005) and low-tech computers (Sinclair, 2009), has developed into the analysis of the effect of more advanced learning systems, such as 3D multi-user virtual environment games (Mallan, et al., 2010; Yong & Ping, 2010).

Previously conducted research analyzed the effectiveness of one type of TEL to gauge whether the TEL program was effective. However, once it is determined that a type of TEL program can be successfully integrated to enhance academic performance, research seems to dissipate without further examination of why the TEL was effective, which could either be due to the type of technology used, or the type of technology used with a particular subject. Since technology is only a tool, certain tools may be used more efficiently to complete certain tasks (Honan, 2010).

Additionally, students may be able to learn a specific type of information easier with one type of tool versus another type of tool (Gitlin, 2002, p. 31).

Definition of Terms

- *Academic performance:* communication and collaboration skills, student motivation, and independent learning.

- *Contingency theory*: Suggests that no particular way to make decisions for, or organize an organization, is best for all because every organization is unique (Daft & Lengel, 1986).

- *Information and communication technology (ICT)*: Technology used as a tool to enhance learning (Bordbar, 2010).

- *Information processing theory:* A cognitive development theory that humans process, rather than simply respond to stimuli, which effects memory and application of information (Fischer, 2010).

- *K-12:* Students enrolled in school in Kindergarten through twelfth grades.

- *Media multitasking:* Using more than one medium at once (Kaiser Family Foundation, 2010).

- *Media richness theory (MRT):* A theory that suggests certain technologies may be more desirable when they feature characteristics that aid in the usability of the technology and dissemination of information (Daft & Lengel, 1986).

- *Meta-Analysis:* A research method that draws conclusions about the strength or consistency of communication effects across studies (Rubin, Rubin, Haridakis, & Piele, 2010).

- *Multi-user virtual environment (MUVE) games*: Gaming systems that enable multiple users to simultaneously participate in shared virtual environments (Mallan, Foth, Greenaway, & Young, 2010).

- *Technology enhanced learning (TEL):* Educational programs that incorporate various technologies with an objective of increasing learning (Dror, 2008).

CHAPTER II

RELATED LITERATURE AND STUDIES

The Literature

Current research on the effects of TEL on the academic performance of K-12 students is quite extensive and is comprised of studies spanning several decades. Due to the recent surge of the use of TEL in the classroom, research including long-term observations and results of incorporating technology in the classroom are not available. Although available research examines different types of TEL, the recommendations for the proper integration and utilization of TEL programs were generally consistent. The general consensus of the findings were that TEL does in fact increase overall academic performance for K-12 children, if properly integrated. Therefore, much of current research discusses the proper way to integrate TEL programs in the classroom and internal and external factors that may help or hinder the process. Analysis of current data, which offers additional insight into the effect of TEL on academic performance, is arranged in the following categories:

1) Teacher and administrator roles in TEL programs;

2) Learning with TEL programs; and

3) TEL and cultural considerations.

Teacher and Administrator Roles in TEL Programs Nearly 100 percent of public schools have Internet access in the United States, and incorporate other types of TEL into the curriculum (Tripp & Herr-Stephenson, 2009, p. 1190). Research has generally supported the notion of student learning being enhanced by the use of computer technology in their classroom activities. In fact, education has for decades, discussed this issue, and has concluded that greater learning would be taking place, if the classrooms had more computer technologies for both students and teachers. (Sinclair, 2006, p. 46)

However, the prevalence of TEL programs and the fact that it is believed that TEL can increase academic performance does not guarantee that these programs will be effective. While digital media and networked technology are increasingly prevalent in the lives of some young people, many still struggle to gain meaningful access to technology (Tripp & Herr-Stephenson, 2009, p. 1203). Due to improper, or lack of meaningful use, of technology in the classroom, "computers are not making the anticipated in roads into assisting students learning, as we previously believed" (Sinclair, 2009, p. 46). A resounding theme in the analyzed research was the pivotal role of teachers in the successful integration of technology into the classroom. A general consensus is that "the teacher"s role is critical in structuring activity in ways that challenge and build upon pupils" implicit conceptualizations, while integrating new scientific ideas" (Hennessy, et al., pp. 283-284). A lack of understanding on the part of teachers of how to use technology in the classroom and the purpose of the TEL program has resulted in TEL programs with lackluster results with minimal impact on overall academic performance. Sinclair"s (2009) summary of Dr. Harold Wenglinsky"s observation of the "One Computer Per Child" program in South Africa studied the link between teacher classroom practices and students" academic performance when TEL was incorporated into the curriculum, finding that the willingness of teachers and administrators to integrate technology into the classroom and learn how to use it competently has a profound impact on the successful integration of TEL programs (p. 47). Despite these findings, Sinclair found that "those teachers who use computers as instructional tools do so infrequently and unimaginatively" (p. 46). Current research, conducted between 2004 and 2010, reveals that the reason behind the infrequent and unimaginative use of technology in the classroom is not simply because teachers are resistant to change or unwilling to incorporate the technology into the classroom. To the

contrary, many teachers do not actually feel competent using the technology themselves or do not completely understand why the technology is being used and the best way to incorporate it into the existing curriculum (Sinclair, 2009; Bordbar, 2010; Venezky, 2004; Hennessy, Deaney, Ruthven, & Winterbottom, 2007). "…technology is used meaningfully when teachers have a good understanding of computer technology and believe that it has the power to influence learning" (Sinclair, 2009, p. 46). Therefore, a great deal of responsibility lies with school administrators to ensure that teachers receive the necessary training to understand how the technology works and how it will aid in students" learning process. However, "instead of formal professional development for teachers, teachers often use practically knowledge and previous experience with incorporating TEL into the classroom" (Bordbar, 2010, p. 181). For the successful integration of TEL, school administrators must first provide teachers who will be using the technology with clear educational objectives, as "poorly stated educational objectives, teachers" experiences and knowledge" increase the likelihood that the technology will not be utilized, or will be used improperly (Sinclair, 2009, p. 47). Another key misconception that the analyzed research reveals is the belief that teacher competency means that teachers must be able to use the technology at an expert level to successfully integrate it into existing curriculum (Sinclair, 2009, p. 48). This misconception has actually hindered the success of TEL programs and made administrators and teachers weary for two reasons: (1) fear that teachers will not be able to learn how to use the technology at an expert level; or (2) the training that would be needed to help teachers learn how to use the technology at an expert level would be too expensive and time consuming (Sinclair, 2009; Venezky, 2004). To the contrary Venezky"s (2004) research, which examines the use of the Internet in K12 classrooms, reveals that teachers must simply be proficient with the technology in order to

utilize it properly and to incorporate it into the curriculum (p. 15). Venezky"s work expands a model that was derived from the Apple Classrooms of Tomorrow (ACOT) program, which incorporates four stages of the integration process for teachers: survival, mastery, impact and innovation (p. 15). While the "mastery" stage could be translated as "expert," the ACOT program views the mastery stage as a point in which teachers understand how to use the technology and can also teach students how to use the technology to increase academic performance. Venezky"s research supports Sinclair"s findings that teachers do not have to expert technology users, but adequate training and support for teachers is critical, because it enables teachers to use the technology as a tool rather than becoming dependent on the technology, cr not

using it at all (2004). As teachers develop in technical competence, general

pedagogical abilities and ability to integrate ICT into the curriculum become more

important. In the innovation stage, the teacher restructures the curriculum and

learning activities, moving beyond the proposed procedures and content. Where a

core set of ICT applications are institutionalized within a school, teachers feel free to

adapt ICT to their own style of teaching. (Venezky, 2004, p. 15) While proper

training of the use of any technology that is incorporated into curriculum is essential,

too much focus on the technology can also be detrimental to the TEL program

(Abbott & Shaikh, 2005, p. 459). Abbott and Shaikh (2005) examined the effect of a

TEL program that incorporated the use of digital imaging technology into the

classroom. Digital imaging technology refers to the use of a digital camera and the

manipulation of the image with imageediting software (p. 455). In the year-long

study, elementary students in a multicultural, urban

area of the UK were taught how to use the technology, and the use of the technology

was incorporated into various academic activities. Abott and Shaikh"s (2005)

findings are as follows: Employing creative ways of learning across the curriculum

using digital technology facilitated greater pupil motivation and achievement in all

participating schools, [and] using digital cameras actively involved pupils in the

decision-making process and pupils took greater responsibility for aspects of their

own learning. (p. 457) Venezky"s research supports Abbott and Shaikh"s findings.

"ICT rarely acts as a catalyst by itself for schooling change yet can be a powerful lever for realizing planned educational innovations (Venezky, 2004, pp. 9-10). According to Venezky"s findings, "ICT can be used as a communication tool, an access path to resources, a facilitator of cooperative activities for teachers or students, or as a variety of other aids," but should essentially be viewed only as a learning tool (2004, p. 10). Therefore, utilizing the best available technologies will not necessarily result in increase academic performance for students. Teachers and administrators must find innovative ways to use technology to develop the most effective TEL programs (Abbott & Shaikh, 2005). School administrators must incorporate "careful planning, involvement of teachers in planning and implementation, [and] appropriate support for staff development" in order to increase the effectiveness of TEL programs (2004, p. 10). Learning with TEL Programs TEL can be effectively utilized in two ways in the classroom: "students learning „from" computers, and students learning „with" computers (Sinclair, 2009, p. 47). When students learn "from" TEL programs, they are learning about various technologies, "such as word processing programs, programming languages, or just exploring the Web" (2009, p. 47). When students learn "with" TEL programs, the "technologies become cognitive tools" (2009, p. 48). Further explanation of learning with TEL programs is as follows: When used as cognitive tools, computer technologies serve, and build students" social skills, cognitive perspective, tolerance, creativity and high order thinking skills. It is within this context that teachers should be able to use computers as agents of support-structures for students learning. It provides and supports fun, curiosity, academic independence and interdependence. (Sinclair, 2009, p. 47) The most successful TEL programs incorporate both aspects—learning from and with technology. However, in order for the program to reach its full potential and increase students" overall academic performance, students must be aware of which activities constitute learning from the technology that is used, and which activities constitute learning with the technology that is used (2009, pp. 47-48). Yong and Ping"s (2010) research, which is based on Yrjö Engeström"s Activity Theory, supports Sinclair"s findings. Basic principles of the Activity Theory are as follows:

Object-orientedness

- The hierarchical structure of activity

- Internalization-externalization with mental processes versus external behavior and interpsychological

- versus intra-psychological Mediation

- Development (p. 25)

- Yong and Ping used the Activity Theory to construct their study, which utilized the 3D MUVE game, Quest Atlantis, to help motivate academically at risk students (2010). While the TEL program did successfully motivate students to use the technology, there were some disturbances noted by teachers who participated in the program, which were attributed to the difference between the expectations of the teachers and that of the students (p. 26). Students successfully learned "from" the technology, by "learning of technology skills and learning of content knowledge," but began to use the technology for non-academic purposes that school administrators, teachers, and parents had not intended (pp. 29-30). Although students were aware of the purpose of the technology, they were naturally tempted to utilize it for other purposes. To rectify the situation of students" and teachers" conflict of interest, students were given more control to help them want to learn "with" the technology. After students become proficient in the use of the technology, the students were given more control of their individual learning. The "student-directed, game-based learning pedagogy" provided a sense of control over the learning process, which resulted in increased motivation to not only use the technology, but use it for its intended academic purpose (pp. 29-30). This student-directed learning approach also ensures that students view the technology as a tool rather than an object, which will help students focus on learning from and with the technology (p. 33). Hennessy et al."s (2007) research, which expounds upon Kenneth Rogoff"s framework of guided participation, supports these findings (p. 283-284). During guided participation, teachers provide students with lessons that include goals that students must reach to move on to the next level or lesson. Student participation is gradually increased as lessons are completed and technology competency increases until the student is largely responsible for his or her learning through increased participation (p. 284). The study examines the way in which teachers were able to effectively integrate the use of interactive whiteboards into the curriculum. Using the guided participation approach, students were given control over their individual learning, which resulted in increased motivation and independent learning (pp. 295-297). Herrington and Kervin (2007) also suggest that who utilizes the technology is more important than the actual technology. Technology presents the opportunity to employ powerful cognitive tools that can be used by students to solve complex and authentic problems. In order for this to occur, however, technology needs to be used in theoretically sound ways, and it needs to be used by students rather than teachers. (Herrington & Kervin, 2007, p. 220) Therefore, students" roles in TEL learning programs is to actively participate in the program and take a proactive role in their own individual learning. However, this is only possible if teachers receive the necessary training from school administrators to teach students how to use the technology in a way that will increase overall academic performance through innovative methods, such as guided participation. TEL and Cultural Considerations Although there were geographical differences in the aforementioned research, location seemed to have no bearing on the impact of TEL programs, as researchers found similar results in an array of geographical locations—the United States, United Kingdom, South Africa, Australia, and Hong Kong. Research was also conducted in urban, rural, affluent, and povertystricken communities, which also did not have a bearing on the effectiveness of TEL programs. However, a commonality between the studies was the focus on culture—not only the culture of individual students, but the culture of the schools integrating the technology as well. Cultural differences do not necessarily change the effectiveness of TEL, but can change certain aspects of the TEL programs, such as the technology used, training, and implementation time. Therefore, a

TEL program that was successful in one school may have completely different results in seemingly similar academic environments (Hayes, 2006). Researchers emphasize that students" cultural differences can impact the approach school administrators and teachers should take when implementing TEL, as well as what kind of TEL should be used. "Social norms and rules influence how media are, and should be used," (Nowak & Rauh, 2004, p. 5). Understanding social norms and rules, key aspects of culture, can help school administrators select technology that is more likely to increase student academic performance. Selwyn"s (2006) study of in-school Internet use of children in the UK found that there was often a "digital disconnection between emerging generations of technology-rich students accustomed to high levels of Internet use and their technology-poor schools" (p. 5). Many K-12 children lead technology-centered lives. This increased exposure has resulted in the need for the use of more advanced technology in the classroom (Selwyn, 2006). To the contrary, Selwyn found that school administrators and teachers often select TEL tools based on the current competency levels of teachers and administrators, rather than selecting the most effective technology for teaching students and then learning how to use the technology themselves. The end result is a disconnection between students and teachers, which can inhibit the learning process (Selwyn, 2006). Similarly, Bulfin and North (2007) conducted an ethnographic case study of Australian adolescents" technology use in contrasting schools. The researchers found that "young people"s language practices and their engagement with various forms of digital culture do not belong to separate domains," (2007, p. 248). Students were more engaged in the learning process when technological skills that are developed at home and other avenues outside of school were also exercised in the classroom (2007). Creating a

distinction between the technology practices of

students non-academic lives and the way technology is used in academic settings is

not conducive to increased learning or academic performance (2007, p. 248).

Therefore, TEL programs should incorporate technology at a level that is suitable for

the majority of students, rather than at levels reflecting teacher competency. Many

schools are comprised of students from different socio-economic statuses, which

could also affect the level of technology exposure students have outside of the

classroom. Therefore, it cannot be assumed that all students require the use of

advanced technology in the classroom. However, as previously mentioned, according

to Dr. Wenglinsky"s study of the "One Computer Per Child" program, socio-

economic factors do not affect to the effectiveness of TEL systems in the classroom

(Sinclair, 2009). When children have varying degrees of technology exposure outside

of the classroom, it is the responsibility of teachers and school administrators to

effectively teach students how to use the technology in a manner that all students

understand its use and can use it proficiently. If time constraints prevent proper

teacher or student training prior to the implementation of technology, administrators

should consider the use of alternative TEL tools (Herrington & Kervin, 2007). In

order to make these decisions, an understanding of student culture is critical. In

addition to cultural influences of individual students, institutional culture should also

be considered when deciding whether to integrate TEL programs into curriculum, as

well as what type of technology is appropriate (Herrington & Kervin, 2007, p. 219).

School administrators should evaluate the school"s existing culture as well as its ideal culture prior to the incorporation of any technology into curriculum, because the integration of TEL programs is likely to change the culture, regardless of intent. "Technology creates its own imperatives and, at

the same time, creates a wide-ranging social system to reinforce its imperative," (Beniger, 1989, p. 105). Venezky"s (2004) research of 94 case studies of K-12 schools that successfully implemented TEL programs in 23 countries supports the concept of the influence of technology on school culture. Technology has the power to alter the learning environment, which could temporarily or permanently transform school culture (2004). A technology that allows every student to advance at his or her own pace in a selected subject may have many applications for lifelong learning and for selected skills at other levels. However, its potential for transforming K-12 education is near zero. (Venezky, 2004, p. 4) It may be advantageous for schools with a culture of being on the cutting edge of technology to select advanced TEL programs, while schools with an undefined technology culture may want to select tools that can be easily integrated into existing curriculum. However, this does not mean that the same TEL tools are appropriate for schools with similar cultures as each institution has unique characteristics that may make certain technologies more desirable than others (Hayes, 2006). Therefore, school administrators and teachers must take a systematic approach when selecting TEL tools to ensure the technology is aligned with the institution"s goals (Venezky, 2004).

AN ANALYSIS OF CHANGING PRICE BY TAX REFORM LAW UNDUR

PRESEDENT RODRIGO ROA DUTERTE

A research paper presented to the faculty of

practical research in Manuel L. Quezon

Senior High School

Submitted by:

Charles Julian B. Cruz

Submitted to:

Dr. Mark Vincent B. Emit

March 2018

CHAPTER I

THE PROBLEM AND ITS BACKGROUND

Background of the Study

President Duterte finally signed into law the tax reform bill earlier on Tuesday, December 19, 2017. The Tax Reform for Acceleration and Inclusion bill (TRAIN) will overhaul the country's 20 year old tax structure, to make the tax system fairer and simpler. The first package of the tax reform bill will be implemented in January 2018, giving more disposable income to every working Filipino who are paying their taxes.

Current tax rates In a nutshell, the Philippines has one of the highest tax rates in Southeast Asia. For one, the corporate tax in the country is 30%, which is applied to all net incomes from the entire tax table sources. Compared to other countries in the region, 30% is extremely steep (refer to the comparison table below). This can be accounted as one of the major factors why foreign investors prefer to do business elsewhere instead of the Philippines. On the other hand, at 32% for the highest income bracket, personal income tax rate is not the highest in the region (which is only next to Vietnam and Thailand at 35%), but it's still in the top three. Below is a complete overview of the progressive personal income tax rates in the Philippines.

The Comprehensive Tax Reform Package of the Department of Finance is part of the Dutertenomics. It aims to provide relief to 99% of the tax paying workers in the Philippines by reducing their monthly income taxes (lessening the overall tax burden of the poor and the middle class). It will redesign the tax system in the country to make it fairer, more efficient, and simpler. At the same time, it's going to help the government raise the resources that it needs to invest further in the country's infrastructure and people.

On the other hand, while it brings down the income tax obligation of all working individuals, it will raise the excise of fuel. his new tax reform is good news for low-income and middle-income earners in the country, which is the majority of the population. The proposed tax reform will be gradually decreasing on the coming years and it will be implemented immediately in 2018 up until 2019. The tax income on 2020 and onwards are expected to be even lower!

Theoretical framework

Maslow's hierarchy of needs is a motivational theory in psychology comprising a five-tier model of human needs, often depicted as hierarchical levels within a pyramid. Maslow (1943, 1954) stated that people are motivated to achieve certain needs and that some needs take precedence over others. Our most basic need is for physical survival, and this will be the first thing that motivates our behavior. Once that level is fulfilled the next level up is what motivates us, and so on.

This five-stage model can be divided into deficiency needs and growth needs. The first four levels are often referred to as deficiency needs (D-needs), and the top level is known as growth or being needs (B-needs).Deficiency needs arise due to deprivation and are said to motivate people when they are unmet. Also, the motivation to fulfill such needs will become stronger the longer the duration they are denied. For example, the longer a person goes without food, the more hungry they will become.

Maslow (1943) initially stated that individuals must satisfy lower level deficit needs before progressing on to meet higher level growth needs. However, he later clarified that satisfaction of a needs is not an"all-or-none" phenomenon, admitting that his earlier statements may have given "the false impression that a need must be satisfied 100 percent before the next need emerges" (1987, p. 69). When a deficit need has been 'more or less' satisfied it will go away, and our activities become habitually directed towards meeting the next set of needs that we have yet to satisfy. These then become our salient needs. However, growth needs continue to be felt and may even become stronger once they have been engaged.

Growth needs do not stem from a lack of something, but rather from a desire to grow as a person. Once these growth needs have been reasonably satisfied, one may be able to reach the highest level called self-actualization. Every person is capable and has the desire to move up the hierarchy toward a level of self-actualization. Unfortunately, progress is often disrupted by a failure to meet lower level needs. Life experiences, including divorce and loss of a job, may cause an individual to fluctuate between levels of the hierarchy. Therefore, not everyone will move through the hierarchy in a uni-directional manner but may move back and forth between the different types of needs.

1. Biological and physiological needs - air, food, drink, shelter, warmth, sex, sleep.

2. Safety needs - protection from elements, security, order, law, stability, freedom from fear.

3. Love and belongingness needs - friendship, intimacy, trust, and acceptance, receiving and giving affection and love. Affiliating, being part of a group (family, friends, work).

4. Esteem needs - which Maslow classified into two categories: (i) esteem for oneself (dignity, achievement, mastery, independence) and (ii) the desire for reputation or respect from others (e.g., status, prestige). Maslow indicated that the need for respect or reputation is most important for children and adolescents and precedes real self-esteem or dignity.

5. Self-actualization needs - realizing personal potential, self-fulfillment, seeking personal growth and peak experiences. A desire "to become everything one is capable of becoming"(Maslow, 1987, p. 64).

Conceptual Framework

This study used I.P.O model. The I.P.O model shows the input, process and output of the research. The step to solve any problem of conducting is called process. The output is the findings of research or results.

According to Business Dictionary, which can be accessed throughhttp://www.businessdictionary.com/definition/input-process-output-diagram.html, a graphical representation of all the factors that make up a process? An input-process-output diagram includes all of the materials and information required for the process, details of the process itself, and descriptions of all products and by-products resulting from the process.

Input	Process	Output

Input	Process	Output

1. What is the profile of respondents?
    1.1 ABM
    1.2 GAS
2. How does train law affects the following?
    2.1 Consumers
    2.2 Producers
    2.3 General Economy
	3. Is there a significant difference between the effects of train law?	4. Based on the findings, what can be recommended?

Statement of the Problem

1. What is the profile of respondents?

    1.1 ABM

    1.2 GAS

2. How does train law affects the following?

    2.1 Consumers

    2.2 Producers

2.3 General Economy

3. Is there a significant difference between the effects of train law?

4. Based on the findings, what can be recommended?

Hypothesis

H_o: There is no significant difference between the effects of train law

Significance of the Study

The researchers are truly believed that this study has significance to the following variables:

Students. This study may help the students to gain knowledge regarding TRAIN law

Teachers. This study will use by the teachers to spread their experiences on how TRAIN law affects them as a teacher.

Parents. This will be used by the parents to share their knowledge and experiences to became aware their children and students about TRAIN law

Scope and limitation

This study scoped the information that gathered by the researchers that may add some knowledge to the readers regarding TRAIN Law. The researcher was interview their selected respondents inside Manuel L. Quezon Senior High School.

This study has a limitation because the students and teachers only in Manuel

L. Quezon Senior High School are involved. The researchers believe that this research will know and focus on An analysis of changing price or Train law by Prseident Rodrigo Roa Duterte.

Definition of Terminologies

TARIN law. Tax Reform for Acceleration and Inclusion (TRAIN) Act, the first package of the Comprehensive Tax Reform Program

Consumer. a person who purchases goods and services for personal use.

Producer. a person responsible for the financial and managerial aspects of making of a movie or broadcast or for staging a play, opera, etc.

General Economy. the wealth and resources of a country or region, especially in terms of the production and consumption of goods and services.

CHAPTER II

RELATED STUDY AND LITERATURE

Related Literature

According to Chrisee Dela Paz (2018) MANILA, Philippines – Royd Agapito (not his real name), a 25-year-old market analyst for a research firm, got what he wanted: higher take-home pay. But what he did not expect is a higher monthly household bill that would offset the gains he would receive from the newly-implemented Tax Reform for Acceleration and Inclusion (TRAIN) law. The administration of President Rodrigo Duterte started 2018 by implementing TRAIN, which reduced personal income taxes but increased those on cars, tobacco, sugar-sweetened beverages, and fuel.

Payroll managers have started adjusting their systems to reflect the new withholding tax rates. Supermarkets, oil retailers, convenience stores, and even sidewalk vendors have begun updating their price lists. A visit to Puregold supermarket on Monday, January 8, showed that a pack of Marlboro Black 20s is more expensive now at P87.50, from last year's P68. gapito, who earns P30,000 monthly, will save P3,438 a month because of the new withholding tax rates. But he said he decided to stick to his old Toyota Vios instead of upgrading to a new car, given the hike in auto excise tax, which mainly hit mass market vehicles. (READ: Honda Philippines raises prices for most cars due to tax reform) "I don't think TRAIN will provide significant impact to an average wage earner. It is like the government is just giving us a new perspective to look at our taxes. You have higher pay, but electricity, transport, grocery bills will also be higher," Agapito said in an interview.

He added that he would also need to cut down on soda to save money. (READ: Existing stocks of sweetened drinks exempt from new tax rates – DTI) Starting mid-January, the retail price of a one-liter bottle of Coca-Cola, for instance, is projected to increase to P43 from the current P31, an increase of P12. This is because of the P12-per-liter tax on drinks using high fructose corn syrup. For drinks using sugar and artificial sweeteners, a P6-per-liter tax has been imposed. However, all kinds of milk, 3-in-1 coffee, natural fruit juices, vegetable juices, and medically-indicated beverages are exempt.

Additional burden While power distributors, oil companies, fuel retailers, and tobacco manufacturers are directly affected by TRAIN, First Metro Investments Corporation vice president Cristina Ulang said they have one thing going for them. "The additional burden is something they can pass on to consumers," Ulang explained. This, however, does not hold true for small-time vendors in the Philippines, like 48-year-old Meanne Reyes, who has two kids. Reyes, who sells sugar-sweetened drinks, snacks, and tobacco along Amang Rodriguez Avenue in Pasig City, said she has fewer stocks due to TRAIN. "Dati P5 per stick lang 'yung Marlboro. Ngayon binebenta ko na ng P7 isa. Dahil mas mahal na 'yung pakete, binawasan ko na lang 'yung pagbili ko ng supplies. Ang taas nang itinaas. Paano naman kaming walang suweldo at pagbebenta ang kabuhayan?" Reyes asked. (Marlboro used to be P5 per stick. Now I'm selling it for P7 each. Since an entire pack is now more expensive, I was forced to buy fewer supplies. The price hike is significant. What will happen to people like me who have no fixed income and depend on sidewalk vending to earn a living?)

Protecting from impact To protect the poor from higher prices of commodities, Finance Secretary Carlos Dominguez III said the Department of Social Welfare and Development (DSWD) is mandated to provide targeted cash transfers to the poorest 10 million households. Each household would get P2,400 per year in 2018, as well as P3,600 per year in 2019 and 2020. Dominguez said the cash transfer will be implemented in the 1st quarter of 2018. "DSWD will identify beneficiaries based on the [list] – the Pantawid Pamilyang Pilipino Program and the social pension beneficiaries. The budget for the unconditional cash transfer is included in the 2018 budget, totaling P25.7 billion," the finance chief said in a Malacañang briefing. Over the course of 5 years, Dominguez said the government will raise over P786 billion in revenues because of TRAIN.

"These revenues will fund the President's priorities: social and infrastructure programs. In package one, Congress passed two-thirds of the needed revenue for 2018 and this is expected to pass the balance in early 2018 to help us achieve our revenue deficit targets," he said. The finance chief added that the 2nd package of the comprehensive tax reform program, which is set to be passed within the month, is seen to lower corporate income taxes and modernize fiscal incentives. All in all, Dominguez said the government targets to raise about P2 trillion from the comprehensive tax reform program to help fund the country's massive P8-trillion infrastructure buildup, which is seen to improve people's lives from all ranks.

According to Dharel Placido (2018) The positive effects of the new tax reform program will outweigh the price hikes that will result from it, Malacañang said Monday. Taxes on certain goods such as fuel will be hiked starting this year, but the government has prepared certain measures to cushion the blow on consumers, Palace Communications Secretary Martin Andanar said to assuage citizen fears of price increases from the passage into law of the Tax Reform for Acceleration and Inclusion (TRAIN). Critics of the tax reform program have warned that while the measure lowers the personal income tax, among others, it will trigger spike in prices of some basic goods and services. "Mas lumalaki po iyong pakinabang, mas malaki po. It outweighs—the positive… The pros outweigh vis-à-vis the TRAIN Law pagka't 'pag mayroon pong malilikom na mas malaking buwis ang ating gobyerno, ito po ay mapupunta rin sa iba't ibang investments ng ating gobyerno at iba't ibang mga proyekto," Andanar said in a radio interview.

Andanar said more jobs will be created as a result of the investments funded by the revenues collected from the tax reform program. He said the government will also distribute a P200 monthly financial assistance to those most affected by the consumer price hike in the first year of the implementation of the tax reform program. This will be raised to P300 in the second and third years. Andanar, meanwhile, said the government welcomes criticisms against the tax reform package, which is expected to create P90 billion in revenues in the first year of its implementation. "Kasama naman 'yan sa demokrasya – iyong mga tumutuligsa, iyong mga critics, and of course kailangan po ay nandiyan ho talaga 'yan, to also keep us in our toes," he said. "Saka 'pag wala po 'yan eh, hindi ho maganda iyong ating demokrasya, kapag hindi po natin hinahayaan ang ating mga kritiko at iyong mga kalaban sa pulitika na tayo po ay i-criticize… iyon ho talaga iyon."

Accordin g to Denisse Shawntel Tan (2018) Last December 19, 2017, President Rodrigo Roa Duterte signed the newly implemented Tax Reform for Acceleration and Inclusion (TRAIN). It officially took effect on the first day of January 2018. The TRAIN aims to simplify the tax system and make it fairer. Under this law, minimum wage earners or those with an annual income not exceeding PhP250,000 are exempted from income tax, hence increasing their take-home pay. From 2018 up to 2022, those earning over PhP250,000 up to PhP400,000 annually will have a tax rate of 20% of the excess over P250,000. While those who earn PhP400,000 to PhP800,000 annually will have a tax rate of PhP30,000 plus 25% of the excess over PhP400,000. Individuals who earn over PhP800,000 to PhP2,000,000 will be taxed PhP130,000 plus a tax rate of 30% of the excess over PhP800,000.

Lastly, those with an annual income of PhP2,000,000 to PhP8,000,000 will have to pay PhP490,000 plus a tax rate of 32% of the excess over PhP2,000,000. If exceeding PhP8,000,000, the tax rate to be paid is PhP2,410,000 plus 35% of the excess over PhP8,000,000. The tax rates will gradually decrease after 2022. However, consumers should brace themselves for the consecutive price hikes of several consumer goods such as tobacco, sweetened beverages, petroleum products, cosmetic procedures, and automobiles as a price increase for these items will offset the lowered tax. An increase of PhP6.00 per liter is sought for beverages with caloric and non-caloric sweeteners, while those with high-fructose corn syrup will have an increase of PhP12.00 per liter. Meanwhile, milk, instant and ground coffee, meal replacement and medically indicated drinks, and drinks that use coco sugar and stevia are exempted from the increase. Several establishments that serve unlimited drinks such as S&R have already stopped their unlimited soda promo in accordance to the sugar tax reform law under TRAIN. Other food commodities that are expected to have a price increase are canned sardines, instant noodles, powdered milk, loaf bread, detergent soap, and coffee refill. These will have a price increase that ranges from 4 to 14 centavos.

According to the computation of the Department of Trade and Industry (DTI), an adjustment range of 4 to 7 centavos can be applied to meatloaf and toilet soap. These computations were derived from factors such as the impact of TRAIN on the transportation and production costs of manufacturers. Meanwhile, fuel price will rise by PhP2.50 per liter in 2018 and will increase by PhP4.50 and PhP6.00 in 2019 and 2020 respectively. For gasoline, there would be a PhP7.00 increase in 2018 and this will go up to PhP9.00 and PhP10.00 per liter in 2019 and 2020 correspondingly. The increased fuel price might make an impact on commuters as fare hikes might be imposed. Jeepney drivers organizations are petitioning for a PhP2.00 or PhP4.00 increase in the minimum fare, while taxi drivers are proposing a PhP50.00 flag-down rate instead of the usual PhP40.00. Transportation Network Vehicle Services (TNVS) company Grab is also planning on submitting a petition to the Land Transportation Franchising Regulatory Board (LTFRB) to ask for a six to ten percent increase from the current fares of Grab cars. Through a domino effect, the prices of local and imported meats would also be affected by the fuel price increase, since transporting these products would use fuel. Meanwhile, Manila Electric Company (MERALCO), the country's leading power supplier, said that consumers should brace themselves for the potential impact of the new tax reform on their monthly bills.

The tax rate of vehicles is also covered in the reform law. Automobiles valued up to PhP600,000 will have a 4% tax rate increase from the previous 2%. On the other hand, 10% will be imposed on vehicles amounting to PhP600,000 to PhP1,000,000; 20% for over PhP1,000,000 up to PhP4,000,000; and 50% of excess over PhP4,000,000. Electric cars and pickups are exempted. Hybrid cars will be taxed half the rates. Smokers can also expect a PhP32.50 increase in tobacco products during the first six months of 2018. Then it will be increased to PhP35.00 from July 2018 to December 31, 2019. After 24 months, it will increase to 37.50 per pack. Meanwhile, a 5% price increase will be applied to cosmetic procedures, surgeries, and aesthetic enhancements. A flat rate of 6% will be allocated on estate tax, while family homes valued up to PhP10,000,000 are exempted from estate tax. 70% of the collected excise tax will fund several of President Duterte's planned infrastructure products while the remaining 30% will be used on the improvement of health, education, targeted nutrition and anti-hunger programs for mothers and children. Along with these are the prioritization of housing, employment, and social protection programs inclined for the poor.

According to Lenie Lectura (2017) CONSUMERS must brace for higher power rates following the passage of the first tax-reform package into law. On December 19 President Duterte signed into law the Tax Reform for Acceleration and Inclusion (TRAIN) bill. The TRAIN law, or Republic Act 10963, is expected to generate P130 billion in revenues. Seventy percent of the revenues will finance the administration's "Build, Build, Build" infrastructure program, while the remaining 30 percent will fund socioeconomic programs. Moreover, the law is expected to reduce personal income tax. "I hope it brings development and progress to our country for the benefit of all," Energy Secretary Alfonso G. Cusi said in a text message on the day the bill was signed. While the TRAIN law will surely bring in revenues, it will, however, impose higher taxes on fuel, cars, tobacco and sugary beverages.

Based on available figures, the initial impact of on power rates will reach P0.04 per kilowatt-hour (kWh). It will then increase to P0.07 per kWh if excise tax on coal reaches P150 per metric ton. Overall, the total impact is P13.2 billion worth of pass-on charges to the consumers. A Senate Ways and Means Committee briefer said the P10 coal-excise tax rate has remained unchanged since 1988, while the local industry has been exempted from paying excise tax since 1976.

Prepare for the worst Manila Electric Co. (Meralco), the country's largest power-distribution firm, said all it could do for now is to "prepare our consumers." Company spokesman Joe Zaldarriaga said Meralco has stated in the past its position about the issue. Preparation, he said, includes a massive information campaign on the impact on power rates. "We really need to prepare our consumers on the rate impact, including possible adjustments in the FIT [feed-in-tariff] and universal charges starting next year," Zaldarriaga said when sought for comment. In its letter addressed to Sen. Edgardo J. Angara, chairman of the Senate Committee on Ways and Means, Meralco said any move toward increasing excise tax on coal would impact significantly on electricity consumers across all sectors—residential, commercial and industrial.

Since more than 50 percent of the country's gross domestic product (GDP) comes from Meralco's franchise area, increasing the excise tax on coal would already be felt by end-users and may reduce competitiveness of industries that are competing in the world market, as well with imports. "Coal is a major fuel source for power generation in the country. Increasing the existing excise tax on coal will only result in higher electricity prices, which will reduce the country's competitiveness vis-à-vis Asean neighbors," said Meralco First Vice President and head of Regulatory Management Office Ivanna de la Peña. Meralco's 6.2 million customers comprise around one-fourth of the Philippine population. Abotiz Power Corp. President Antonio Moraza, in a text message, also said consumers should face the inevitable.

"I am sure the government is happy with the results. They raised a substantial amount of money," Moraza said. "For the private sector, opinions will differ, for sure. In our case, unfortunately, power rates will go up." AboitizPower is the holding company for the Aboitiz Group's investments in power generation, distribution and retail electricity services. It also owns distribution utilities that operate in high-growth areas in Luzon, the Visayas and Mindanao, including the second- and third-largest private utilities in the country. The power firm is on track to meeting its 4,000-megawatt (MW) net attributable capacity target by 2020. It is set to add some 500 MW of attributable capacity next year. Moreza said the additional power projects are on track and should be mostly online in the first half of 2018. For Alsons Consolidated Resources Inc. (ACR), company vice president for business development Joseph Nocos stressed that coal still accounts for a significant portion of the power generated in the country because of its reliability and affordability.

"Given the crucial role that coal plays in the power industry, it is imperative for us and our fellow power generators to closely study the implications of this new tax measure," Nocos said in a text message. Alsons's power projects are in Mindanao. It operates three diesel power facilities: the 103-MW Mapalad Power Corp. diesel plant in Iligan City, the 55-MW Southern Philippines Power Corp. facility in Alabel, Sarangani, and the 100-MW power plant of the Western Mindanao Power Corp. in Zamboanga City. Three more power projects are set for construction by the middle of 2018. These are the second 105-MW coal plant of Sarangani Energy Corp.(SEC) , the 105-MW San Ramon Power Inc. (SRPI) base-load coal-fired power plant in Zamboanga City and the 15.1-MW Siguil hydropower project in Sarangani Province. Once finished, these three projects will bring ACR's power-generation portfolio to around 588 MW of generating capacity, which is approximately 25 percent of

Mindanao's projected peak power demand in 2021. Meanwhile, Semirara Mining and Power Corp. (SMPC), the country's largest coal producer, said the tax adjustment should cover all types of fuel."If coal should have additional tax then natural gas should be taxed, as well," DMCI Holdings Chairman Isidro Consunji said in a text message.

SMPC is a subsidiary of DMCI. "In the short run, it favors Semirara," Consunji added. "Our contract specifies we are exempt from all taxes except income tax until end of our coal operating contract." Meanwhile, the National Electrification Administration (NEA) also expressed grave concern. The NEA chief feared the proposal to raise the coal tax would lead to higher electricity rates. "I believe this will discourage investors in putting up generation facilities that are not friendly to environment," NEA chief Edgardo Masongsong said. "With more than 50 percent of energy source coming from coal, I am afraid we will be paying more for our electricity consumption."

Pass-on SEN. Sherwin T. Gatchalian, chairman of the Senate Committee on Energy, said the excise tax would become a "pure pass-on charge," resulting to an additional P13.2 billion in electricity costs that consumers inevitably would have to shoulder. "Despite my affirmative vote, I would like to put on record that I still maintain my reservations regarding the massive increase in the excise tax on coal that has made it into the final version of the law for the President's signature," Gatchalian said. The two chambers of Congress agreed on a compromise tax rate of P150 per metric ton on coal, divided into tranches over the next three years upon its enactment. This means the excise tax would be P50 per metric ton in 2018, P100 in 2019 and P150 in 2020. The original Senate version proposed a "100-200-300" hike scheme.

Gatchalian explained the negative implications of the tax hike. "The tax hike up to P150 after three years will result in an average monthly rate increase of P14.348 for a 200-kWh household served by a 100-percent coal-contracted distribution utility," he said. "This is equivalent to the price of half a kilogram of rice for 2.7 million households," While proponents of the coal-tax increase may downplay it as negligible, Gatchalian pointed out that Filipinos are already struggling through the pain of paying the highest power rates in Southeast Asia. With this, Gatchalian stresses its supporters "miss the point entirely." Meawnhile, Laban Konsyumer Inc. President Vic Dimagiba appeals to businessmen never to take advantage of the looming higher excise taxes by manipulating a supply situation on basic goods and services with the end in view of creating windfall profits for themselves.

"Consumers deserve protection of their universal right of access to goods and services at justified prices," Dimagiba said. "Thus, we enjoin government agencies…to protect and safeguard the well-being of the consumers and strengthen monitoring and enforcement activities and file cases against businessmen who may commit profiteering and hoarding at the expense of the consumers." The consumer group, he added, may take legal action to question the legality of the higher excise tax.

How to mitigate power-rate hikes ON the other hand, higher excise tax on coal will promote the development of renewable energy (RE) sources. "It should be favorable for RE," said SN Aboitiz Power President President Joseph Yu, who agreed that the tax adjustment will encourage the utilization of RE in the country. He said that for those who are not using coal as fuel, this will "have a lifting effect on profitability, which will then make RE projects more viable."

The power-generation arm of Meralco is "seriously" looking at venturing into wind energy, amid an impending rise in coal taxes.

"We've been asked to look at wind proposals," Meralco PowerGen Corp. (MGen) CEO Rogelio Singson said. "When coal tax kicks in, wind will be competitive."

Meanwhile, Gatchalian called on the DOE to fast-track the implementation of the Retail Competition and Open Access (RCOA) circular to mitigate the effects of projected electricity-rate hikes.

The circular, which seeks to finally implement the RCOA provision of the 16-year-old Electric Power Industry Reform Act of 2001 (Epira), is expected to foster competition among electricity suppliers by giving consumers the freedom to select from where and what kind of electricity to purchase. This is expected to drive down electricity costs and promote transparency in the energy sector.

"With the coal tax in place, all the more that we need to implement RCOA to democratize our power sector. The RCOA will help lower costs to protect consumers from the inflationary effects of the coal tax," Gatchalian said. "Once you give the consumers the power of choice, they can choose whether they want coal, renewable energy or geothermal, whichever is cheaper for them."

The lawmaker reiterated the expected impact of the coal tax on consumers. He estimates an increase of P10 in the monthly electricity bills of average households in 2018, P20 by 2019 and P28 by 2020, noting that these estimates are bound to grow as new coal plants come online in the near future.

The DOE, meanwhile, assured that the legal hurdles of RCOA will be settled as soon as the revised circular is approved by the Energy Regulatory Commission and signed by the agency's secretary. "I highly commend the Department of Energy for its initiative to implement RCOA," Gatchalian said. "Our end goal here is to drive down the price of electricity for the benefit of energy consumers."

The National Renewable Energy Board (NREB), the advisory body tasked with the effective implementation of RE projects in the Philippines, meanwhile, commented that the government needs to fully implement the mandate of the RE Act of 2008, which include the issuance of the rules on Renewable Portfolio Standards (RPS) for on-grid and off-grid areas and Green Energy Option Program.

The RPS requires distribution utilities (DUs) to source a portion of their power supply from eligible RE sources. The Green Energy Option, meanwhile, is a mechanism to provide end-users the option to choose RE as their source of energy.

"NREB already endorsed all three draft rules for approval of the DOE," NREB Chairman Jose Layug said. "NREB is set to endorse the RE market rules to the DOE for approval by the end of the year after finishing the public consultation."

Yes to higher coal taxes

ENVIRONMENT advocates like members of Greenpeace laud the members of the Senate and the House of Representatives for pushing efforts toward what they say is "a fairer tax scheme on coal."

"We will continue to work with partners to expose the true costs of coal, and to empower communities and the government in transforming our energy systems to renewable sources, which are the real cheaper, safer and cleaner alternatives," Greenpeace said in a statement. "The vision is to power the country's development with 100-percent renewable energy."

The group added, "While the tax adjustment is a historic victory, the fight is far from over in ending the age of coal and limiting global temperature increase to 1.5 degrees Celsius."

"We owe this to every Filipino who are at the forefront of climate impacts. And the coal industry still owes a lot."

Meanwhile, WWF-Philippines said the passage of the coal-tax hike is necessary to help protect Filipinos and environment from the devastating impacts of coal consumption.

"Companies need to embrace sustainability as a business imperative," said Angela Consuelo Ibay, WWF-Philippines head of climate and energy program.

"Extreme weather events, climate disasters, resource depletion, ecosystem loss and pollution can cause major disruptions on businesses' value chain and productivity, and can debilitate our economy."

According to the group, they believe that "taxing coal and other fossil fuels is a way of climate-proofing our assets and industries."

"Consumers have become more socially and environmentally aware and demand companies to make lasting contributions to our people and planet's overall well-being."

The group said that the coal tax pooled together with fossil-fuel taxes from diesel, kerosene and natural gas can bring valuable fiscal benefits for the country.

"Why do we continue to allow the dirtiest fossil fuel to enjoy exemptions from taxes, which they have been enjoying for more than 30 years?" Ibay added. "Our people deserve better."

According to Rhick Lars Vladimer Albay (2018) ILOILO City – The Department of Trade and Industry (DTI) Region 6 is girding for the full impact of the Tax Reform for Acceleration and Inclusion (TRAIN) Law, as it closely monitors the prices of prime commodities in Western Visayas

"[DTI] secretary [Ramon Lopez] is warning all of us to look and closely monitor the suggested retail prices (SRP) of products and services in the region, because as of this time wala pa dapat price increases," related DTI OIC-regional director Rebecca Rascon on Friday.

Rascon further explained that the higher excise taxes under TRAIN should only be implemented on basic and prime commodities produced and acquired from Jan. 1, 2018 onwards – hence old buffer stocks should not be subject to price hikes. "Ang amun instruction from the head office is to closely monitor basic and prime commodities and their SRPs in the outlets, be it supermarkets or grocery stores," explained the Trade official.

"Sa subong may mga inventories pa, so what we see in the outlets and shelves of supermarkets and grocery stores are old stock, [because] usually may buffer ang dealers and distributors, even ang manufacturers, [so as of now] dapat wala pa effect ang TRAIN on prices."

However, Rascon sees that Western Visayas consumers may begin to experience the full impact of TRAIN's higher excise taxes on Jan. 15 – as the old stock from last year starts to be depleted.DTI secretary Lopez earlier dismissed fears of consumers on the impact of TRAIN on prices of basic goods. Lopez said in a press conference Thursday that the new tax law imposing excise taxes has minimal effect on prices of basic commodities. He said that based on computation of economists and even the DTI, the excise tax on fuel will hike prices of goods by less than one percent. From DTI's computation, the new law only translates 0.4 percent increase in prices of goods.

According to a table of adjusted prices released by DTI, a 50-gram pouch of instant coffee is set to increase only by P0.08 – from P39.40 to P39.48. Meanwhile, 150-gram powdered milk will see a hike from P50 to P50.10, as instant noodles go up from P7.30 to P7.33./PN IAN PAUL CORDERO/PN Jhoanna Ballaran (2018) An economic expert criticized on Saturday the government's downplaying of the effects of the Tax Reform for Acceleration and Inclusion (Train) Law, warning that the measure could bring dire effects to the economy. An economic expert criticized on Saturday the government's downplaying of the effects of the Tax Reform for Acceleration and Inclusion (Train) Law, warning that the measure could bring dire effects to the economy.

Ibon Foundation Executive Director Sonny Africa took a swipe at the Department of Finance's (DOF) "deceitful" pronouncements that the law would only have a slight impact to the economy. Africa pointed out that inflation rose and gross domestic product (GDP) growth slowed down in the last two rounds of oil tax increases: in 1996, when the government imposed for the first time the excise tax on oil; and in 2005, when the expanded value-added tax (E-VAT) was implemented.

"In these two years, on the basis of one tax measure alone on oil products, tumaas ang inflation rate, tumaas ang prices ng basic goods and services (the inflation rate increased, the prices of basic goods and services increased.) So I think it is very unfair for the government to say na walang epekto to (that this has no effect)," Africa said during a news forum at Annabel's Restaurant in Quezon City.

Citing government data, Africa said that inflation rate increased from 8 percent in 1995 to 9.1 percent in 1996; and GDP growth went down from 5.8 percent in 1996 to 5.2 percent in 1997. GDP growth, on the other hand, went down from 6 percent in 2004 to 5.1 percent in 2005 when the E-VAT was implemented.

"It doesn't make sense. Kasi kung walang epekto, ibig sabihin, walang kikitain ang gobyerno (If there is no effect, that means, the government will not earn anything). So I think it is self-contradictory for the DOF to say na walang epekto 'to kasi (it has no effect because) if the government wants to generate revenues, it comes from somewhere, revenues come from people's pockets," he added. Tax the rich more Africa said that the government is using the lowering of income taxes as a "smoke screen" the actual effect of the Train Law to the majority of the population. He explained that the government's revenue losses from income tax exemption would be shouldered by the poorest 15 million Filipino families.

"'Yung reality ng Train nagbibigay siya ng income tax benefits maybe, at most, to six to seven million Filipinos pero pinapatawan ng taxes all 23 million Filipino families. Ibig sabihin the poorest 15 million Filipino families na wala namang income tax benefits will pay higher taxes," he added.
(The reality of Train is it gives income tax benefits maybe, at most, to six to seven million Filipinos but imposes taxes on all 23 million Filipino families. That means the poorest 15 million families that have no income tax benefits will pay higher taxes.)

Instead of imposing higher taxes to the general public, the government should improve its collection of corporate income tax, which is about P300 to P400 billion annually according to the National Tax Research Center (NTRC), Africa said. "I think kung icocompute talaga 'yung (if we're going to compute the) amount of economic activity, amount of potential revenues, ang laki at ang clear ng gap (there is a huge and clear gap) between actual collections and potential revenues," he added.

The expert also pushed for higher tax rates to the country's richest families, saying that a mere additional 10 to 20 percent income tax could generate an additional P90 billion in revenues, according to Ibon Foundation's computation.

"Just taxing the richest 20 percent families a little bit more, pwede siya kumita ng P90 billion. Para sa amin, 'yung tamang tax system sa Pilipinas ay dapat bumatay doon sa hindi pagiging pantay ng income at assets ng mga tao," Africa said.

CHAPTER III

RESEARCH METHODOLOGY

Research Design

This study conducted according to the experimental design of Quantitative research. In the Experimental design, it tries to emphasize objective measurements and the statistical analysis of data collected through questionnaires

Sampling procedure

Slovin's Formula is used to calculate the sample size (n) given the population size (N) and a margin of error (e).It's a random sampling technique formula to estimate sampling size this method will be used to get the number of responderts in this study to gather a data An analysis of changing price by tax reform law undur presedent rodrigo roa duterte -It is computed as n = N / (1+Ne^2).

Whereas:

n = no. of samples

N = total population

e = Margin of error

Instrument of the study

The researchers used survey questionnaire for their instrument to gather a data that was used for this study. The survey questionnaire was divided into two parts which are the profile of the students and the survey regarding to An analysis of changing price by tax reform law undur presedent rodrigo roa duterte. According to Dave Vannette 2015 a survey is a method of gathering information from a sample of people, traditionally with the intention of generalizing the results to a larger population. Surveys provide a critical source of data and insights for nearly everyone engaged in the information economy, from businesses and the media to government and academics.The survey is the collection of information regards to the kind, action or opinion of large group of people that define as one population or widepart of research that made of variety of styles under the questions for respondents.

Data Gathering

Data gathering procedure is a process of collecting information from the respondents surveying actually involves gathering responses from the topic of the study through a written medium. The researchers will distribute the survey questionnaires to their selected respondents for the needed answer regarding An analysis of changing price by tax reform law undur presedent rodrigo roa duterte. The researchers used Stratified random sampling is a method of sampling that involves the division of a population into smaller groups known as strata. In stratified random sampling, the strata are formed based on members' shared attributes or characteristics. A random sample from each stratum is taken in a number proportional to the stratum's size when compared to the population. These subsets of the strata are then pooled to form a random sample.

Data Analysis Techniques/ Statistical Treatment

According to Ronald Fisher 2012 Analysis of variance or also known as ANOVA is a collection of statistical model used to analyze the differences among group means and their associated procedures.

The researchers will be use analysis of variance test to determine the result independent variables have on the dependent variable into the middle regression study. The researchers utilize ANOVA test results in an F-Test to generate additional data that aligns with the proposed regression model.

Formula:

$$\bar{x} =$$

Notations:

$\bar{x}$ just stands for the "sample mean"

Σ means "add up"

xi "all of the x-values"

n means "the number of items in the sample"

AN ANALYSIS OF THE NUMBERS OF EMPLOYEES WHO ARE IN FAVOR

AND DID NOT FAVOR ON WAGE HIKE

A research paper presented to the faculty of

practical research in Manuel L. Quezon

Senior High School

Submitted by:

Ryan Christopher B. Demapanag

Submitted to:

Dr. Mark Vincent B. Emit

March 2018

CHAPTER I

THE PROBLEM AND ITS BACKGROUND

Background of the Study

The Employers Confederation of the Philippines (ECOP) maintained its opposition to the proposed P125 a day across-the-board wage hike, claiming that only few of the country's total labor force will benefit from it.In its perspective paper, ECOP stressed that the proposed wage increase will only benefit 16 percent of wage and salary workers in the formal sector."The rest who will not benefit will suffer from unintended consequences. It would aggravate the discrimination and inequity between this protected sector and the rest of the labor force," it added.The employer's position paper was a response to the urgent memorandum of Department of Labor and Employment (DOLE) Secretary Silvestre Bello III who ordered consultations on legislative measures proposing a P125 across-the-board wage increase for private sector workers.Citing 2014 data, ECOP said the formal sector only has 7.78 million workers employed by 946,988 registered establishments.In contrast, micro and small establishments employ 4,281,910 wage and salary workers or 55 percent of the total number of wage employment in the formal sector, ECOP said. Implementing the P125 wage hike will cost P166 billion annually, which will be massively shouldered by micro, small and medium enterprises (MSMEs). The brunt of this massive increase amounting to over P166 billion annually or 56 percent of the total will be borne by micro and small establishments," ECOP said. Emphasizing the impact of wage increase, ECOP noted that "a striking characteristic of the formal sector is that it is mostly constituted of MSEs numbering 938,971 or 99.15 percent out of the total of 946,988."It also took note that the implementation of the P125 across-the-board daily wage increase would cost P972,473,625.00 a day (P125 x 7,779,789 total employment), which only covers direct cost.The group added that the wage increase will place upward pressure on 2017 inflation rate by 7.7 points."With this across-the-board daily wage increase which is not productivity-based, cost of production of goods and services would rocket sky-high," ECOP said.Enterprises could not just simply pass on the increased cost of goods to the market primarily because of the competition offered by low-cost imports and smuggled goods. Inexorably, the increased price of goods and services would lead to cost-push inflationary spiral," it added.

Statement of the Problem

The study aims to answer the following questions:

1. What is the profile of the workers?

1.1 Number of employees who are in favor to Train Law

1.2 Number of employees who are not in favor to Train Law

2. What are their works?

3. What is the distribution of the scores of employees who are in favor and not in favor to wage hike

4. Is there significance between the both groups

5. Based on the findings, what can be recommended for improvement?

Significance of the Study

The result of the study is significant to the following individuals: Employees the respondents who are affected to Wage Hike Scope and Limitations The study will be confined to the parents of the ABM students of Manuel Luis Quezon Senior High School who are minimum wage earners The study will cover the number of the employees who are in favor and not in favor of Wage Hike.

Definition of Terms

The following words are defined for better understanding of the study:

• Minimum Wage- the lowest wage permitted by law or by a special agreement (such as one with a labor union)

• Employees- a person employed for wages or salary, especially at nonexecutive level

CHAPTER II:

REVIEW OF RELATED LITERATURE

Related Literature

Since 2008 the big questions about raising minimum wage became more focused on when, where and why rather than generally asking which the effects are on labor market. Some recent studies explain why the researchers have difficulties to prove the adverse effects of minimum wage raise on unemployment (Addison, Blackburn, & Cotti, 2013). Regarding US economy the authors show that because minimum wage has fallen in real terms and relative to the average of the economy, the increases directly affect smaller number of low wage worker and the effects on unemployment are smaller. Minimum wage elasticities for teenagers seem to have increased substantially particularly in states where unemployment rate was particularly high. Stronger evidence of a disemployment effect for low wage workers and teenagers are relevant in states with high unemployment rates. Some authors manage to prove that changes in the legal minimum wage affect only those workers whose initial wage is close to the minimum (20%) (Alaniz, Gindling, & Terrell, 2011). Their conclusion is based on a broader approach, because they study the impact of changes in legal minimum wages on a host labour market outcomes including: wages and employment; transition of workers across jobs (in the covered and uncovered sectors) and employment status (unemployment and out of the labour force); transitions into and out of poverty. The studies on the impact of minimum wages include the impact on average wages and the distribution of wages; employment, unemployment and hours worked; the distribution of wages and employment between the formal and informal sectors; the effects of minimum wages on tipped workers and social welfare; firms location decisions and minimum wages; the behavioural effect of minimum wages. (Alaniz et al., 2011; Amine & Lages Dos Santos, 2011; Azar, 2012; Boeri, 2012; Méjean & Patureau, 2010; Wang, 2012). Anyway, the general opinion is the effect of minimum wage on employment should be studied focusing on labour market outcomes in specific sectors of the economy that tend to pay workers at or close to the minimum. Consequently, many studies focus on fast-food restaurant sector and retail. Mainly, all these studies supported the idea that minimum wages slightly lower employment. Addison et.al. (Addison, Blackburn, & Cotti, 2009) study shows that the general impact of the minimum wage in the retail sector is not consistent with the reductions in employment suggested in prior research for the retail trade sector as a whole. Their conclusion is based on a study focusing on employment effects of minimum wage in specific subsectors of the retail trade sector. Using data from 1995-2005, they examine how employment levels vary with the current minimum wage in every particular state. The results provide little support for the presence of disemployment effects. Many of their estimated elasticity suggest that increasing the minimum wage may modestly increase sectorial employment. The arguments could be monopsony and efficient-wage. The mobility of labour force in the sectors with a large number of employees with minimum wage is high, so a higher minimum wage tends to stabilize the workers; they are not migrating to other sectors. Also, we could estimate a positive demand effect, if the minimum wage raises the purchasing power of these groups of workers. Often, minimum wage is perceived as an issue related to developing countries. Indeed, the study of the impact of minimum wages in developing economies include articles on Nicaragua, Brazil, Chile, Colombia, Costa Rica, Honduras, Indonesia, Kenya, Trinidad and Tobago, Turkey and South Africa (Alaniz et al., 2011; Bird & Manning, 2008; Dinkelman & Ranchhod, 2012; Gindling & Terrell, 2009, 2010; Lemos, 2009; Magruder, 2013). In the same time, we found important contributions related to developed countries, like Canada, USA, OECD countries or European countries as groups (Addison et al., 2009; Autiero, 2008; Bellou & Kaymak, 2012; Sen, Rybczynski, & Van De Waal, 2011). Nicaragua is a very interesting case because the country has a relatively high level of minimum wages compared to average wages, which means that minimum wages have potential to affect a large fraction o Chapter III: Methodology Research Design This section presents the research methodology of this study. It is a quantitative research. It is quantitative in knowing the researcher wants to analyse who are in favor and not in favor on wage hike. Population and Sampling Procedure The subject of this study is analysis who's favor and in favor on wage hile . The researcher will use Stratified Random Sampling to get the population of the employees Research Instruments The researcher will classify the respondents into two groups, first group is who are in favor to train Law and the second group is those who are not in favor to train law. The researcher uses a checklist of questionnaire in getting the relevant information for the study. It is adopted from the questionnaire used by Lauretta (2006) and Tacti (2013). The questionnaire is slightly modified to suit the purpose of the study. Data Gathering Procedure A letter of request signed by the researcher and noted by the adviser was submitted to the respective department heads, in to gain appropriate institutional approval to collect data and distribute questionnaires to the intended respondents. The researcher personally distributed the questionnaires to the respondents. The respondents were specifically instructed to answer all the questions as honestly as possible or as closely as possible to their recall of their actual experience. Furthermore, the respondents were assured that their responses would be treated with strict confidentiality and would be used only for the intended purpose of the study. The researcher retrieved the accomplished questionnaires.

CHAPTER III

METHODOLOGY

Research Design

This section presents the research methodology of this study. It is a quantitative research. It is Experimental or Non- Experimental in nature because the researcher wants to the effects of social media as a source of information influence to the students of MLQSHS.

Population and Sampling Procedure

The subject of this study is analysis on how An Analysis of the numbers of employees who are in favor and did not favor on Wage Hike

The researcher will use Stratified Random Sampling to get the population of employees.

Research Instruments

Data collection instruments refer to devices used to collect data such as questionnaires (Seaman 1991:42). Polit and Hungler (1997:466) Define a questionnaire as "a method of gathering information from respondents about attitudes, knowledge, beliefs and feelings". The questionnaire was designed to gather information about the effect of the taxation to the living of the Filipino.

Data Gathering Procedure

The researcher personally distributed the questionnaires to the respondents. The respondents were specifically instructed to answer all the questions as honestly as possible or as closely as possible to their recall of their actual experience. Furthermore, the respondents were assured that their responses would be treated with strict confidentiality and would be used only for the intended purpose of the study. The researcher retrieved the accomplished questionnaires.

THE EFFECTS OF MOBILE PHONES TO THE STUDENTS

OF MANUEL LUIS QUEZON

SENIOR HIGH SCHOOL

A research paper presented to the faculty of

practical research in Manuel L. Quezon

Senior High School

Submitted by:

Chris Webber F. Dy

Submitted to:

Dr. Mark Vincent B. Emit

March 2018

CHAPTER I

THE PROBLEM AND ITS BACKGROUND

Background of the study

Mobile phone is a portable telephone that can make and receive calls over a radio frequency link while the user is moving within a telephone service area. Modern mobile telephone services use a cellular network architecture, and. Therefore, mobile telephones are often also called cellular telephones or cellphones. In addition to telephony, 2000s-era mobile phones support a variety of other services, such as text messaging, MMS, Email, Internet Access, Short-range wireless communications (Infrared, Bluetooth), Business application, gaming and digital photography. Mobile phone which offer these and more general computing capabilities are referred to as smartphones.

Does mobile phone affect the student academic performance? Does mobile phone help student to make their life easy? Does mobile phone take a big part of the student's life?

In this study, we will examine the impact of mobile phone usage, during class lecture, on student learning. Participants in three different study groups (control, low-distraction, and high-distraction) watched a video lecture, took notes on that lecture, and took two learning assessments after watching the lecture. (Titsworth,2013) Students who were not using their mobile phones wrote down 62% more information in their notes, took more detailed notes, were able to recall more detailed information from the lecture, and scored a full letter grade and a half higher on a multiple choices test than those students who were actively using their mobile phones.

Mobile phones can be a helpful academic tool, or a hurtful academic disruption depending upon the attitude and use pattern of the student owner. The biggest lament of teachers with regards to cell phones is that they lead to student distraction and off task behavior. Cell phones can ring during class, drawing everyone's attention away from the lesson and disrupting the flow of learning. Many teachers worry that this added distraction negatively impacts students' school performance as it stops them from dedicating their full attention to their studies. (Schreiner 2017) The impacts to the students in using their cellphone during class can cause so many worried about their academic subjects. And their attention to the lecture is disturbed by use of mobile phones.

The cell phone is one of the most rapidly growing new technologies in the world (Rebello, 2012). Young adult students and non-students alike own a wide range of gadgets. They believed that these mobile phones are helpful to them. "an incredible distraction, and makes it much more difficult to teach" (Matchan,2015), some educators believed that these mobile phones are distraction to student studies lifestyle. Educators don't agree on much when it comes to digital devices in classrooms except that they aren't going away. Some 88 percent of American teens ages 13 to 17 have or have access to a mobile phone, majority of teens (73 percent) have smartphones, according to a Pew Research Center study released in April. Ninety-two percent of teens report going online daily; with more than half saying they're online several times a day. Twenty-four percent say they do so "almost constantly." The results suggest that low-achieving students are more likely to be distracted by the presence of mobile phones while high achievers can focus in the classroom regardless of the mobile phone policy," (Matchan,2015) she believes that mobiles phones really bring good and bad effect to student's lifestyle.

Conceptual Framework

(IPO)

Input	Process	Output
Profiles of the respondents 1.1Number of students who use mobile phone 1.2Number of students who don't use mobile phone	2. Survey questionnaires 3. Analysis of Data	4. Recommendations

Statement of the Problem

The study aims to answer the following questions:

1.What is the profile of the students?

        1.1number of students who use mobile phone?

        1.2 Number of students who don't use mobile phone

2. What are the main reasons of the student's use of mobile phone.?

3.what are the academic performance of students who use and don't use mobile phones?

4. Is there a significant difference of the scores of students who use and don't use mobile phones?

5.Based on the findings, what can be recommended for improvement?

Significance of the Study

The result of the study is significant to the following individuals:

        Students-They will learn how to manage their time using their mobile phones in relation to their academic performances.

        Teachers- They will know if using mobile phone inside the classroom is effective in student's learning.

Scope and Limitations

The study will be confined to the students of Manuel Luis Quezon Senior High School. The study will cover the analysis of the effects of mobile phone use of students in relation to their academic performance.

Definition of Terms

The following word are defined for better understanding of the study.

Academic- relating to education and scholarship.

Mobile Phone- a telephone with access to a cellular radio system so it can be used over a wide area, without a physical connection to a network.

Cellular- denoting or relating to a mobile telephone system that uses many short-range radio stations to cover the area that it serves, the signal being automatically switched from one station to another as the user travels about.

Infrared- (of electromagnetic radiation) having a wavelength just greater than that of the red end of the visible light spectrum but less than that of microwaves. Infrared radiation has a wavelength from about 800 nm to 1 mm, and is emitted particularly by heated objects.
particles, especially high-energy particles that cause ionization.

Cyberbullying- bullying that takes place using electronic technology. Electronic technology includes devices and equipment such as cell phones, computers, and tablets as well as communication tools including social media sites, text messages, chat, and websites.

CHAPTER II

REVIEW OF RELATED LITERATURE

Related Literatures

The mobile phone is one of the greatest inventions in 20th century. We cannot imagine how our life without the mobile phone is. It is an obvious truth that the mobile phone gives us benefits in some aspects of life. Using mobile phone distributes our communication to make it easier than before. Besides a mobile phone can provide us with a lot of functions like relaxing with music, chatting or playing games... However, today people especially young people are becoming addicted to using the mobile phone. They cannot stay away from their phones, even for a minute. Perhaps, because of the benefits of the mobile phones, most people do not realize lots of negative effects that the mobile phone has brought to us. Using mobile phones too much not only affects our health seriously but also causes some personal problems and limiting communication face to face adoption of cell phones by young generation has been a global phenomenon in recent years.

In the 21st century, students use their mobile phones not just in their own entertainment but also for their academic matters. Teens say phones make their lives safer and more convenient. Yet they also cite new tensions connected to cell phone use (Pew Research Center, 2013). Recent advances in digital technology have transformed the modern cellular/mobile telephone (cell phone) from a device once singular in function into a multi-function device with capabilities like to an internet-connected computer. At almost anytime and anyplace, today's cell phones allow users to call, send and receive text messages, update social networking sites (e.g., Facebook), stream videos and live events, play video games, and search the internet mobile phone use is banned or regulated in some circumstances. Despite recognized safety concerns and legal regulations, some people do not refrain from using mobile phones. Historically, these types of activities have been defined as sedentary behaviors. "96% of undergraduate college students and 89% of non-students of the same age own a cell phone" (PEW Research Center,2013) Based on this report, the high rate of cell phone ownership and use among today's college students and their generational peers has led to the development of the term "hyper-connected" to describe this population. Because the cell phone is so pervasive among students, this population makes a logical starting point for investigating the potential relationship between cell phone use, physical and sedentary activity, and physical fitness. Problematic cell phone use has been linked to depression, anxiety, low self-esteem, and unhealthy lifestyle practices such as skipping meals, multiple sexual partners, poor sleep habits, alcohol consumption, smoking, and illegal drug use. It is important to expand our understanding of the potential health impact these devices may have on users.

The cell phone is one of the most rapidly growing new technologies in the world (Rebello, 2012). Young students and non-students alike own a wide range of gadgets. They believed that these mobile phones are helpful to them. "an incredible distraction, and makes it much more difficult to teach" (Matchan,2015), some educators believed that these mobile phones are distraction to study lifestyle. Educators don't agree on much when it comes to digital devices in classrooms except that they aren't going away. Some 88 percent of American teens ages 13 to 17 have or have access to a mobile phone, majority of teens (73 percent) have smartphones, according to a Pew Research Center study released in April. Ninety-two percent of teens report going online daily; with more than half saying they're online several times a day. Twenty-four percent say they do so "almost constantly." The results suggest that low-achieving students are more likely to be distracted by the presence of mobile phones while high achievers can focus in the classroom regardless of the mobile phone policy," (MAtchan,2015) she believes that mobiles phones really brought good and bad effect to student's lifestyle.

"Cellphones may wind up being an escape mechanism from their classrooms. For some, cellphones in class may provide a way to cheat," Roberts said.it is also one of the negative effects of having a cellphone of students. Sometimes during their examinations, it is their way to pass the examination knowing that they have internet access. "Too much use of cellphones may cause depression and anxiety" (Donell,2016) For such people, losing a phone or having its battery die could cause anxiety or panic. Too much phone use can interfere with normal activities or cause conflicts with family and other people.

They study of adolescents, in which 548 students were asked to fill out a questionnaire regarding their cell phone use. The results of the questionnaires were that just under 89% believed they were average cell phone users, while 8.4% believed they were heavy users and only 2.9% percent believed they were addicted to their cell phone. This study found that gender, texting, monthly charges, impulsiveness, recreational reasons and cultural reasons were all influential to cell phone addiction. (Hyun Young Koo and Hyun Sook Park, 2013). Based on the results of the questionnaires the students have been addicted to their mobile phone that influence them.

Measured student perceptions of the effects of cell phone use on class performance (Kennedy and Smith, 2014) Recently the cellphone being use in the classroom and they make an article that students will show they're perceptions about the effects of it.

"When a mobile phone rings during class, it is a serious distraction" and any quantity of information loss. (Campbell, 2013) Using the mobile phone in the classroom can distract with the lessons.

In this study, we will examine the impact of mobile phone usage, during class lecture, on student learning. Participants in three different study groups (control, low-distraction, and high-distraction) watched a video lecture, took notes on that lecture, and took two learning assessments after watching the lecture. (Titsworth,2013) Students who were not using their mobile phones wrote down 62% more information in their notes, took more detailed notes, were able to recall more detailed information from the lecture, and scored a full letter grade and a half higher on a multiple choices test than those students who were actively using their mobile phones.

Mobile phones can be a helpful academic tool, or a hurtful academic disruption depending upon the attitude and use pattern of the student owner. The biggest lament of teachers with regards to cell phones is that they lead to student distraction and off task behavior. Cell phones can ring during class, drawing everyone's attention away from the lesson and disrupting the flow of learning. Many teachers worry that this added distraction negatively impacts students' school performance as it stops them from dedicating their full attention to their studies. (Schreiner 2017) The impacts to the students in using their cellphone during class can cause so many worried about their academic subjects. And they're attention to the lecture is disturbed using mobile phones.

The use and abuse of the mobile phones have adverse impact on the academic performance of the students. Negative Effects in Studies they can store answers in the phones and they can sneak text messages to friends seeking answers to questions in exams (Phaneendra,2016) The students cheat their way out of tests and other activities by using they're mobile phones and search for the answer

"However, none of these supposed advantages can overcome one very basic disadvantage: Cell phones distract students from schoolwork and class activities." (Earl, 2014). He emphasizes the importance of encouraging the learner to focus and concentrate on the class subject, not their cell phone screen. He provides information about how student's IQ will decrease by 10 points. This is due to the student being distracted, by their cell phones, from their studies.

"Using Cell Phones in the Classroom" discusses the transition a teaching veteran has worked to make his classroom mobile device friendly. (Graham,2014) He discuss to about provide apps and websites for the students and their parents to use, which has increased the total amount of students that do his homework assignments and has allowed parents to be more involved in the student's school and homework practice.

"Many students who may perform poorly on academic measures seem to see their devices as useful for a narrow range of tasks—most of which involve passive consuming of entertainment or knowledge-level content," (Crowley, 2013) If all students are to be successful using smartphones and other technology for learning, then it's clear that different students may need different activities

"The isolation squanders opportunities for students to learn to engage and communicate with empathy." The cellphones and easy access to social media are also at the root of much of the student disruption and conflict that happens on campus and the teachers are having a tougher time figuring out how smartphones might support learning. (Meyer, 2014) The fact that so many students have below grade-level reading skills.

"We find that mobile phone ban has very different effects on different types of students," (Beland and Murphy, 2015) It depends on how the students use the mobile phones but there are so many aspects that can influence the students to be lazy.

The usefulness of that measure; they would prefer to evaluate learning based on more varied, deeper measures, such as student projects. (Crowley, 2016) The

Use of earpiece in the school and at home forgetting their academic work which is supposed to be their priority Analysis of performing an art/creative work and playing mobile phone revealed that 50% can play mobile phone games very well, 27% can do their art/creativity work well while 23% can neither do the art/creative work nor play games well. In order words, the academic works suffers it most. (Patrick, 2014)

The impact that cell phones have made on high school and college students has been both positive and negative. For example, the advancements of cell phones and tablets have played a major role in the utilization of education in the classroom. In the 1990s, cell phones and tablets did not exist in the classroom, students had to rely solely on computers that were usually placed in a computer lab, or in the library. Furthermore, students had to rely on reading material out of the library which slowed down the research process for writing papers and/or thesis'. Now, here we are in the twenty-first century and classrooms are filled with a large variety of laptops, cell phones and tablets. With the availability to the internet being near limitless, but the technology can be very distracting to the students. The student's distraction, is thus distracting to the teachers or professors and to the student's fellow classmates. Over the last 50 years modern advancements in technology have played a crucial role in the development of education in both negative and positive aspects. "Do Cell Phones belong in the Classroom?" Robert Earl discusses the use of cell phones by students during their classes. He talks about how some schools allow cell phones for safety reasons, but the students are not permitted to be on their cell phones during lectures. However, many students continue to use their cell phones during classes. Robert Earl provides statistics pertaining to these students. He identifies several reasons cell phones can be useful, and provides evidence that cell phones can be an advantage to high school and college age students. He still believes that cell phones do not belong in the classroom, stating "However none of these supposed advantages can overcome one very basic disadvantage: Cell phones distract students from schoolwork and class activities." Robert Earl encourages teachers and professors to be aware of the use of cell phones during class. He emphasizes the importance of encouraging the learner to focus and concentrate on the class subject, not their cell phone screen. Robert Earl provides information about how student's IQ will decrease by 10 points. This is due to the student being distracted, by their cell phones, from their studies. In the second article that supports the thesis, "The Etiquette of In-Class Texting" there are many authors that discuss the use of cell phones in college classrooms and the affect that cell phones have on students, their teachers and their peers. The cell phones are portrayed as positive and negative attributes to the college students. The journal includes a study that provides proof that college students are distracted by their cell phones, and their distraction is proven to be just as distracting to their professors. The journal provides the perceptions of cell phone use affecting student's ability to learn. "Negative consequences and concerns about cell phone use include poor spelling, bad grammar, and distracted attention," (Etiquette, 3). The authors provide negative attributes of the cell phone to demonstrate why teachers and professors feel that they need to ban cell phones and other technology, (such as tablets) in their classrooms. The article finishes by explaining how this type of technology connects students to each other and the world. "Do Cell Phones belong in the Classroom?" and "The Etiquette of In-Class Texting" the two sources were effective in strengthening the thesis. This was done by providing examples of many of the negative consequences that occur due to using cell phones during class or too often. The weaknesses that are in the third source "Using Cell Phones in the Classroom," include the teacher's lack of acknowledging that some students do not abide by his cell phone rules. There are students that do not want to have their phones out at the teacher's permission, so they will lie and are in this way able to text during class while the teacher is out of the classroom or while they are helping another student. Another weakness is that Graham does not acknowledge any arguments or negative feedback he may have gotten. His article is written solely for encouraging cell phone use in class rooms the effect of cell phones on college and high school students has been primarily negative. Over the last 50 years modern advancements in technology have played a crucial role in the development of education in both negative and positive aspects. The two supporting sources have provided proof to how cell phones make available some positive advantages to the student's access to internet and therefore also access to faster research opportunities. The third opposing source provided information to how useful cell phones can be to students learning and the increase in the amount of work that gets done when students can use their phones, but there are always students that do not want to follow the teacher's rules, and therefore mess it up for all the other students. "Because although technology and the wealth of information that it can provide has the potential to shrink achievement gaps, I am actually seeing the opposite take place within my classroom." The phone could be a great equalizer, in terms of giving children from all sorts of socioeconomic backgrounds the same device, with the same advantages. But using phones for learning requires students to synthesize information and stay focused on a lesson or a discussion. For students with low literacy skills and the frequent urge to multitask on social media or entertainment, incorporating purposeful smartphone use into classroom activity can be especially challenging. The potential advantage of the tool often goes to waste. "It's like giving kids equal access to cigarettes and candy," Freed said. "There is a reason that adults have tried to limit and regulate young people's behavior, given that teens are not as adept at understanding risk and cause and effect." "High levels of smartphone use by teens often have a detrimental effect on achievement, because teen phone use is dominated by entertainment, not learning, applications,"- Meyer (2013). Struggling students (from all backgrounds) seem to be more susceptible than their higher-achieving peers to using their smartphones for noneducational purposes while in school.

He also added that "The isolation squanders opportunities for students to learn to engage and communicate with empathy." The cellphones and easy access to social media, according to Meyer, are also at the root of much of the student disruption and conflict that happens on campus.

However, Crowley believes teachers must adapt classroom instruction to the modern world. "If educators do not find ways to leverage mobile technology in all learning environments, for all students, then we are failing our kids by not adequately preparing them to make the connection between their world outside of school and their world inside school," she said.

Society has come to a point where the idea of living without cell phones seems ludicrous. Students desire cell phones to sustain contact with friends. The parents of students want their children to have them for security purposes. Cell phones carry multiple benefits, but with this technology lies a dualism that teeters precariously between the benefits and negative effects of cell phone usage -- especially with students. Children, teens and even young adults are prone to distraction with cell phones. In the classroom and out of school, cell phones provide students an instant network of communication and entertainment. Inside the classroom, students are distracted from the lessons to text, play games and, if they are very daring, call other people. Cell phone ringers, alarms and ring tones disrupt the flow of lessons and the attention of every student in the room and the teacher. According to the National School Safety and Security Services, text messaging can be an aid for cheating students. Also, the camera in a cell phone can be used to photograph exams. The camera also can be used to photograph other students in a way that is a violation of privacy. In case of school emergencies, cell phones can prove more of a hindrance than a help. Cell phones have been used to call in bomb threats. In many districts, tracking a cell phone is not easily done. Also, students' use of cell phones in a school emergency can possibly trigger a real bomb if an explosive device is on the school's property.

Cell phone usage by students during a school emergency can obstruct public safety personnel from controlling the event. Parents can be alerted to the emergency before public safety personnel have a chance to contain the situation. Parents can inadvertently increase the chaos by showing up at an imprudent time.

Cell phone systems are prone to overload during a real crisis. This has been proven during disasters like the World Trade Center attacks and the Columbine shootings. Several students using cell phones all at once can add to the overload and paralyze a system that may be needed by crisis teams, public safety personnel and school administrators. This may in turn magnify the crisis and increase the chance of tragedy.

Here's a list of negative effects caused to a student with excessive use of mobile phones:

1. Lack of concentration

According to report published in the *Daily Mail*, a new study claims that

- Heavy internet and mobile phone users are prone to lack of concentration and forget things easily

- This also affects their awareness and eventually lead to passive mind

- Moreover, this also leads to weak focus and attention

2. Stress

Parents want to give all the facilities to their children at a tender age to help them carve a perfect career path. They purchase the most expensive and latest smartphone for their children for this, which is the origin of all the problems apparently.

- Students generally have peer pressure to maintain their image. Even if they do not want to buy an expensive mobile phone, they will do it for their friend circle

- Children get stressed trying to maintain a proper communication level with parents, teachers and friends on phone

3. Low grades

Of course, use of technology has direct implication on education, be it positive or negative. If a teacher is using technology in the classroom, it will benefit a student. However, if a student chatting for long hours on phone, it will leave a negative impact on him/her.

According to a report published in the *Guardian*, a research done by Louis-Philippe Beland and Richard Murphy, published by the Centre for Economic Performance at the London School of Economics, says: "I'll Communication: The Impact of Mobile

Phones on Student Performance" found that after schools banned mobile phones, the test scores of students aged 16 improved by 6.4%. The economists reckon that this is the "equivalent of adding five days to the school year".

Why are mobile phones affecting kids negatively?

Despite knowing about education-related apps, kids spend most of their time doing following activities:

- Listens to music frequently

- Playing mobile games

- Chatting and calling friends

- Following social media

In short, excessive use of mobile phones is becoming a distraction for students and is wasting their time. They are delved into the virtual world to an extent that they forget all other important things

4. Lack of vision

Anxiety, stress and depression are some of the problems faced by students due to 24-hour connection with friends and other people. According to a study, students fail to set goals for themselves due a confused state of mind.

What leads to a confused state of mind? Teenagers get deep into a delirious state of mind once they start keeping their phone next to them always.

- They do not sleep

- They constantly check their phone

- Despite sleeping, they are not stress free

5. Cyber bullying

According to recent survey by Microsoft Corporation, India ranks third on the highest rate of cyber bullying, after China and Singapore. As many as 7,600 children between the age group of 8-17 years are the victim of cyber bullying.

"What is cyber bullying can vary between different cultures, and even among different individuals. In addition, cyber bullying, as a term, is not recognized worldwide. To address this, the study explored the issue by asking children about negative experiences they've had online - from their point of view (being called mean names, being teased, etc.). While such experiences may not be viewed as bullying by all who experience it, these behaviors may be considered by some as having potentially adverse effects," noted the report.

Impacts of cyber bullying:

- Rising student suicides

- Increase of aggression in students

- Loss of self confidence

- Depression

- Increase in student drug intake

"Sending or receiving relevant messages may allow students to engage in similar processes as those that occur during note-taking. Specifically, relevant <u>messages</u> may allow students to encode lecture content in a manner like the processes that occur during note-taking (Peverlyet.al.2013)." The frequency of messaging was also found to be a factor in the interruption of learning: students who tweeted with higher frequency on content not related to the class took lower quality notes than those who tweeted less frequently on non-classroom related subjects, and   scored up to 17 percent lower than the control group on multiple-choice tests.

While many instructors assume that mobile devices interrupt learning processes in the classroom even when they are related to material being studied this research points to the value that such devices may impart. That said, the study suggests that texting about content external to the lesson, or texting at a very high frequency, can, indeed, interrupt learning. In addition to helping guide campus and classroom mobile device policies, this research contributes to the growing body of research on how the brain processes information when confronted with multiple, simultaneous sources of input.

There is no doubt that the mobile phone is a very useful tool and today, mobile phones are a major part of society. It eases communication with colleagues, friends and relatives. But every technology that provides such benefits comes with a consequent price. The impact of mobile phones on youth and society is astronomical. It is this area that requires attention, when you are giving your teen a cell phone. Here's how cell phones affect teenagers.

1.Teen Tendonitis (TTT):

What is the impact of mobile phones on young people's social life? Teenagers are totally addicted to texting. Excess messaging can lead to Teen Tendonitis (TTT). It can cause pain in the hands, back and neck due to poor posture. It can also lead to impaired vision and even arthritis down the line.

2. Stress:

Having a cell phone will tempt your teen to spend all day talking or texting, instead of doing anything productive. Studies have proven that teens who spend too much of their time with their cell phones are more prone to stress and fatigue. It can also lead to psychological disorders in some cases.

3. Sleep Loss:

Most of the teens keep their cell phones nearby while sleeping to respond to texts and calls. They feel pressurized to remain reachable around the clock. It leads to sleep interruption and disruption. Teens also become irritable when they are sleep deprived.

4. Accidents:

Teens are more likely to respond to calls, text while driving, and riding than adults. They talk and text on the phone without realizing that it can cost their lives. Even the U.S. Government Website for Distracted Driving has proven that traffic crashes are the leading cause of death in teens

5. Increases Anxiety:

Relying on texting as a primary mode of communication can increase anxiety in teens. Texting is instantly gratifying, but it also produces anxiety. The instant replay by the friend can bring joy and elation. But in case of delayed response or no response, this same pleasure turns into disappointment.

Cell phones don't provide much more of a distraction than students already have, and students should be learning to embrace the technology as a learning tool. This is great if kids are *using* the device as a learning tool and not just stealthy texting their friends all day. It's important to embrace technology and teach our kids to do the same, but the fact that we finally have research pointing to the effect the phones are having on academic performance should be enough for us to collectively decide that there needs to be more restrictions. Just because something is becoming the new norm, doesn't mean it can't be re-evaluated.

Researchers found that students sending and receiving messages while studying scored lower test results and were less effective at tasks such as note taking.

The study examined how a generation of "voracious texters" might be affected by so many online distractions.

It found that when students did not use mobiles, they were better at being able to recall information.

"It is a common occurrence to observe students who are physically present, yet mentally preoccupied by non-course-related material on their mobile devices.

"As mobile devices have deeply saturated the college student population, this problem will likely continue to pose a significant obstacle," says the study, by Jeffrey Kaseko, Stevie Munoz and Scott Sigsworth.

The study showed students video lectures, while getting them to use mobile phones in different ways - such as asking them questions related to their social life or sending a link to a photo or asking a question related to the lecture.

There were also experiments with the impact of different numbers of texts and messages. When the students were tested on their ability to recall information and in multiple-choice questions, there were significantly better results for those who had "abstained" from using mobile devices.

"Perhaps one of the biggest challenges instructors face in the 21st Century college classroom is the struggle of retaining student interest and engagement while students remain connected to the outside world through their mobile devices''- (bjorsern,2015) He suspect that the average cell phone use during a typical college class is four to five times, which is enough to predict a change in a student's GPA, "said Bjornson" Some students probably underreported their cell phone use, but that just makes the results even stronger." Even when students with higher GPAs use their cell phone in class, their test scores are lower than when they don't, said Bjornson. "It's not that GPA doesn't matter, but even when you take GPA into account, cell phone use is an independent and significant predictor of test scores. Above and beyond GPA, cell phone use still predicts changes on test scores." "The overall trend was that when cell phone use is higher, test scores are lower, for everybody, within each period before a test," said Bjornson.

The results did not surprise Bjornson. "If students aren't paying attention, they're not getting the information. An A student can't necessarily pay attention to two things at the same time any better than a D student. Students may assume that cell phone use isn't related to their test scores, or they just can't help themselves because it's what they're now accustomed to doing all day long."

CHAPTER III

METHODOLOGY

Research Design

This section presents the research methodology of this study. It is a qualitative research. It is qualitative in nature because the researcher wants to analyze the effects of mobile phone use of students in relation to academic performance.

Population and Sampling Procedure

The subject of this study is the analysis of the effects of mobile phone use of students in relation to academic performance. The list of the students can be achieved in the students' master list of the enrollees in School Year 2017-2018.

The researchers used Stratified Random Sampling to get the population of grade 11 and grade 12 respondents

Research Instruments

The researchers classify the respondents into two groups, first group is who make use of mobile phones and second group is who don't make use of mobile phones. The researcher uses a checklist of questionnaire in getting the relevant information for the study. It is adopted from the questionnaire used by Lauretta (2006) and Tacti (2013). The questionnaire is slightly modified to suit the purpose of the study.

Data Gathering Procedure

A letter of request signed by the researcher and noted by the adviser was submitted to the respective department heads, in to gain appropriate institutional approval to collect data and distribute questionnaires to the intended respondents.

The researcher personally distributed the questionnaires to the respondents. The respondents were specifically instructed to answer all the questions as honestly as possible or as closely as possible to their recall of their actual experience. Furthermore, the respondents were assured that their responses would be treated with strict confidentiality and would be used only for the intended purpose of the study. The researcher retrieved the accomplished questionnaires.

AN ANALYSIS OF THE EFFECT OF CYBERBULLYING IN MLQSHS IN THE

ACADEMIC PERFORMANCE

A research paper presented to the faculty of

practical research in Manuel L. Quezon

Senior High School

Submitted by:

Margie G. Abogado

Submitted to:

Dr. Mark Vincent B. Emit

March 2018

CHAPTER 1

THE PROBLEM AND ITS BACKGROUND

Background of the Study

Cyberbullying or cyberharassment is a form of bullying or harassment using electronic means. It has become increasingly common, especially among teenagers. Harmful bullying behavior can include posting rumors, threats, sexual remarks, a victims' personal information, or pejorative labels. Bullying or harassment can be identified by repeated behavior and intent to harm. Victims may have lower self-esteem, increased suicidal ideation, and a variety of emotional responses, including being scared, frustrated, angry, and depressed. Cyberbullying may be more harmful than traditional bullying. Awareness in the United States has risen in the 2010s. due in part to high-profile cases. Several US states and other countries have laws specific to cyberbullying. Some are designed to specifically target teen cyberbullying, while others use laws extending from the scope of physical harassment. In cases of adult cyberharassment, these reports are usually filed beginning with local police. Research has demonstrated a number of serious consequences of cyberbullying victimization. Internet trolling is a common form of bullying over the Internet in an online community (such as in online gaming or social media) in order to elicit a reaction, disruption, or for someone's own personal amusement. Cyberstalking is another form of bullying or harassment that uses electronic communications to stalk a victim; this may pose a credible threat to the victim. Not all negative interaction online or on social media can be attributed to cyberbullying. Research suggests that there are also interactions online that result in peer pressure, which can have a negative, positive, or neutral impact on those involved

In Social Media, Cyberbullying can take place on social media sites such as Facebook, Myspace, and Twitter. "By 2008, 93% of young people between the ages of 12 and 17 were online. In fact, youth spend more time with media than any single other activity besides sleeping." The last decade has witnessed a surge of cyberbullying, bullying that occurs through the use of electronic communication technologies, such as e-mail, instant messaging, social media, online gaming, or through digital messages or images sent to a cellular phone.

There are many risks attached to social media sites, and cyberbullying is one of the larger risks. One million children were harassed, threatened or subjected to other forms of cyberbullying on Facebook during the past year,[when?] while 90 percent of social-media-using teens who have witnessed online cruelty say they have ignored mean behavior on social media, and 35 percent have done so frequently. 95 percent of social-media-using teens who have witnessed cruel behavior on social networking sites say they have seen others ignoring the mean behavior, and 55 percent have witnessed this frequently.

According to a 2013 Pew Research study, eight out of ten teens who use social media now share more information about themselves than they have in the past. This includes their location, images, and contact information. In order to protect children, it is important that personal information such as age, birthday, school/church, phone number, etc. be kept confidential.

Two studies from 2014 found that 80% of body-shaming tweets are sent by women, while they also accounted for 50% of misogynistic tweets.

Cyberbullying can also take place through the use of websites belonging to certain groups to effectively request the targeting of another individual or group. An example of this is the bullying of climate scientists and activists.

Conceptual Framework

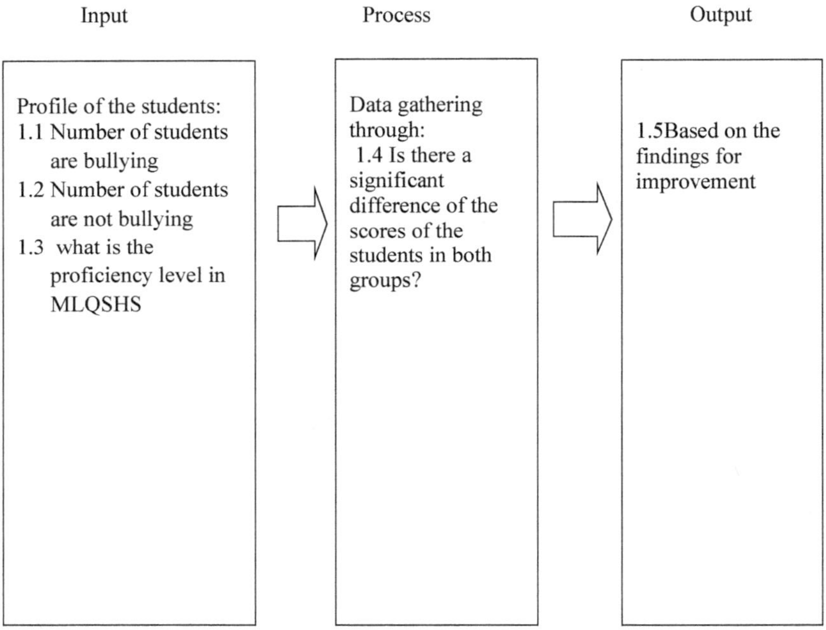

Input	Process	Output
Profile of the students: 1.1 Number of students are bullying 1.2 Number of students are not bullying 1.3 what is the proficiency level in MLQSHS	Data gathering through: 1.4 Is there a significant difference of the scores of the students in both groups?	1.5Based on the findings for improvement

Figure 1 'CONCEPTUAL FRAMEWORK'

Figure 1 presents the paradigm of the study is illustrating the conceptual frame of the study.

The components are INPUT, PROCESS AND OUTPUT. Under input there profile of the numbers of students are bullying and number of students are not bullying. Which will undergo the data gathering significant difference of the scores of the students in both groups, the findings for improvement, the academic performance of the students in both groups and output is the recommendation for academic performance are bullying.

Statement of the Problem

This study will determine the comparison of the effect of cyberbullying in MLQSHS in the academic performance.

The study will address the following question:

1. What is the profile of the students in terms of?

    1.1 Number of students are bullying

    1.2 Number of students are not bullying

2. What is the proficiency level in MLQSHS of the students in both groups?

3. Is there a significant difference of the scores of the students in both groups?

    4. Based on the findings for improvement?

Hypothesis

The hypothesis of the study is:

There is no significant difference of the scores of the students in both groups.

Scope and Limitations

The study will be confined to the students of Manuel Luis Quezon Senior High School. The study will cover the analysis of the effect of cyberbullying in MLQSHS in the academic performance.

Significance of the Study

The result of the study is significant to the following individuals:

Teachers- If they can't explain their topics through verbal discussion about cyberbullying there they can easily search the topic and easily present it to the class

Students - An important part of education is student's learning. Good quality education is based mainly on how well student attain the knowledge. One way to achieve that is to simplify the content and make it as intuitive as possible.

Hypothesis- an idea or theory that is not proven but that leads to further study or discussion.

Scope and Limitations

The study will be confined to the students of Manuel Luis Quezon Senior High School. The study will cover the analysis of the effect of cyberbullying in MLQSHS in the academic performance

Definition of Terms:

Bullying - is equated to the concept of harassment, which is a form of unprovoked aggression often directed repeatedly toward another individual or group of individuals.

Cyber - is a prefix used in a growing number of terms to describe new things that are being made possible by the spread of computers. Anything related to the Internet also falls under the cyber category.

Cyberstalking - refers to the crime of using the Internet, email, or other types of electronic communications to stalk, harass, or threaten another person. Cyberstalking most often involves sending harassing emails, instant or text messages, or social media posts, or creating websites for the sole purpose of tormenting the victim.

CHAPTER II

REVIEW OF RELATED LITERATURE

Related Literature

The Cyberbullying Research Center is dedicated to providing up-to-date information about the nature, extent, causes, and consequences of cyberbullying among adolescents. Cyberbullying can be defined as "Willful and repeated harm inflicted through the use of computers, cell phones, and other electronic devices." It is also known as "cyber bullying," "electronic bullying," "e-bullying," "sums bullying," "mobile bullying," "online bullying," "digital bullying," or "Internet bullying." The Center also explores other adolescent behaviors online including sexting, problematic social networking practices, and a variety of issues related to digital citizenship. This website serves as a clearinghouse of information concerning the ways adolescent use and misuse technology. It is intended to be a resource for parents, educators, law enforcement officers, counselors, and others who work with youth (as well as for youth themselves!). Here you will find facts, figures, and detailed stories from those who have been directly impacted by online aggression. In addition, the site includes numerous resources to help you prevent and respond to cyberbullying incidents. All of the information on this site is informed by over fifteen years of research. The Cyberbullying Research Center is directed by Dr. Sameer Hindu (Florida Atlantic University) and Dr. Justin W. Patching (University of Wisconsin-Eau Claire). They have been studying cyberbullying since 2002 and first launched this web site in 2005.

They founded the Center as a means to further their mission of bringing sound research about cyberbullying to those who can benefit most from it.

- Social Networks such as Facebook,

- Twitter,

- Instagram,

- YouTube,

- Myspace, etc.

- Instant Messaging (IMs) and Text messaging.

- Email.

- Chat rooms/forums/blogs.

CHAPTER III

METHODOLOGY

Research Design

This section presents the research methodology of this study. It is a qualitative research. It is qualitative in nature because the researcher wants to an analysis of the effect of Cyberbullying in MLQSHS in the academic performance.

Population and Sampling Procedure

The subject of this study is the analysis of the effect of Cyberbullying in MLQSHS in the academic performance.

The list of the students can be achieved in the students' master list of the enrolees in School Year 2017-2018.

Research Instruments

The researchers classify the respondents into two group first group is who are cyberbullyingand second group is who are not cyberbullying. The researcher uses a checklist of questionnaire in getting the relevant information for the study

Bibliography

https://en.wikipedia.org/wiki/Cyberbullying

https://nobullying.com/what-is-cyberbullying/

https://cyberbullying.org/about-us\

Dr. Sameer Hindu (Florida Atlantic University) and Dr. Justin W. Patching (University of Wisconsin-Eau Claire).

THE EFFECTS OF TAX REFORM FOR ACCELERATION
AND INCLUSION (TRAIN LAW)
IN SMALL BUSINESSES

A research paper presented to the faculty of

practical research in Manuel L. Quezon

Senior High School

Submitted by:

Haicel T. Aurelio

Submitted to:

Dr. Mark Vincent B. Emit

March 2017

CHAPTER I

THE PROBLEM AND ITS BACKGROUND

Background of the Study

According to Claire Jiao, (2018) Micro, small and medium enterprises (MSME) are the biggest winners in the government's tax reform program, according to new research by several firms.

Experts said the most important change was the raising of the tax threshold from ₱1.5 million to ₱3 million. MSMEs with gross sales below the threshold can opt to pay a flat tax of just 8% instead of paying the regular income tax.

This change makes the tax system "simpler and more favorable" to entrepreneurs, a report by Chinabank Securities read.

According to its simulation, entrepreneurs earning up to ₱1.5 million annually will see their disposable incomes increase by as much as 12.7% this year.

The change is even more significant for those earning between P1.5 million and ₱3 million a year — the newly tax-exempt. Their disposable incomes are expected to jump by 27-28.2%.

Even though consumer prices are expected to go up because of higher taxes on fuel and coal, Chinabank Securities said inflation will still be outpaced by the rise in entrepreneurs' income.

For those earning up to ₱1.5 million annually, inflation will not erode their income gains until 2021. For those earning between ₱1.5 million and ₱3 million, they have until 2025, the bank said.

Cutting tax in half

Tax consultancy Abrea Consulting Group, meanwhile, said that even if MSMEs don't avail of the 8% flat tax, they will still benefit from the overall lowering of income tax rates.

Under the Tax Reform for Acceleration and Inclusion (TRAIN) law, all income ₱250,000 and below will be exempt from tax. Tax rates were also lowered for most taxpayers, except those earning ₱2 million and above.

In a sample case, Abrea Consulting Group showed that a typical sari-sari store (mom and pop shop) making P500,000 in gross sales a year would have to pay ₱52,500 in taxes under the old rules. With the new rules, the store's tax bill will go down to ₱25,000 using the lower income tax or ₱20,000 using the flat tax.

"They'll be saving at least half of what they're paying right now," Abrea Consulting Group President Mon Abrea said in an interview on Monday. "So that's really good tax relief for our small businesses."

Simplifying rules

The simplified tax procedures should also benefit MSMEs that often don't have the time or money to hire accountants to go over their books, Abrea said.

The TRAIN law cut down the income tax returns from 12 pages to four. It also extended the deadline for taxpayers to pay the second installment of their tax liabilities from July 15 to October 15.

"I think that's the ultimate objective of the TRAIN law, simplifying the rules to encourage compliance for small businesses," Abrea said.

"I don't think the government should run after the few taxes of the small businesses. We just want them to comply so they be part of the formal economy."

What is Train Law? The Tax Reform for Acceleration and Inclusion (TRAIN) is the first package of the comprehensive tax reform program (CTRP) envisioned by President Duterte's administration, which seeks to correct a number of deficiencies in the tax system to make it simpler, fairer, and more efficient. It also includes mitigating measures that are designed to redistribute some of the gains to the poor.

Through TRAIN, every Filipino contributes in funding more infrastructure and social services to eradicate extreme poverty and reduce inequality towards prosperity for all. TRAIN addresses several weaknesses of the current tax system by lowering and simplifying personal income taxes, simplifying estate and donor's taxes, expanding the value-added tax (VAT) base, adjusting oil and automobile excise taxes, and introducing excise tax on sugar-sweetened beverages. What will the tax reform fund?

Manuel L. Quezon High School
Senior High School

1. Education

The tax reform will be able to fund investments in education, achieving a more conducive learning environment with the ideal teacher-to-student ratio and classroom-to-student ratio:

- Achieve the 100% enrollment and completion rates

- Build 113,553 more classrooms

- Hire 181,980 more teachers between 2017 and 2020

2. Healthcare Services

With the tax reform, we can invest more in our country's healthcare by providing better services and facilities:

- Upgrade 704 local hospitals and establish 25 local hospitals

- Achieve 100% PhilHealth coverage at higher quality of services

- Upgrade and/or relocate 263 rural and urban health units to disaster-resilient facilities

- Build 15,988 new barangay health stations

- Build 2,424 new rural health units and urban health centers

- Between 2017 and 2022, hire an additional 2,424 doctors, 29,466 nurses, 1,114 dentists, 3,288 pharmacists, 2,682 medical technologists, 911 public health associates, and 2,497 UHC implementers

3. Infrastructure Programs

The additional revenue raised by the tax reform will be used to fund the infrastructure program of the Department of Public Works and Highways (DPWH), which consists of major highways, expressways, and flood control projects. Funding these major infrastructure projects is possible with tax reform for our country to sustain high and inclusive growth.

The TRAIN will provide hefty income tax cuts for majority of Filipino taxpayers while raising additional funds to help support the government's accelerated spending on its "Build, Build, Build" and social services programs.

This tax reform package corrects a longstanding inequity of the tax system by reducing personal income taxes for 99 percent of taxpayers, thereby giving them the much needed relief after 20 years of non-adjustment of the tax rates and brackets. This is the biggest Christmas and New Year gift the government is giving to the people.

The proposed tax reform program aims to provide the needed additional revenues that would fund our country's investment needs, promoting better lives for Filipinos. There are so many benefits that we receive but if we focus on the small businesses it will have an effect of Tax Reform for Acceleration and Inclusion (TRAIN LAW) in Small Businesses?

Conceptual Framework

IPO (Input, Process, and Output) Models of teamwork that examine relationships between variables people bring with them to an interaction (inputs), the interaction among people (process, and the subjective and objective outcomes of this interaction (output). A graphical representation of all the factors that make up a process. An input-process-output diagram includes all of the materials and information required for the process, details of the process itself, and descriptions of all products and by-products resulting from the process. The researcher uses this model to easy determine and they use this to easy understand what the flow of the research was:

Input	Process	Output
1. What is the profile of the respondents? 1.1 Name (Optional) 1.2 Age 1.3 Gender 1.4 Types of Business 2. What is the effect of Tax Reform for Acceleration and Inclusion	4. Will there be any tax savings or benefit from the TRAIN law?	5. Based on the findings, what can be recommended for improvement?

(TRAIN LAW) in Small Businesses? 3. What are the benefits to the TRAIN Law to the small businesses?		

Statement of the problem

1. What is the profile of the respondents?

    1.1 Name (Optional)

    1.2 Age

    1.3 Gender

    1.4 Types of Business

2. What is the effect of Tax Reform for Acceleration and Inclusion (TRAIN LAW) in Small Businesses?

3. What are the benefits to the TRAIN Law to the small businesses?

4. Will there be any tax savings or benefit from the TRAIN law?

5. Based on the findings, what can be recommended for improvement?

Significance of the Study

The result of the study is significant to the following individuals:

Owner of the Business

The owner of business gets knowledge about the effect of TRAIN Law in their small businesses and there are benefits that they get from the TRAIN Law.

Community

They can get also knowledge about the Effect of the TRAIN Law.

Scope and Limitations

The study will be confined to the people who have a small business along Blumentritt. The study will cover the effect of TAX REFORM FOR ACCELERATION AND INCLUSION (TRAIN LAW) in Small Businesses.

Definition of Terms

The following words are defined for better understanding of the study.

TRAIN Law - The Tax Reform for Acceleration and Inclusion (TRAIN) is the first package of the comprehensive tax reform program (CTRP) envisioned by President Duterte's administration, which seeks to to correct a number of deficiencies in the tax system to make it simpler, fairer, and more efficient. It also includes mitigating measures that are designed to redistribute some of the gains to the poor.

Tax - a compulsory contribution to state revenue, levied by the government on workers' income and business profits or added to the cost of some goods, services, and transactions.

Consumer - a person who purchases goods and services for personal use.

Revenue - income, especially when of a company or organization and of a substantial nature.

Small Business - small business is an independently owned and operated company that is limited in size and in revenue depending on the industry.

CHAPTER II

RELATED LITERATURE

Related Literature

According to Chrisee Dela Paz January 09, 2018

MANILA, Philippines – Royd Agapito (not his real name), a 25-year-old market analyst for a research firm, got what he wanted: higher take-home pay. But what he did not expect is a higher monthly household bill that would offset the gains he would receive from the newly-implemented Tax Reform for Acceleration and Inclusion (TRAIN) law.

The administration of President Rodrigo Duterte started 2018 by implementing TRAIN, which reduced personal income taxes but increased those on cars, tobacco, sugar-sweetened beverages, and fuel.

Payroll managers have started adjusting their systems to reflect the new withholding tax rates. Supermarkets, oil retailers, convenience stores, and even sidewalk vendors have begun updating their price lists.

A visit to Puregold supermarket on Monday, January 8, showed that a pack of Marlboro Black 20s is more expensive now at P87.50, from last year's P68.

By mid-January, motorists will also have to brace for higher fuel prices, once existing petroleum stocks of retailers are used up. (READ: Filipinos to feel impact of higher fuel tax starting mid-January)

Higher fuel prices will also have a trickle-down effect on public transport service providers, which have started seeking fare hikes. (READ: Grab files petition for 5% fare hike and Fare hike? Uber to gauge impact of new taxes first)

Trickle-down effect

Agapito, who earns P30,000 monthly, will save P3,438 a month because of the new withholding tax rates. But he said he decided to stick to his old Toyota Vios instead of upgrading to a new car, given the hike in auto excise tax, which mainly hit mass market vehicles. (READ: Honda Philippines raises prices for most cars due to tax reform)

"I don't think TRAIN will provide significant impact to an average wage earner. It is like the government is just giving us a new perspective to look at our taxes. You have higher pay, but electricity, transport, grocery bills will also be higher," Agapito said in an interview. He added that he would also need to cut down on soda to save money. Starting mid-January, the retail price of a one-liter bottle of Coca-Cola, for instance, is projected to increase to P43 from the current P31, an increase of P12.

This is because of the P12-per-liter tax on drinks using high fructose corn syrup. For drinks using sugar and artificial sweeteners, a P6-per-liter tax has been imposed. However, all kinds of milk, 3-in-1 coffee, natural fruit juices, vegetable juices, and medically-indicated beverages are exempt.

Additional burden

While power distributors, oil companies, fuel retailers, and tobacco manufacturers are directly affected by TRAIN, First Metro Investments Corporation vice president Cristina Ulang said they have one thing going for them.

"The additional burden is something they can pass on to consumers," Ulang explained.

This, however, does not hold true for small-time vendors in the Philippines, like 48-year-old Meanne Reyes, who has two kids.

Reyes, who sells sugar-sweetened drinks, snacks, and tobacco along Amang Rodriguez Avenue in Pasig City, said she has fewer stocks due to TRAIN.

"Dati P5 per stick lang 'yung Marlboro. Ngayon binebenta ko na ng P7 isa. Dahil mas mahal na 'yung pakete, binawasan ko na lang 'yung pagbili ko ng supplies. Ang taas nang itinaas. Paano naman kaming walang suweldo at pagbebenta ang kabuhayan?" Reyes asked.

(Marlboro used to be P5 per stick. Now I'm selling it for P7 each. Since an entire pack is now more expensive, I was forced to buy fewer supplies. The price hike is significant. What will happen to people like me who have no fixed income and depend on sidewalk vending to earn a living?)

Protecting from impact

To protect the poor from higher prices of commodities, Finance Secretary Carlos Dominguez III said the Department of Social Welfare and Development (DSWD) is mandated to provide targeted cash transfers to the poorest 10 million households.

Each household would get P2,400 per year in 2018, as well as P3,600 per year in 2019 and 2020.

Dominguez said the cash transfer will be implemented in the 1st quarter of 2018.

"DSWD will identify beneficiaries based on the [list] – the Pantawid Pamilyang Pilipino Program and the social pension beneficiaries. The budget for the unconditional cash transfer is included in the 2018 budget, totaling P25.7 billion,' the finance chief said in a Malacañang briefing.

Over the course of 5 years, Dominguez said the government will raise over P786 billion in revenues because of TRAIN.

"These revenues will fund the President's priorities: social and infrastructure programs. In package one, Congress passed two-thirds of the needed revenue for 2018 and this is expected to pass the balance in early 2018 to help us achieve our revenue deficit targets," he said.

The finance chief added that the 2nd package of the comprehensive tax reform program, which is set to be passed within the month, is seen to lower corporate income taxes and modernize fiscal incentives.

All in all, Dominguez said the government targets to raise about P2 trillion from the comprehensive tax reform program to help fund the country's massive P8-trillion infrastructure buildup, which is seen to improve people's lives from all ranks.

According to Mon Abrea November 30, 2017

The Senate has already passed its version of the Tax Reform for Acceleration and Inclusion (TRAIN) bill. Will small businesses benefit from TRAIN? Were your proposals considered to make sure we support the fast-growing micro, small, and medium enterprises (MSMEs) in the country?

Yes. I am very happy to say that our government listens to us taxpayers. When we proposed a simple and lower tax for small businesses, the Department of Finance (DOF) already included it in the pipeline for comprehensive tax reform.

Our initial proposal is to introduce a flat 10% tax based on gross from small businesses. In the Senate version of TRAIN which was approved on final reading on November 28, they proposed an 8% flat tax in lieu of business and income tax for small businesses.

However, after further study of our proposal, I realized that some large corporations are only paying an effective rate of 5% or lower due to tax planning or tax avoidance schemes, while the Bureau of Internal Revenue (BIR) is using as well a 5% threshold for value-added tax (VAT) and income tax payment. So, why not allow small businesses – which we proposed to be those making P5 million and below in annual gross sales – to pay a flat 5% tax to be filed and paid annually to encourage voluntary compliance?

Further, as reiterated in our letter to our senators, we are proposing an exclusive Salary Tax table so we can collect more from self-employed individuals and professionals with the simple and lower tax rate of 5% and 15%, respectively.

In an interview, you were quoted as saying that self-employed individuals and professionals are not paying the right taxes. Is it true that only employees are burdened by our high income tax rate?

Based on the presentation of Marikina 2nd District Representative Miro Quimbo during our Tax Forum early this year, he highlighted that 99% of employees are paying taxes while only less than 50% of self-employed individuals and professionals were complying.

Based on the 2015 annual report of the BIR, 82% of our income tax collections are coming from withholding taxes of employees. This clearly shows that due to the high income tax rate, our hardworking employees have been burdened for the last 20 years while self-employed individuals and professionals have chosen either not to register or not to pay their taxes correctly.

Since you are working closely with BIR Commissioner Caesar Dulay on tax administration reforms, have there been significant improvements which directly benefit our small businesses? Will the Seal of Honesty (SOH) Certification Program really help stop corruption in the BIR?

Yes. I am proud to say that we have a very honest and good BIR chief. Commissioner Dulay has been very open to all our proposals for simplifying tax compliance, broadening the taxpayer base, and increasing voluntary compliance to stop corruption in the BIR.

He has released several issuances, from the suspension of the tax audit in his first 3 months to assess its efficiency and impact on our revenue collections, to the

reduction of documentary requirements to speed up transactions in the BIR, and creation of the medium-size taxpayer group to focus on assisting small businesses in the Revenue District Offices.

As reiterated by Commissioner Dulay during the launch of the Seal of Honesty, we need to help collect the right taxes and stop bribing examiners to promote integrity and honesty in the BIR. We need to pay our taxes correctly and on time.

According to Dominik Banzon January 23, 2018

Recently implemented by President Rodrigo Duterte's 2018 resolutions is to implement a new tax reform that will benefit all. Introducing the Tax Reform for Acceleration and Inclusion or TRAIN law is set to affect the life of millions of Filipinos this 2018.

Simply explained TRAIN Law, this law means that workers who earn an annual income of P 250, 000 will be exempted from paying Income Tax. Those earning above the said price will be slapped with the increased tax and burden. But being it a new tax reform system, the country is still yet to experience the effects of the TRAIN Law.

Mon Abrea, TRAIN Law advocate and the Consulting Group President for this law, says that: "Small businesses are likewise expected to benefit from the TRAIN law." Many articles have been talking about the individual effect of the new tax system, but how will the Train Law affect business in the Philippines?

1. Price hike in oil prices

Though there is an increase in take home pay for earners under P20, 000 people will still experience additional spending. An increase in oil prices also means an increase in transportation of goods throughout the country.

2. Increase in product prices

DTI Secretary Ramon Lopez assured the public that TRAIN will have minimal effect on prime commodities such as canned goods, rice, milk, and bread. But there will still be an increase on cars, sugar-sweetened products like soft drinks, and tobacco.

3. Decrease in certain product stocks

For those who sell sugar-sweetened products like soft drinks and such or tobacco, since there is an increase in their price buyers and even owners will think twice about buying such items regularly.

4. VAT Exemption from Small Businesses

The previous P1.9 million thresholds have increase to P3 million, making small businesses earn and save more. This will also encourage interested entrepreneurs to create and transform their business ventures even more.

There are positive and negative effects of the TRAIN Law that will affect consumers and of course, SME's. This is a big challenge to businesses and companies to step up. Not only upgrade their current services and offers, but also their digital presence to be able to convert leads into actual clients.

The internet and social media offers a place to market your product. Just narrow down on your target market and research on the latest online trends to keep up with the fast changing times!

Running a business is hard work. If you need help with your digital marketing, we are offer premium digital service to small and large businesses. Let us help you reach your 208 Business Goals with our services!

According to Mon Jocson January 12, 2018

The Bureau of Internal Revenue (BIR) admits having difficulty in determining if small and medium enterprises are paying proper taxes.

According to the BIR, they can ensure that employees are paying proper taxes as it can be done automatically, unlike those who are self-employed or those with businesses."But the self-employed pay voluntarily, we relied on voluntary filing and payment," BIR Asst. Commissioner Atty. Marissa Cabreros said. However, with the implementation of the tax reform law, the BIR is confident that many self-employed will pay their taxes. Based on the TRAIN law, small medium enterprise owner and the self-employed have the liberty to choose the manner in which they pay their taxes. Under the tax reform, all self-employed and businesses earning below P300-million yearly should pay an 8 % tax, or through a graduated income tax rate. "Your gross receipts is 8%, it's easier. You should file. You will not worry if you will collect it and keep your gross receipts. Another option is the gross receipts you collect, and it has deduction," Cabreros said. The BIR said the process has been easier under the

TRAIN law that's why they are expecting more tax payments. For Maricar Cruz, who owns a laundry shop, she is happy with the tax reform the government implements. She vows to always pay her taxes on time. "The 8% tax is okay. I hope it could help for the progress of the country," Cruz said. However, Laban Konsyumer President Vic Dimagiba said although the process has been simplified, small medium enterprises cannot hugely benefit from the tax reform law. "They should pay VAT that's for sure. They can no longer benefit. They have additional payments. They will pass on to their customers all the increases in fuel and electricity and other hikes," Dimagiba said. The BIR said everyone might feel burdened because of the tax reform, but notes that many will benefit in the long run. The agency said additional taxes collected from the tax reform will be allocated to the projects of the government that will further improve the Philippine economy.

According to Ted Cordero December 27, 2017

The simplified tax filing and payment process under the recently enacted Tax Reform for Acceleration and Inclusion (TRAIN) law will make doing business easier for small entrepreneurs, Senator Sonny Angara said on Wednesday. Angara said that under the Republic Act 10963 or the TRAIN compensation, income earners as well as professionals and self-employed individuals with small businesses, whose annual taxable income do not exceed P250,000, are exempted from income taxes and are no longer required to file income tax returns (ITRs). Currently, even if self-employed and professionals have no tax due, they are still required to file ITRs for record and monitoring purposes of the Bureau of Internal Revenue (BIR). Those with annual gross sales or earnings of above P250,000 but below P3 million can choose between a flat tax of 8 percent or the schedular personal income tax rates where they can deduct their business operation costs and expenses.

"Marami talaga sa ating self-employed at professionals ang nahihirapang makasunod sa mga regulasyon ng pagbubuwis. Minsan nga, mas malaki pa ang gastos nila sa pag-comply sa tax rules kesa sa mismong babayaran nilang buwis. Kaya minabuti nating padaliin na ang sistema lalo na para sa mga maliliit na negosyante," Angara said.

The TRAIN also increases the value-added tax (VAT) threshold from the current P1.9 million to P3 million. This means that those earning below P3 million will be exempt from the 12 percent VAT and will be subject to the 3 percent percentage tax only if they opt for the schedular personal income tax rates. In the present, VAT and percentage tax are filed and paid every month. With the tax reform, such filing and payment will be made quarterly. The TRAIN law likewise provided that only those who have annual sales or earnings of above P3 million—from the current P600,000—will be required to have their books of accounts audited by certified public accountants. The tax reform law also mandates the BIR to cut the ITR form from the current 12 pages to four pages only.

The tax reform law also states that the BIR commissioner must simplify the business registration and tax compliance requirements of self-employed individuals and professionals. "We are hopeful that these reforms would not only incentivize our self-employed and professionals to pay correct taxes, but also encourage more Filipinos to engage in business. Kapag maraming naengganyong mag-negosyo, mas dadami ang trabaho sa bansa at may dagdag-kita upang makatulong guminhawa ang pamilya," Angara said. In the Doing Business report of the World Bank, the Philippines slipped to 113th this year from 99th last year among 190 countries.

The World Bank said to start a business in the Philippines, an entrepreneur would need to make 20 different tax and contribution payments and visit multiple agencies in person.

CHAPTER III

METHODOLOGY

Research Design

This section presents the research methodology of this study. It is a quantitative research. It is quantitative in nature because the researcher wants to know The Effects of Tax reform for Acceleration and Inclusion (TRAIN LAW) in Small Businesses.

Population and Sampling Procedure

The subject of this study is analysis on how The Effects of Tax reform for Acceleration and Inclusion (TRAIN LAW) in Small Businesses. The researcher will use Stratified Random Sampling.

Research Instruments

Data collection instruments refer to devices used to collect data such as questionnaires (Seaman 1991:42). Polit and Hungler (1997:466)

Define a questionnaire as "a method of gathering information from respondents about attitudes, knowledge, beliefs and feelings". The questionnaire was designed to gather information about the effect of the taxation to the living of the Filipino.

Data Gathering Procedure

A letter of request signed by the researcher and noted by the adviser was submitted to

the respective department heads, in to gain appropriate institutional approval to collect data and distribute questionnaires to the intended respondents.

The researcher personally distributed the questionnaires to the respondents. The respondents were specifically instructed to answer all the questions as honestly as possible or as closely as possible to their recall of their actual experience. Furthermore, the respondents were assured that their responses would be treated with strict confidentiality and would be used only for the intended purpose of the study. The researcher retrieved the accomplished questionnaires.

THE EFFECTS OF SOCIAL MEDIA AS A SOURCE OF INFORMATION INFLUENCE TO THE STUDENTS OF MLQSHS

A research paper presented to the faculty of

practical research in Manuel L. Quezon

Senior High School

Submitted by:

Rizza O. Baduria

Submitted to:

Dr. Mark Vincent B. Emit

March 2018

CHAPTER I

THE PROBLEM AND ITS BACKGROUND

Background of the Study

Social media are increasingly being used as an information source, including information related to risks and crises. The current study examines how pieces of information available in social media impact perceptions of source credibility.

Newer communication technologies have increased the possibilities for how people can send and receive information. Social media are one such technology that has seen increased usage as an information source. Social media has also seen a great deal of usage by those seeking health information, with 59% of adult Americans (80% of internet users) reporting that they have accessed this type of information online (Fox, 2011). As this Pew Report suggests "people use online social tools to gather information, share stories, and discuss concerns" (Fox, 2011, p. 5). Similarly health professions and organizations are seeing the advantages of adopting social media because it is seen as an information equalizer allowing access to health care information to populations who, in the past, would not have this access. It provides a sense of privacy for the information seeker in that he/she does not have to disclose personal information in order to obtain health related information.

However, a major question surrounding the use of social media as an information source is how people assess the source credibility of this information.

This question becomes especially important to answer for users of social media, as the gatekeeping function switches from producers to consumers of information for newer technologies. These newer channels provide new pieces of information not available in "legacy" channels which may be used to make credibility judgments, such as the ability to see how quickly and recently a page host updates their page. The current study examines how this piece of information impacts a viewer's cognitive elaboration and their perceived credibility of the source.

. Technologies are a key factor in gaining a competitive edge and in ensuring the profitability and survival of a company. Within the last decade a paradigm shift occurred that has placed external sources at the center of identifying technologies. Developments in information technologies have created new external sources of information such as social media, which have enlarged the organizational search field. Social media possess some characteristics which could make them a promising source for technology information. The importance of social media for companies in technology identification has, however, not been examined empirically. This study therefore analyses social media as a source for technological information. The findings of this study show that social media play in comparison to other external sources only a minor role for companies. Additionally, the evaluation of social media does not vary depending on internal or external factors.

Social media are increasingly being used as an information source, including information related to risks and crises. The current study examines how pieces of information available in social media impact perceptions of source credibility.

Specifically, participants in the study were asked to view 1 of 3 mock Twitter.com pages that varied the recency with which tweets were posted and then to report on their perceived source credibility of the page owner. Data indicate that recency of tweets impacts source credibility; however, this relationship is mediated by cognitive elaboration. These data suggest many implications for theory and application, both in computer-mediated communication and crisis communication. These implications are discussed, along with limitations of the current study and directions for future research.

Conceptual Framework

IPO (Input, Process, and Output) Models of teamwork that examine relationships between variables people bring with them to an interaction (inputs), the interaction among people (process, and the subjective and objective outcomes of this interaction (output). A graphical representation of all the factors that make up a process. An input-process-output diagram includes all of the materials and information required for the process, details of the process itself, and descriptions of all products and by-products resulting from the process.

Input	Process	Output
1. What is the profile of the respondents? 1.1 Age 1.2 Gender 1.3 Strand 2. How do social media influence the students? 2.1 Learn new things 2.2 social benefits 2.3 job opportunities 2.4 information 3. What are the effects of Social Media as a source of Information?	4. Is there a significant difference between the effects of Social Media as a Source of Information?	5. Based on the findings, what can be recommended for improvement?

Statement Of The Problem

1. What is the profile of the respondents ?

    1.1 Age

    1.2 Gender

    1.3 Strand

2. How does social media influence the students?

    2.1 Learn new things

    2.2 Social benefits

    2.3 Job opportunities

    2.4 Information

3. What are the effects of Social Media as a Information

4.. Is there a significant difference between the effects of Social Media as a Source of Information?

5. Based on the findings, what can be recommended for improvement?

Significance of the Study

The result of the study is significant to the following individuals:

Students

Social Media helps the students to source the information that they need on their paper works.

Teachers

They will also get information on social media that they can apply on their lesson to make it easy.

Scope and Limitations

The study will be confined to the ABM & GAS students of Manuel Luis Quezon Senior High School. The study will cover the effects of social media as a source of information influence to the students of MLQSHS.

Definition of Terms

The following words are defined for better understanding of the study.

Social Media: Websites and applications that enable users to create and share content or to participate in social networking.

Influence: The capacity to have an effect on the character, development, or behavior of someone or something, or the effect itself.

Information: Facts provided or learned about something or someone.

Source: A place, person, or thing from which something comes or can be obtained.

CHAPTER II

RELATED LITERATURE

Related Literature

The following related literature and studies are attempt to discuss the effects of social media as a source of information influence the students of MLQSHS.

According to (Cole, 2009; Väljataga & Fiedler, 2009) Social Media can increase student learning through student interactions, challenges arise when social media are incorporated into an academic course. The assumption that students are familiar with and agreeable to using certain types of social media can cause educators to inadvertently fail to provide the resources or encouragement necessary to support student usage and learning (Cole, 2009; Väljataga & Fiedler, 2009).

Also, Arnold and Paulus (2010) found that even when social media is used for an educational purpose, students incorporate the technology into their lives in a way that may differ from the intentions of the course instructor. For example, off-topic or non-academic discussions occur on social media because of its primary design as a social networking tool (Lin et al., 2013). Further, as a student's age increases, the frequency of off-topic discussions also increases (Lin et al., 2013).

Hence, This indicates that while social media may encourage broader discussions of course content, older students may spend more time than younger students engaging in unrelated discussions. Social media can also negatively affect student GPA as well as the amount of time students spend preparing for class

(Annetta et al., 2009; Junco, 2012b). One explanation for this impact is that social media provides too much stimulation and therefore can distract students from completing their coursework (Hurt et al., 2012; Patera et al., 2008).

Furthermore, Another reason for this may be that students who spend more time on social media may have difficulty balancing their online activities and their academic preparation. Social media can also be a challenging instructional strategy to incorporate because it attempts to balance the authority of the educator with the active participation of the students. Collaboration through social media supports more of a constructivist approach to learning, where students and educators can work together to co-create understanding of a particular topic, rather than an approach that emphasizes individual contributions (Stevens, 2009).

Moreover, As a result, students and educators become equal participants in the knowledge sharing process. Though this seems beneficial for creating and disseminating knowledge, social media can also become a privacy concern (i.e. cyber-plagiarism) as well as an outlet for abuse and cyber-bullying (Chen & Bryer, 2012; Frye et al., 2010; Jackson, 2011; Smailes & Gannon-Leary, 2011). This suggests that establishing standards for social media use should include behavior and attitude guidelines similar to those enforced in the classroom.

According to Kuppuswamy and Shankar (2010) social network websites grab attention of the students and then diverts it towards non-educational and inappropriate actions including useless chatting. Based on the above statement we can say that social networking sites may badly affect the academic life and learning experiences of the student. Trusov, Bucklin, and Pauwels (2009) noted that the Internet is no doubt evolution of technology but specifically social networks are extremely unsafe for teenagers, social networks become hugely common and well-known in past few years.

Consequently, This research is conducted to explore the affect of social networking websites and its impact on academic life and learning experiences of students. As Kuppuswamy and Shankar (2010) explained that the social networks grabs the total attention and concentration of the students and diverts it towards non educational, unethical and inappropriate actions such as useless chatting, time killing by random searching and not doing their jobs.

In the other hand, Students and teenagers mostly use social networks for time killing and sake of enjoyment but it has been analyzed that internet use for education purpose and any appropriate task including online tutorials, online lectures and education material downloading is very good but use of internet for only social network is very useless perhaps dangerous.

Gafni and Deri (2012) used the term "social absorption" for students, where they emphasized the role of social networks in socializing and opening new channels for discovering more academic resources. Ahmed and Qazi (2011) found that social network sites promote interactions among students and teachers. Rouis(2012) performed a study on 161 Tunisian students and concluded that academic performance was improved because of their satisfaction with their family and friends' relations and consecutiveness.

Also, With regard to uses and activities of children on social networking, <u>Ito et al., 2009</u>identified a number of positive activities that children undertake. The technologies involve several positive activities mostly related to involvement in interest-driven communities. Ahn (2011) added that "Social network sites provide a platform for the youth to participate in communities that help them to learn and practice skills within a particular knowledge area." Similarly, a study by Fishman et al., 2005 indicated that "college students produce tremendous volume of writing through various social media tools such as blogs, emails, and other social media environments."

Hence, In terms of educational benefits, a number of researchers have found positive outcomes in online community engagement among children and their peers. Tiene (2000) showed that "written communication on cyberspace enables students to take part in discussions at a time convenient to them and articulate their ideas in more carefully thought-out and structured ways." Deng and Tavares (2013) concluded that "web-based discussions can contribute to the development of students' reflective ability and critical thinking skills." The authors also add that relative to face-to-face communication, "children are more willing to voice their views (agreements or disagreements) and are more attuned to others' opinions in online discussions."

According to Apeanti and Danso (2014), students think that it is more fun for their teachers to use social media. The authors also note that children think their academic performance would be better if they could contact their colleagues and teachers through social media. The authors noted also that teachers should offer class hours on social media. Researchers have tackled different methods and ways where social networking could be utilized in education. These methods included gaining more vocabulary and writing skills (Yunus et al., 2013), exchanging assignments, discussions, and resources with fellow students (Asad et al., 2012), formulating group discussions, communicating, and exchanging ideas with fellow students (Salvation and Adzharuddin, 2014).

Moreover, Other benefits involve teachers being able to share course related materials with their students, create student groups, collaborate on projects, providing peer support and facilitating teaching (English and Duncan-Howell, 2008). on projects, providing peer support and facilitating teaching (English and Duncan-Howell, 2008).

Paul and Gelish (2011) noted that students' social network use is related to their personality and, hence, attitude toward social networking. They elaborated that "some students are influenced more than others depending on their personality."Burak (2012) addressed the issue of risk-taking behavior when using social networking. The study concluded that multitasking would lead to "higher risk-taking behavior." Fowler and Nicholas (2008) reported that clusters of happy and unhappy people were visible in the social network as well as separation of friends.

Tartari (2015) showed that social media had a positive effect on children and teenagers. A positive impact was noticed with regard to communication abilities, information research, technical skills development, and effective use of new technology. Results also showed negative effects of risk, depression, cyberbullying, and sexual harassment. Ito et al., 2009 reported that social media may influence aspects such as romance, friendship, social status, and sharing music, movies, video games, and other aspects of adolescent culture. Boyd (2007) suggested that social media enhances children's view of self, community, and the world. Staying connected by social media helps children to stay connected with friends and family and to make new friends, share pictures and videos, and exchange new ideas (O'Keeffe and Clarke-Pearson, 2011).

Deng and Tavares (2013) concluded that "web-based discussions can contribute to the development of students' reflective ability and critical thinking skills." The authors also add that relative to face-to-face communication, "children are more willing to voice their views (agreements or disagreements) and are more attuned to others' opinions in online discussions."

According to Apeanti and Danso (2014), students think that it is more fun for their teachers to use social media. The authors also note that children think their academic performance would be better if they could contact their colleagues and teachers through social media. The authors noted also that teachers should offer class hours on social media. Researchers have tackled different methods and ways where social networking could be utilized in education. These methods included gaining more vocabulary and writing skills (Yunus et al., 2013), exchanging assignments, discussions, and resources with fellow students (Asad et al., 2012), formulating group discussions, communicating, and exchanging ideas with fellow students (Salvation and Adzharuddin, 2014). Other benefits involve teachers being able to share course related materials with their students, create student groups, collaborate on projects, providing peer support and facilitating teaching (English and Duncan-Howell, 2008).

Furthermore, Social network is a strong tool for social interaction and connection, where it can improve family ties and friends in a rich social context. A study on 161 Tunisian students concluded that performance was improved because of students' satisfaction with their family and friends relations (Rouis, 2012). The author emphasized the role of multitasking as a moderator of such relationships, where multitasking and students interest in university will help enhance performance based on Facebook use.

In the other hand, The research on social media and children usually focuses on many aspects or dimensions. Most empirical studies dealt with the relations between using social networking and academic performance (Alwagait et al., 2015; Hawi and Samaha, 2016). Some studies attempted to shed light on the learning aspects of using social networking (Zhang et al., 2015; Mao, 2014). Many studies focused on the negative things that could occur in children using social networking (Maddena et al., 2016; Koutamanis et al., 2015; Li, 2017). Some studies attempted to focus on the reasons why children use social networking (Samaha and Hawi, 2017), while others studied the children's attitudes toward social networking related to being connected (Miller et al., 2015; Tomczyk and Kopecky, 2016). Some studies touched on the sensitive role of the involvement of parents in their children's use of social networking (Lovea et al., 2016).

Consequently, Empirical studies showed mixed results with regard to the impact of social media on academic performance. Studies have found that the participation of students on social networks may have both positive and negative impacts on their academic performance. Mehmood and Taswir, 2013 noted that "the use of social media networks and the Internet is one of the most important factors that can influence educational performance of students positively or adversely."

Hence, Several studies in different cultures and countries on the use of social media and academic performance found no significant relations. In Ethiopia, Ndaku et al. (2013) found no significant relation between time spent on social networks and students' grade point average. In a study in Pakistan, Ahmed and Qazi (2011) also noted that there was no significant relation between time spent on social media networks and students' academic performance. In Nigeria, Akanbi and Akanbi(2014) found no evidence of a correlation between social media usage and academic performance. Meanwhile, through studies in the United States, Paul and Gelish

(2011) and <u>Kolek and Saunders (2008)</u> found that the use of social networks was not related to academic performance.

Also, Social media can provide rich tools for teaching innovation and compiling ways to engage students effectively (APA, 2011). Results of some empirical studies show that educators should embrace social media (Ito et al., 2009). Some suggested that high school students use it to connect with other students for homework and group projects (Boyd, 2008). Some teachers use blogs as teaching tools, where they reinforce skills in English, written expression, and creativity (Borja, 2005). Social media also allow students to get together outside the class to collaborate and exchange ideas about projects and assignmentsO'Keeffe and Clarke-Pearson, 2011.

Moreover, A similar study conducted by Hyllegard, Ogle, Yan, and Reitz (2011) sought to understand students' motivation in using Facebook and fanning, or liking, particular brands on the social networking site. The researchers found students use the site to establish personal connections with others and use the site to create affiliations with brands that define who they are and help them establish a sense of self (Hyllegard et al., 2011). Thus, these motives are similar to the "social benefits" motive discovered by Hennig-Thurau et al. (2004), the desire to display their personality discussed by Casteleyn et al. (2009), and the desire for self-expression cited by Pempek, Yermolayeva, and Calvert (2009).

In addition, Hyllegard et al. (2011) found that students "fanned" companies and brands to become market mavens who could receive and disseminate information about brands. This motivation discovered by Hyllegard et al. (2004) is consistent with the "concern for others" motive and "self-enhancement" motives discovered by Hennig-Thurau et al. (2004), as students could improve their knowledge about a product (self-enhancement), and then share this information with friends (concern for others). In 2011, Smock, Ellison, Lampe, and Wohn applied the uses and gratification approach to analyze why individuals use Facebook in general, as well as why they use certain functions on the website.

Besides, The researchers found that users who update their status are motivated chiefly by a desire for expressive information sharing, whereas individuals who post comments do so for relaxing entertainment, companionship, and social interaction. However, individuals who posted on friends' walls did so for professional 6 advancement, social interaction, and habitual pass time. Two motives, professional advancement and social interaction, were discovered as underlying reasons why users sent private messages. Smock et al. also found social interaction was the only significant motive discovered in the usage of Facebook's chat feature. Finally, the usage of groups on the site was positively influenced by expressive information sharing, and negatively by social interaction.

According to the Merriam-Webster, social media are forms of electronic communications through which users create online communities to share information, ideas, personal messages and other content such as videos. Over the course of several years, social media has changed dramatically. Because of social media, people today can exchange ideas, feelings, personal information, pictures and videos at a truly astonishing level. Social networking is one of the most active web-based activities in the Philippines, with Filipinos being declared as the most active users on a number of web-based social networks such as Facebook, Instagram, Snapchat, and Twitter. The use of social media has become so extensive in the Philippines that the country has been tagged as "The social networking capital of the world," and has also become part of Filipino cyberculture (Wikipedia). The effects of these social media can be considered positive but also has some negative consequences. It increases student collaboration, improves participation, content rich resources and they are useful for team projects. These sites have also caused some potential harm to society The students become victims of social networks more often than anyone else. This is because when they are studying or searching their course material online, they get attracted to these sites to kill the boredom n their study time, diverting their attention from their work and they are more likely to drink and use drug.

At present, whether social media is favourable or unfavourable, many students utilize these sites on a daily basis. As social media sites continue to grow in popularity it is our belief that technology is a vital part of today's students' success equation (Wang, Chen & Liang, 2011). Many researchers have been looking into a considerable amount of research on how social media influences student academic performances at colleges. Many parents are worried that their children are spending too much time on Facebook and other social media sites and not enough time studying.

According to john hopskin ()Be Social media can provide instant news faster than traditional news outlets or sources and can be a great wealth of information, but there is also an ever increasing need to verify and determine accuracy of this information. Here are some items to consider that can help determine authenticity: Location of the source - are they in the place they are tweeting or posting about? Network - who is in their network and who follows them? Do I know this account? Content - Can the information be corroborated from other sources? Contextual updates - Do they usually post or tweet on this topic? If so, what did past or updated posts say? Do they fill in more details? Age - What is the age of the account in question? Be wary of recently created accounts. Reliability - Is the source of information reliable?

Information on social media platforms suffers from a relative lack of professional gatekeepers to monitor content. How to evaluate the information credibility on social media platform has become an important issue for today information consumers. Despite its importance, little research has empirically examined what factors influence the information credibility on social media platforms, which limits our understanding of the determinants of online information assessment. To fill this gap, this study examines the factors that influence individuals' perceived information credibility on social media platforms. Drawing on the persuasion theory—the Elaboration Likelihood Model (ELM), we identify that five factors from two dimensions of credibility (medium and message credibility) are key ingredients in the online information assessment, and develop a research model that predicts individuals' perceived information credibility on social media platforms. We test and validate the proposed model with empirical data from 135 users of the Facebook page. The results show that interactivity, medium dependency from the medium credibility dimension and argument strength from the message credibility dimension are main determinants of the information credibility. However, we did not observe any moderating effect of personal expertise between two credibility dimensions and information credibility, which suggested from ELM.

CHAPTER III

METHODOLOGY

Research Design

This section presents the research methodology of this study. It is a quantitative research. It is Experimental or Non- Experimental in nature because the researcher wants to the effects of social media as a source of information influence to the students of MLQSHS.

Population and Sampling Procedure

The subject of this study is analysis on how effect of social media as a source of information influence to the students of MLQSHS. The researcher will use Stratified Random Sampling to get the population of ABM & GAS respondents.

Slovin's Formula is used to calculate the sample size (n) given the population size (N) and a margin of error (e).It's a random sampling technique formula to estimate sampling size this method will be used to get the number of respondents in this study to gather a data regarding the capability level of Manuel L. Quezon Senior High School students in managing a business.

-It is computed as $n = N / (1+Ne^2)$. Whereas:

n = no. of samples

N = total population

e = Margin of error

Research Instruments

Data collection instruments refer to devices used to collect data such as questionnaires (Seaman 1991:42). Polit and Hungler (1997:466) Define a questionnaire as "a method of gathering information from respondents about attitudes, knowledge, beliefs and feelings". The questionnaire was designed to gather information about the effect of the taxation to the living of the Filipino.

Data Gathering Procedure

A letter of request signed by the researcher and noted by the adviser was submitted to the respective department heads, in to gain appropriate institutional approval to collect data and distribute questionnaires to the intended respondents.

The researcher personally distributed the questionnaires to the respondents. The respondents were specifically instructed to answer all the questions as honestly as possible or as closely as possible to their recall of their actual experience. Furthermore, the respondents were assured that their responses would be treated with strict confidentiality and would be used only for the intended purpose of the study. The researcher retrieved the accomplished questionnaires.

AN ANALYSIS OF THE PERCEPTION OF SENIOR HIGH STUDENTS

IN TEACHING SEX EDUCATION TO

SECONDARY LEVEL AT SCHOOL

A research paper presented to the faculty of

practical research in Manuel L. Quezon

Senior High School

Submited by:

Shania G. Cantila

Submitted to:

Dr. Mark Vincent B. Emit

March 2018

CHAPTER 1

INTRODUCTION

Background of the Study

According to the Philippines Statistics Authority that Early pregnancy and motherhood varies by education, wealth quintile, and region. It is more common among young adult women age 15 to 24 with less education than among those with higher education (44 percent for women with elementary education versus 21 percent for women with college education). Early childbearing is also more common in Caraga (38 percent) and Cagayan Valley (37 percent) than other regions. The proportion of young adult women who have begun childbearing is higher among those classified as belonging to poor households than those in wealthier households (37 percent for young women in the lowest wealth quintile versus 13 percent for women in the highest wealth quintile). Also, Initiation of sexual activity before age 18 is more common among young adult women with less education and those in poorer households. Over 40 percent of young adult women with some elementary education, compared with only 7 percent of those with college education, reported having their first intimate sexual act at age 18 (Table 2). Similarly, 36 percent of young adult women in the lowest wealth quintile, compared with only 10 percent of those in the highest wealth quintile, had their first intimate sexual act before age 18. Across regions, the proportion ranges from 11 percent in Cordillera Administrative Region to 27 percent in Davao. The proportion of young adult women reporting first intimate sexual act before age 18 is 22 percent for rural areas and 17 percent for urban areas. Among young women age 15 to 24, 2 percent reported initiating their sexual activity before turning 15. In addition with this, a survey reveals that one in five (19 percent) young adult Filipino women age 18 to 24 years had initiated their sexual activity before age 18. Some of them would have had their first intimate sexual act before marriage. The survey reveals that 15 percent of young adult women age 20 to 24 had their first marriage or began living with their first spouse or partner by age 18. This proportion is lower than the proportion (19 percent) earlier cited regarding initiation by young women of an intimate sexual activity. Age at first marriage hardly changed over the years. A slightly higher proportion (17 percent) of older cohort of women (age group 40-49) had their first marriage at age 18.

On the other hand, Health officials have recorded an 18 percent increase in the number of new cases of human immunodeficiency virus (HIV) in 2016 compared to the year before. And there were 9,200 Filipinos who tested positive for the virus, while in 2015 there were only 7,829. This brings the total number of people living with HIV (PLHIV) in the Philippines to 37,653. (Department of Health, 2016). According to a survey done by DOH within January – December year 2016, there are 1,113 cases of AIDS with 26 people are diagnosed per day, 9 out of 10 are asymptomatic, and 63 women are living with HIV are pregnant. Also, DOH released a table about the age range of people with HIV: Less than 15 y/o 22 are positive, 15-

24 y/o 2625 are positive, 25-34 y/o 5921 are positive, 35-44 y/o 1510 are positive, and above 50 y/o 186 are positive.

Given this alarming information, the government through the Department of Education feels it is Sex Education must be included in the curriculum of schools, especially to Middle School and High School students because they belong to the age group considered "vulnerable." According to psst.ph article released in March 2017, Sex Education is probably one of the sensitive topics as far as the Philippines is concerned. It has been a subject of debate whether to incorporate this in the school curriculum. The reason behind it is to address the problems of pre-marital sex and teenage pregnancies among teenagers, and to check the spread of sexually-transmitted diseases (STDs).

Statement of the Problem

The study will analyze the perception of the senior high school students in implementing sex education to be taught in secondary level. Definitely the study will address the following questions:

1. What is the profile of the students in terms of:

   1.1 Name;

   1.2 Strand;

   1.3 Gender;

1.4 Age:

2. What are the numbers of students who think teaching sex education in secondary level?

1.1 Appropriate

1.2 Inappropriate

3. What are the effects of teaching sex education at school?

3.1 Positive Effects

3.2 Negative Effects

4. What is the main reason in approving teaching sex education at schools?

5. What can be recommended based on the findings?

Significance of the study

The result of the study is significant to the following individuals who are related to teaching sex education in secondary levels at school:

Students. They will understand more whether teaching sex education is of good use or not.

Teachers. They will know the perception of the students in teaching sex education and have new strategic ideas in teaching sex education.

Parents. They will know how to teach sex education on their children in accordance to the teachings of the school.

Youth. They will understand more the importance of being knowledgeable in sex education.

General Public. They will be informed on the increase of early teenage pregnancy and sexually transmitted diseases and how sex education affects it.

Future Researchers. Baseline data for a related or duplicated study of the analysis of the perception of senior high students in teaching sex education on secondary level at school.

The Researchers. Will have a better and deeper understanding in teaching sex education to secondary level students.

Scope and Limitations

The study is confined to the Senior High School Students studying in Manuel Luis Quezon High School located at Tondo, Manila. Specifically, grade 12 students both ABM (Accountancy, Business, and Management) and GAS (General Academic Strand) Strands.

Definition of Terms

HIV. A virus spread through certain body fluids that attacks the body's immune system, specifically the CD4 cells, often called T cells. Over time, HIV can destroy so many of these cells that the body can't fight off infections and disease. These special cells help the immune system fight off infections. HIV stands for human immunodeficiency virus.

AIDS. AIDS stands for Acquired Immune Deficiency Syndrome: Acquired means you can get infected with it; Immune Deficiency means a weakness in the body's system that fights diseases. Syndrome means a group of health problems that make up a disease.

STD. A sexually transmitted disease (STD) is an infectious illness that is transmitted through unprotected sexual activity including vaginal, anal and oral sex, or skin-to-skin contact with an infected area.

Sex Education. Sex education is a broad term used to describe education about human sexual anatomy, sexual reproduction, sexual intercourse, and other aspects of human sexual behavior.

Secondary Level of Education. Also known as High School (both junior and senior high school).

Vulnerable. High risk or prone to sexual activities.

CHAPTER II

REVIEW OF RELATED LITERATURE AND STUDIES

According to the University of Nairobi Research Archive, sometime in 2015, The controversy surrounding the teaching of sex education has ranged the world over, with different schools of thought imposing their attitudes and perception towards sex and the teaching of the same with little if any consideration of the views and needs of youth in dynamic society. This dynamism has propagated divergent perception ranging from reactionary to liberal thought. Consequently, the youth have been left at crossroads regarding issues of sexuality with no choice but to scavenge for information on sex from their peers, graffiti, the media and other sources, as others rather than themselves debate their fate. It is in this light that this study investigated students' perception of sex education in Kikuyu Division. Particularly, the study sought to establish the extent to which students in secondary schools were exposed to sex education, the extent to which students in secondary schools considered the teaching of sex education appropriate. Additionally it sought to identify students' sources of knowledge in sex education, the perceptions of sex education held by students from various socio-cultural backgrounds and finally assess if boys and girls differed in their perception of sex education The literature reviewed gave remarkable insights into the concept of perception. In addition, sexuality was 'presented as a factor affecting all area of life including relationships and academic performance. Signals got from external stimuli on sexuality and sex education were also presented as a factor that influenced and colored perception throughout life, leading to certain behavior more so III adolescence. A sample of 360 students was utilized in the study. Three methods of selecting the sample were used. These were stratified, purposive and simple random sampling. The research instrument employed for the study was a student' questionnaires. Descriptive and inferential statistics were used for analysis of data obtained. In particular, descriptive statistics used included frequencies, percentages and means while the inferential statistic used was the t-test. From the findings, it was revealed that: students were not adequately exposed to an organized school based sex education and that though some aspects of sex education were being taught in carrier subjects, like biology and SEE; the students got the bulk of sex information from other sources apart from the school. Additionally, peers and media were identified as the most popular source of sex information, in comparison to parents, church and teachers. Moreover, married teachers of 30 to 40 years of age were ranked highest in a list of the preferred sex educators. It was also established that school based sex education was regarded appropriate by an overwhelming majority of the students. Moreover, it was noted that different socio-cultural backgrounds and gender difference were not responsible for difference in perception, towards of sex education In view of the above, certain recommendations were made based on the findings of the study. Among them were: 1. A review of the existing sex education curriculum should be done to ensure relevance to students in a dynamic society. 2. A component of life skills be incorporated in the school curriculum to approach to empower the youth in having a positive perception towards their sexuality Finally, the researcher presented some suggestions for further study among them were: An investigation on the perception of pupils in primary schools to the teaching of sex education needs to be carried out. An evaluation of the existing sex education curriculum in terms of content and methodology needs to be carried out. An investigation into 'the possibility of a life skills approach toward the teaching of sex education in schools.

According to a blog posted in word-doodling, a word press media, around May 2011, "I can't be the only one in this country with that sort of experience. Somewhere out there, hundreds of teens are learning the ins and outs of sex from their hormonally-fueled peers and pornos, seeing how much reward there is to the act without being taught the many realities that come along with it. Our parents, teachers, elders and priests are all fine and dandy trying to help us maintain the illusion that sexual obliviousness equals spiritual innocence, all the while allowing us to learn about a fundamental aspect of our humanity from the most unreliable sources possible. It's ridiculous to assume that an educational lecture on the topic in a controlled, academic environment would contribute to the decay of our morality more than what's going on now."

The blogger also added "This brings us to the meat of this admittedly-long piece: why sex education, one of the major provisions of the RH Bill, can make us all smarter about sex and reduce unplanned/teen pregnancies, and even make us more responsible about our sexual activity. You've read this far, so I'll make it easier for you to read from here on by using numbered points: Details Desexualize Sex. Try telling a fourth-grader how sex is performed. Odds are, the most common reaction is "Eeeww, I pee out of there!" They're not going to want to try sex just because you tell them how it works; in fact, it might even discourage them for a few years. Things get even less sexy when you go into the details of gamete production and menstrual cycles. It Doesn't Clash with Religious Beliefs. Contrary to the beliefs of some anti-RH Bill folks, sex educators don't go around telling students to have premarital sex. It's fact-based education that explains in detail the inner workings of the human body, which many religious people believe is a temple of God. Sex itself is believed to be a spiritual union blessed by the Lord Almighty. For the religious, sex education is something that allows them to more fully appreciate this divine gift. It Talks about Contraceptives, but Doesn't Force Kids to Use Them. Another misconception running rampant is that knowledge about condoms makes people more promiscuous. We can make the following conclusions based on this logic: knowledge of sharp objects makes people more murderous, knowledge of stars makes people astronauts, and knowledge of wind patterns makes us windmills. Knowledge does not cause inevitable action. In fact, knowledge about contraceptives is beneficial to people regardless of their stance on this issue. They can learn the pros and cons behind contraceptives, learn about success rates and side effects, and make an informed decision on whether or not to use them. Those who cry foul about contraceptive use increasing promiscuity, therefore increasing unplanned pregnancies due to contraceptive failure and the abortions that "inevitably" follow need to realize one thing: majority of contraceptive failures arise from improper use. In short, contraceptives fail because people don't know how to use them. They don't know how to use them because they were never taught. The Realities of Sex Make Sex a Less-Attractive Prospect for the Unprepared. Other than the whole "Eeeeww" argument, there are two more details about sex that makes kids think twice about sticking their wee-wees into their hoo-hoos: pregnancy and sexually-transmitted diseases (STDs). Sex education doesn't talk about the fairy-tale pregnancies that have women jumping for joy and giving birth without a hitch; it details the many ups and downs a woman can encounter while pregnant. Along with the happiness that comes about with bringing a new life into the world, there's also a lot of nausea, vomiting, hunger pangs and mood swings. There are aches and pains and certain lifestyle prohibitions to ensure the developing fetus' health. Feet are going to swell, breasts are going to hurt, and mornings are going to be a bitch. That's not even mentioning the incredible costs incurred during and after a pregnancy, or the many responsibilities of parenthood. STDs, on the other hand, can lead to rashes, pus-filled boils, and burning sensations. They can lead to the weirdest, most uncomfortable discharges from the worst places imaginable. They can kill. Even worse, they can make your life a long, agonizing spiral of worsening quality. It Teaches People to be Responsible about Sex.

All this information, both the good and the bad, helps build maturity and a sense of responsibility. After all, having sex involves more than just the person himself; other people's health and overall quality of life hang on the act. It may not force kids to use contraceptives or have sex, but it does force them to do one thing: think first. That's what education gives us – the ability to consider the effects, costs, and benefits of our actions. Sex education will not lead to a collapse of morality, but an enlightenment of our humanity and our responsibility for the future."

According to a blog created by Aaron Ronquillo in psst.com on March 3, 2017, Sex Education is probably one of the sensitive topics as far as the Philippines is concerned. It has been a subject of debate whether to incorporate this in the school curriculum. The reason behind it is to address the problems of pre-marital sex and teenage pregnancies among teenagers, and to check the spread of sexually-transmitted diseases (STDs). Most recently, the Department of Health announced a plan to distribute condoms to high school students. They said this is in conjunction with introducing sex education to these students in order to address the aforementioned problems. This move was met with strong if not harsh criticism from the conservatives of society. While the aforementioned measure will address the said problems, the issue here is whether the youth are mature enough to understand the nature of sex. The concern of these groups is that these youths might be further encouraged to engage in (pre-marital) sex since these condoms are an assurance they can do it safely without the risk of transmitting STDs or getting their partner pregnant. According to the data collated by the Philippine Statistics Authority (PSA), among 10 Filipinas aged between 15 and 19 years old, one has gotten pregnant: 8% have become mothers and 2% are pregnant with their first child. From the Department of Health (DOH), the data they have gathered showed there have been over 30,000 AIDS /HIV cases recorded between 1984 and 2016. It can be gleaned from these statistics that the factors that have contributed to these problems are the apparent misguided notions the youth have about sex. It can be further inferred they lack parental guidance when exposed to media not suited to their ages. This is especially true if pornography is involved. Without proper guidance, their understanding of sex is they can get pleasure from it but are unaware of the real consequence – the process of procreation. Girls are often the ones who pay for the consequences when they get pregnant. Their lack of maturity makes them vulnerable when pressured by their boyfriends to have sex as a way to demonstrate their love. But the moment they get pregnant, they are the ones who often run away from potential responsibilities of being a parent. This is because they have not reached that stage where they can fully grasp the meaning of love. Given this alarming information, the government through the Department of Education feels it is Sex Education must be included in the curriculum of schools, especially to Middle School and High School students because they belong to the age group considered "vulnerable." Emphasis will be placed on educating the youth on how the reproductive system works. Despite this move, this must be supplemented by proper upbringing at home. Parents need to supervise children on the media they are exposed, especially pornographic materials. They must be prepared to answer any query (tactfully) regarding sex if their children ask them. This is perhaps a better solution than giving condoms to teenagers in school.

According to an article in Philippine Daily Inquirer written by Jeannnette Andrade on August 26, 2016 that sex education is not about sex, but about matters that affect one's personal safety, hygiene and well-being. She added "This, according to a Department of Education (DepEd) official, was the primary aim of sexuality education in the K-12 curriculum, that detractors of the Responsible Parenthood and Reproductive Health Law of 2012 (RH Law) have denounced for supposedly teaching adolescents and grade-school pupils about the sex act. Teaching age-appropriate sexuality education in public schools is one of the provisions of the RH Law whose full implementation President Duterte has pushed for."

She cited Rosalie Masilang, DepEd Adolescent Reproductive Health focal person and supervising education program specialist, in her article, "said teaching sex education in school was meant "to equip and empower learners in making informed choices and decisions on issues that affect their personal safety and well-being." Masilang said that as early as Grade 1, pupils are taught the difference between a "good touch" and a "bad touch," to help them avoid falling prey to people with impure intentions. "We tell the kids that they have the right to say 'no!' to being touched. Children should learn the kind of touch that is innocent and that with malice," the DepEd official said. Children, she added, are most vulnerable to exploitation, mainly from people related to them, and sexuality education can help them note the warning signs and avoid abuse. Masilang debunked the misconception among conservative groups that sexuality education was just about sex, and said that children would also learn the science of reproduction, physical care and hygiene and puberty. Also included are discussions on gender and sexuality, correct values and the norms of interpersonal relations to discourage premarital sex and teenage pregnancy.

According to estimates by the United Nations Population Fund, more than 60 percent of Filipino women from 2000-2010 became mothers before they reached the age of 20. Masilang said sexuality education can be integrated in the curriculum either through natural or purposive means. Natural integration means it would be taught as part of Science, Health, Araling Panlipunan (Social Studies) and Edukasyon sa Pagpapakatao (Values Education) subjects. Purposive integration can be done through Mathematics and Language subjects. The DepEd official said teachers and guidance counselors teaching sexuality education were equipped with adequate knowledge and skills to competently handle the subject."

Neil Kokemuller, an active business, finance and education writer and content media website developer, cited in his article four (4) positive impact of sex education. First is STD Awareness. Sex-ed programs often include significant coverage of various types of sexually transmitted diseases. For many students, this is the first time they go through a thorough review of causes and results of STDs. Regardless of the overall teaching philosophy, STD awareness can either help motivate student abstinence or at least cause them to take precautions when engaging in sexual behavior to prevent diseases. Second is Reduced Sexual Activity. For people who believe that teenagers should not be sexually active, data compiled by the Advocates for Youth organization revealed positive news. In a 2009 compilation of studies, the organization shows that 40 percent of participants in high school sex-education programs either delayed sex or had fewer partners. Additionally, 30 percent noted that while they engaged in sexual activity, they either reduced frequency or stopped after their experience in a program. Third is Better Protection. High school students that continued or intended to continue sexual activity at least seem to get the message that protection is important. The Advocates for Youth site also indicated that 60 percent of sex-education program participants stopped or reduced the amount of unprotected sex they were having. Many sex-ed programs include discussion of various types of contraception used to prevent STDs and lower pregnancy risks. And lastly is Reduced Pregnancies. Teen pregnancy is a major concern in high schools and homes across America. A correlation often exists between the amount of education and the rate of teen pregnancy. A study from the National Survey of Family Growth showed that students are half as likely to get pregnant between the ages of 15 and 19 after going through a sex-education class. The Advocates for Youth site pointed out that programs that teach prevention techniques tend to have the most success in this area.

A commentary by Fr. Cecilio Magsino in Inquirer on Mach 2014 states that "Some 10 years ago, I joined a group of high school students to do a "work camp" in Gasan, a small town in the western coast of Marinduque. The young boys repainted the physical structure of the public school and did some repairs. While looking at the work they were doing, I happened to go inside a classroom that was used by third-year high school students. There were piles of books the students would use for their studies, and I browsed through one they used for the subject "Health and Home Economics." The author of the book devoted a chapter to pregnancy. I don't recall the name of the author who I think was a woman. She gave wise advice to the young: Getting pregnant is best reserved for marriage, marriage must be prepared for, courtship done at the right time in one's life, dating and choosing one's spouse require mature judgment and so forth.

Here we have a case of a school in a small town of a small province of the Philippines giving its students education about love and responsibility years before the Reproductive Health (RH) Law was passed. I recalled this experience upon reading Michael Tan's Feb. 14 column. Tan advocates the application of the RH Law because in his view "right now most schools are totally silent when it comes to issues of sexuality, and teachers are too scared to talk about it." Tan did not present any statistics to support his claim."

He added, "I myself worked as a chaplain for a girls' school for seven years and a boys' school for five years; and it was not as if these schools did not teach its students matters about sexual conduct and ethics, not to mention biology. It is also arguable that if a small school in a small town of a small province of the Philippines is educating its young people about love and life, then there could be other schools that are doing the same. It might be true that there are teachers or schools who are silent about the matter. But it is also usually a fallacy to generalize. The problem, as I perceive it, is that education about human sexuality is "ambivalent": It can be the bearer of two values, good and bad. The root of this ambivalence is the nature of human sexuality itself; it is at the same time a physical and natural event, and also a personal and spiritual event. And it so happens that the two are united so as to form one reality. If these two components were separated then the so-called "sex education" does not really become education but simply "information." And as everyone knows, information can be mishandled and can end up with sad and catastrophic consequence. Here we have the negative value of such "education."

Also, "people who know a bit of history know that this is what happened in the "sexual revolution" of the 1960s and 1970s. Schools started giving their students sex education with the resultant alarming progressions in teenage pregnancies and abortions despite information about how to avoid pregnancies through contraceptives. What I think will really contribute to the good of young people is education about love, life and responsibility, an education which will not only give them the "facts of life" but also the entire context within which these facts contribute to human fulfillment. And that context is the calling to marriage, true love, chastity and mature responsibility, things those young students in that little town of Gasan were being taught. So we must not just give information about facts but rather move into the sphere of educating the youth in virtues.

Parents indeed have the primary duty of carrying out this education because of its very personal and intimate nature. Schools can collaborate with them in this task."

In a research conducted by Odekunmi Funke Beatrice around November – December 2013 entitled The Effect of Sex Education on Teenage Pregnancy among Secondary School Students in Ibadan Metropolis, he concluded that "The results of this investigation on incidence of teenage pregnancy among adolescents in Ibadan metropolis revealed the reality of the teenage pregnancy in the area of study. The adolescent preferred information from parents, medical practitioners, and sexual clinics compared to that from any other source. Though the level of sex education is considerably high, what is evident is that the sex education available is not good enough to address the problems of teenage pregnancy in the region. The result demonstrated that there is high rate of teenage pregnancy among the adolescents sampled in this study. Thus more is needed to be done regarding the type and quality of sex education in Nigeria. Evidently, lack of quality sex education plays a significant prominent role in the perpetration of this social problem. A comprehensive sex education is the type that will emphasize the value of abstinence, but also to provide teenagers with the tools and knowledge that are more likely to lead to more responsible behavior should they decide to have sex at all."

Odekunmi Funke Beatrice recommended that paucity of human and material resources has undermined efforts to redress this social malady. Saying, "the implication of this result is that the parents need to do more in giving sex education to their children as more children prefer to be taught by their parents. More also medical practioners and sexual clinics should be involve in giving sex education to children as more students also prefer this source of information to other sources. According to American Psychological Association (2005) teens that have parents who are diligent in instilling their values and expectations in their children are more likely to wait to have sexual intercourse, and to have it less often and exercise some safety."

Onlymyhealth website posted this article some time in 2013 "Sex education in schools is being given increasing importance as it is known to inform students about issues related to sex and sexual health. It is considered important for societies that its individuals are well-informed about sex, sexual practices, child sexual abuse and sexually transmitted diseases. A school plays an important role in implementing effective sex education to growing children. Various studies suggest that effective sex education in schools prevents adolescents experimenting with sex. These sex education programmes also encourage the teenagers to use protection while indulging in any kind of sexual act. According to the WHO, sex education should be imparted on the children who are 12 years and above. It is estimated that 34 percent of the HIV infected persons are in the age group of 12 to 19. However, like all ideologies, sex education in schools too has its own pros and cons.

Pros of Sex Education in Schools

- Sex education in schools can help children understand the impact of sex in their lives. It dispels myths related to sex and broadens their horizon.

- It can also answer all the questions that they have regarding their changing body and hormonal surges.

- Children are often inquisitive about the other gender. Sex education in school can help them understand the differences and keep the desire to explore things for themselves in check.

- Child sexual abuse is a social malice that is afflicting thousands worldwide. Sex education in schools can play an active role in curbing the incidence of abuse as through this medium children can be made aware of the difference between good and bad touch.

- It is much better to teach children about sexual health in school rather letting them use other resources, such as pornographic material and the internet. This is important because avenues, such as the internet have a huge store of information that might be misleading.

- With problems, such as teenage pregnancies and transmission of STDs on the rise, it is only appropriate that sex education is made accessible in school so that the most number of children can be made aware.

- It transforms children into responsible adults. It is a known fact that teenagers today turn sexually active, therefore, sex education can help them understand the benefit of abstinence in the early years or it can at least teach them how to be responsible sexually active people.

Cons of Sex Education in Schools

4. Mostly teachers who are given the task of teaching sex education to students are not experts and have vague ideas about sexual health themselves. This is even more harmful as incorrect information is extremely lethal as it can actually leave a wrong impression on the students. Children have an impressionable mind and incorrect information imparted at an early age can actually transform them into ignorant adults.

5. Students may still be subject to embarrassment or excitable by subject matter. If not taught properly, sex education in school can become a matter of ridicule and students may not take any interest in it.

6. The fact that in most schools sex education is treated like an extracurricular course and not a primary one. If the authorising body is not serious about it then they cannot expect that students and teachers will be interested in it.

7. Sex education at school may be at odds with the religious ideologies. Unless these disparities are sorted out by someone, who is aware of the two ideologies, sex education at school can actually confuse the students more."

CHAPTER III

METHODOLOGY

This chapter focuses primarily on the techniques used and the methodology employed in collecting data for the study. It gives a description of how data was collected. It discusses the design, the population, sample and sampling procedure, data collection techniques and instruments used in analysing data.

Research Design

This section presents the research methodology of this study. It is a descriptive analytic research with field survey. It is descriptive in nature because the researcher wants to know the reason behind students' perception in teaching sex education in secondary level at school. It is a field survey since questionnaire is administered to the respondents.

Population and Sampling Procedure

The target population of this research is Manuel Luis Quezon Senior High School students – grade 12 ABM and GAS students with a population of 123 students.

The researcher will use Stratified Random Sampling to get the sample population with a confidence level of 95% (alpha level of 0.05).

Step 1: Find the sample size

$$n = \frac{N}{(1+Ne^2)}$$
where: n = Sample Size

$$n = \frac{123}{(1+123*0.05^2)}$$
N = Population Size

$$n = \frac{123}{1.3075}$$
e = Margin of Error

n=94.07

Step 2: Find the Sampling Proportion

$$p = \frac{n}{N}$$
where: p = Sampling Proportion

$$p = \frac{94.07}{123}$$
n = Sample Size

p = 0.7647
N = Population Size

p = 0.77

Step 3: Find the sample respondents for each section

GAS 1   Male18 (0.77) = 13.86

             Female 23 (0.77) = 17.71

GAS 2   Male- 16 (0.77) = 12.32

             Female-22 (0.77) = 16.94

ABM 1   Male -12 (0.77) = 9.24

             Female -9 (0.77) = 6.93

ABM 2   Male -13 (0.77) = 10.01

             Female -10 (0.77) = 7.7

TOTAL: 95

Research Instruments

A Structured questionnaire titled Students Perceptionon SEx Education Questionnaire (SPSEQ)which was designed by the researcher was used in collecting data for the study. The instrument was divided into two parts. Part A sought information on the school and sex of the respondents while part B consists of items on sex education using a 4 point likert scale of strongly agree (SA), Agree (A),

Disagree (B), and Strongly Disagree (SD) with scoring value of 4, 3, 2, And 1 respectively for positive items while 1,2,3 and 4 was used for negative statements.

Reliability of the Instrument

Cronbach's Alpha was used to obtain a reliability coefficient of 0.95 from the pilot test which involved 95 students with the population of interest.

Data Gathering Procedure

A letter of request signed by the researcher and noted by the adviser will be submitted to the respective department heads, in order to gain appropriate institutional approval to collect data and distribute questionnaires to the intended respondents.

The researcher will personally distribute the questionnaires to the respondents. The respondents will be instructed to answer all the questions as honestly as possible or as closely as possible to their recall of their actual experience. They were given three (3) days to accomplish the questionnaires. Furthermore, the researcher will assure that the responses of the respondents will be treated with strict confidentiality and will be used only for the intended purpose of the study. The researcher will retrieve the accomplished questionnaires after the time given.

Data Analysis Techniques/Statistical Treatment

The data collected based on the survey questionnaire was analyzed with the use of sample mean and standard deviation. Any item with a mean value of 2.5 and above was regarded as positive perception which is considered acceptable while those items with a mean value below 2.5 were considered to be negative and not accepted.

Bibliography

http://blogs.edweek.org/edweek/finding_common_ground/2015/06/should_sex_educa tion_be_taught_in_schools.html

https://psa.gov.ph/content/one-ten-young-filipino-women-age-15-19-already-mother-or-pregnant-first-child-final-results

http://cnnphilippines.com/news/2017/02/01/HIV-cases-increase-2016-DOH.html

http://erepository.uonbi.ac.ke/handle/11295/20439

https://worddoodling.wordpress.com/2011/05/09/why-sex-education-is-important-especially-in-the-philippines/

Kokemuller, Neil. "Positive Impact of Sex Education." Synonym, http://classroom.synonym.com/positive-impact-sex-education-3959.html.

http://www.onlymyhealth.com/sex-education-in-schools-pros-cons-1310535352.

http://iosrjournals.org/iosr-jhss/papers/Vol17-issue4/L01745964.pdf.

Survey Questionnaire

English Proficiency Test –answer

Part I: English Grammar

1. Juan ___ in the library this morning.

A. is study   B. studying   C. is studying D. are studying

2. Alicia __________ the windowplease. It's too hot in here.

A. opens   B. open   C. opened   D. will open

3. The movie was _______________the book.

A. as   B. as good   C. good as   D. as good as

4. Ell's hobbies include jogging, swimming, and_______________.

A. to climb mountainsB. climb mountains   C. to climb   D. climbing mountains

5. Mr. Hawkins requests that someone _______________the data by fax immediately.

A. sent B. sends   C. sends   D. to send

6. Who is _______________, Marina or Sachiko?

A. tallestB. tallC. tallerD. the tallest

Manuel L. Quezon High School
Senior High School

7. The concert will begin_______________ fifteen minutes

A. inB. onC. withD. about

8. I have only _________________ Christmas cards left to write.

A. fewB. fewerC. lessD. little

9. Each of the Olympic athletes _______________ for month, even the years.

A. have been trainingB. were trainingC. has been training D. been training

10. Maria _________________ never late to work.

A. amB. areC. wereD. is

11. The company will upgrade _______________ computer information system next

months.

A. thereB. theirC. it'sD. its

12. Cheryl likes apples _________________ she does not like oranges.

A. soB. forC. butD. or

13. You were _________________ the New York office before 2 p.m.

A. suppose callB. supposed to callC. supposed callingD. supposed call

14. When I graduated from college next June, I_______________ a student here

for five years.

A. will have beenB. have beenC. has beenD. will have

15. Ms. Guth _______________ rather not invest that money in stock market.

A. has to B. couldC. would D. must

Part II. English Grammar

The majority to the news is about violence or scandal

A. TheB. ToC. NewsD. Violence

16. Takeshi swimmed one hundred laps in the pool yesterday.

A. SwimmedA. HundredB. InC. Yesterday

17. When our vacation, we plan to spend three days scuba diving

A. When   B. Plan C. Days D. Diving

18. Mr. Felnauer does not take critical of his work very well.

A. DoesB. CriticalC. HisD. Well

19. Yvette and Rinaldo Send E-mail messages to other often.

A. and B. SendC. OtherD. Often

20. Mr. Olsen is telephoning a America Red Cross for help.

A. Is B. aC. RedD. For

21. I had a enjoyable time at the party last night.

A. aB. TimeC. AtD. Last

22. The doctor him visited the patient's parents.

A. The B. HimC. Visited D. Patient's

23. Petra intends to starting her own software business in a few years.

A. IntendsA. Starting B. SoftwareC.Few

24. Each day after school, Jerome run five miles.

A. EachB. AfterC. RunD. Miles

Part III.

1. The Rate of __________ has been fluctuating wildly this week.

A. MoneyB. BillsC. CoinsD. Exchange

2. The bus _________ arrives late during bad weather.

A. every weekB. LaterC. yesterdayD. always

3. Do you _______ where the nearest grocery store is?

A. KnowB. noC. nowD. not

4 Jerry seinfeld, the popular American comedian, has his audiences _______.

A. putting too many irons in the fireB. keeping their noses out of someone's businessC. rolling in the aislesD. Going to bat for someone

5. The Chairperson will _______ members to the subcommittee.

A. appointB. DisappointC. appointmentD. Disappointed

6. The critics had to admit that the ballet _________ was superb.

A. procrastinateB. PerformanceC. pathologyD. psychosomatic

7. Peter says he can't _________ our invitation to tonight.

A. angelB. acrossC. acceptD. almost

8. We were_______ friends in that strange but magical country.

A. UponB. amongC. towardD. in additon to

9. The hurricane cause _______ damage to the city.

A. extendB. extendedC. extensiveD. extension

10. Many cultures have special ceremonies to celebrate a person's __________ of

passage into adulthood.

A. rightB. riteC. WritD. Write

11. He goes never to the company softball games.

A. NeverB. TheC. SoftballD. Games

12. Do You know the student who books were stolen?

A. DoB. KnowC. WhoD. Were

13. Jean-Pierre will spend his vacation either in Singapore nor the bahamas.

A. WillB. HisC. norD. Bahamas

14. I told the Salesman that i was not innteresting in buying the latest model.

A. ToldB. thatC. InterestingD. Buying

15. Frederick used work for a multinational corporation when he lived in malaysia.

A. Used WorkB. MultinationalC. WhenD. Lived in

Part IV.

Directions to Erik's house

Leave interstate 25 at exit 7s, follow that road(elm street) for two miles. After one mile, you will pass a small shopping center on your left. At the next set of traffic lights, turn right into maple Drive. Erik's house is the third house on your left. it's number 33, and it's while with green trim.

1. What is Erik's address?

A. interstate 25B. 2 Elm streetC. 13 erika streetD. 33 maple drive

2. which is closest to Erik's house?

A. The traffic lightsB. the shopping centerC. exit 7SD. a greenhouse

3. The main focus of the presentation will be ______.

A. monthly expendituresB. monthly salary figuresC. monthly sales figuresD. Staff meeting presentations

4. Who will give the presentation?

A. the company presidentB. Megan fallermanC. Steven RobertsD. future customers

The B&B Tour

Spend ten romantic days enjoying the lush countryside of Southern England. The counties of Devon, Dorset, Hampshire, and Essex invite you to enjoy their castles and coastline, their charming bed breakfast inns, their museums and their cathedrals. Spend lazy days watching the clouds drift by or spend active days hiking the glorious hills. These fields were home to Thomas Hardy, and the ports launched ships that shaped world history. Bed and breakfast abound, ranging from quiet farmhouses to lofty castles. Our tour begins August 15. Call or tax us today for more information 1-800-222-XXXX. Enrollment is limited, so please call soon.

5. Which of the following counties is not included in the tour?

A. DevonB. CornwallC. EssexD. Hampshire

6. How many people can go on this tour?

A. 10B. an unlimited numberC. 2-8D. a limited number

7. What can we infer about this area of southern England?

A. The region has lots of vegetation.B. The coast often has harsh weather.C. The sun is hot and the air is dry.D. The land is flat

Anna Szewcyzk, perhaps the most popular broadcaster in the news media today, won the 1998 Broadcasting Award. She got her start in journalism as an editor at the Hillsville County Times in Missouri. When the newspaper went out of business, a colleague persuaded her to enter the field of broadcasting. She moved to Oregon to begin a master's degree in broadcasting journalism at Atlas University. Following graduation, she was able to begin her career as a local newscaster with WPSU-TV in Seattle, Washington and rapidly advanced to national television. Noted for her quick wit and trenchant commentary, her name has since become synonymous with Good Day, America! Accepting the award at the National Convention of Broadcast Journalism Held in Chicago, Ms. Szewcyzk remarked, "I am so honored by this that I'm not at a total loss for words!" Who would ever have believed it?

8. What is the purpose of this announcement?

A. to invite people to the National Convention of Broadcast JournalismB. To encourage college students to study broadcastingC. To recognize Ms. Szewcyzk's accomplishmentsD. To advertise a job opening at the Hollsville County Times

9. The expression " to become synonymous with" means

A. to be the same as.B. to be the opposite of.C. to be in sympathy with.D. to be discharged from.

10. What was Ms. Szewczyk's first job in journalism?

A. She was a T.V announcer in Washington.B. She was a newscaster in Oregon.C.

She was an editor for a ewspaper in Missouri.D. She was a talk show host in C

AN ANALYSIS OF THE IMPACT OF EDUCATION OCCUPATION MISMATCH

EFFECTS ON WAGES OF FILIPINO WORKERS YEAR 2018

A research paper presented to the faculty of

practical research in Manuel L. Quezon

Senior High School

Submitted by:

Jhona Suzane Dagcasin

Submitted to:

Dr. Mark Vincent B. Emit

March 2018

CHAPTER 1

THE PROBLEM AND ITS BACKGROUND

Introduction

It is an evident that the distribution of income in an economy is related to the amount of education people have accumulated. The educational attainment cf a person will greatly reflect oh his/her career and the job he'she will pursue that will significantly amount the income fitted for his labor. A mismatch exists in the labor market in the form of educational or the skills of msimatch. According to Allen & van der Velden (2001) these are reported to have serious effects on wages and the associated with negative negative labor market outcomes. The basic idea is although a higher education raises the productivity in general, the actual level of productivity realized that is also determined by the match between educational and job level. There are different kinds of mismatches. A spatial mismatch by Buchan & Calman (2004) when the health workers typically prefer to live and work in larger cities that offers greater job opportunites and infrastructure resulting in greater shortage in rural settings and an unemployment or underemployment in urban settings. The skills mismatch refers to the situation where the workers" skills and education are not adequate for the demands of jobs in the current economy. There are a mismatch between skills workers possess and what the jobs will be require, what the economists calls an imbalance between the supply of and demand for human capital. The skills mismatch can describe situations in which workers skills exceed cf log behind these employees seek is said by Handel (2003). An example of this, in setting of Philippine is the oversupply of nurses and lack of demand for them. The Filipino nurses may have difficulty entering the US labor market until 2020 since the shortage of nurses in America ended in 2020 and now, they have ample supply of US-educated nurses. The government is pushing for the new legislation that would establish a special local jobs plan for idle Filipino nurses, now estimated at more than 300,000. The focus of this research is to specifically analyze the education-occupation mismatch and its impact on wages and need to look on the issues of mismatches since it affects the labor market. In the case of the Philippines there is indeed a need to look and review labor mismatch because of this causes has high unemployment rate. The evident reason observed, is that available job vacancies and the specific fields they should be placed on that is already occupied. Therefore, they will be left unemployed. Department of Labor and Employment said that many of the graduates do not satisfy what the economu needs. They are either not ready for the jobs or they don't possess the skills needed or knowledge needed for the work they applied for. Mismatch can also be noticed when workers and jobs are randomly assigned to labor markets. Each labor market clears at each instant but some have more workers than jobs, hence unemployment and some have more ore jobs than workers. According to Shimer (2005). As workers and jobs move between labor markets, some unemployed workers lose or leave their job and become enemployed. This research will focus also analyze the Beveridge Curve (ratio of vacant jobs and unemployed workers) that will be important in understanding the existence of mismatch on the Philippine labor market.

Theoretical Framework

A. Impact of Education-Occupation Mismatch on Wage. In the recent studies of education and wage determination are almost always embedded in the framework of Mincer's (1974) a human capital earnings functions (HCEF). According to this model, the log of individual earnings (y) in a given time period can be decomposed, where S represents year of completed education, X represents the number of years an individual has worked since completing schooling, and e is a statistical residual. In the absence of direct information on the experience of Mincer proposed the use of potential experience" the number of years an individual of age A could have worked, assuming he started school at the age 6, finished S years and began working immediately thereafter: X=A-S-6.

Theory

The unemployment and vacancy rates are dependent on the exogenous number of workers per market M and endogenous number of jobs per market N. Therefore, the unemployment and the vacancies are being effected by productvity shocks due to the unemployment and vacancies" impact on the number of jobs per market. The following proposition demonstrates how: the unemployment rate u, is increasing in the number of workers per labor market M and decreasing in the number of jobs per labor market N. The vacancy rate v is decreasing in the number of workers per labor market N and increasing in the number of jobs per labor market N. There a lot of implications, first is a higher productivity encourages firms to produce more jobs, and therefore this would raise the number of jobs per labor market N, and hence diminishes unemployment rate and upsurges vacancy rate. Thus, it presents to us that the impact of productivity shocks cause a downward-sloping vacancy-unemployment (v-u) focus movement. Second, the unemployment and vacancy rates decreases whenever there is a proportional increase in both M and N. Doubling M and N is equivalent to merging randomly selected pairs of labor markets. If both markets have unemployment, this merger does not affect the university of unemployment or vacancy rates, and similarly if both markets have vacancies. But merging a market with unemployment and a market with vacancies reduces the unemployment and vacancy rate in both. The measurement in the United States (US), the Bureau of Labor Statistics (BLS) has measured a job vacancies using the JOLTS. The measurement is said that is the most reliable time series for vacancies in the U.S. In accordance to the prerequisities of job earnings, the Bureau of Labor Statistics specified that job opening entails first, there is a specific slot of position that occurs, second, within 30 days, the work could start, and third, to fill in the vacant position, the employer is enthusiastically hiring outside the institution itself. The active recruiting pertains to the commitment of the institution in rendering contemporary efforts in fulfilling the opening through advertisement and other methods of publicity. The time preferential such as full-time, part-time, permanent , temporary, and short-term openings are incorporated. The vacancy rate is measured as the ratio of vacancies to vacancies plus employment, in order to measure the unemployment rate of each month. The Bureau of Labor Statistics (BLS) uses the Current Population Survey (CPS) wherein it entails a measurement procedure of using household and outside questionnaire. An unemployment rate is measured as a ratio of unemployment to the sum of unemployment and employment.

Conceptual Framework

A. The Model used by the researchers in the An Analysis of the Impact of Education Occupation Mismatch effects on Wages of Filipino workers years 2018.

This section provides a framework for the regression model to be estimated: no formal model of wage determination is presented: the researchers draw from the previous theoretical and empirical studies (Mincer's Model) in analyzing the likely effects of certain variables on wages. The researchers will use the Mincer's human capital earnings function as the basis to the impacts of education occupation mismatches on wages, the researchers will use this function: _ _ _ _ = _ + _ _ _ _ _ + _ where: _ _ _ _ = log _ _ _ _ _ _ _   _ _ _ _ _ / _ _ _ _ _ _ _ _

MATCH= the field of study and occupation category 1= matched 0= not matched.

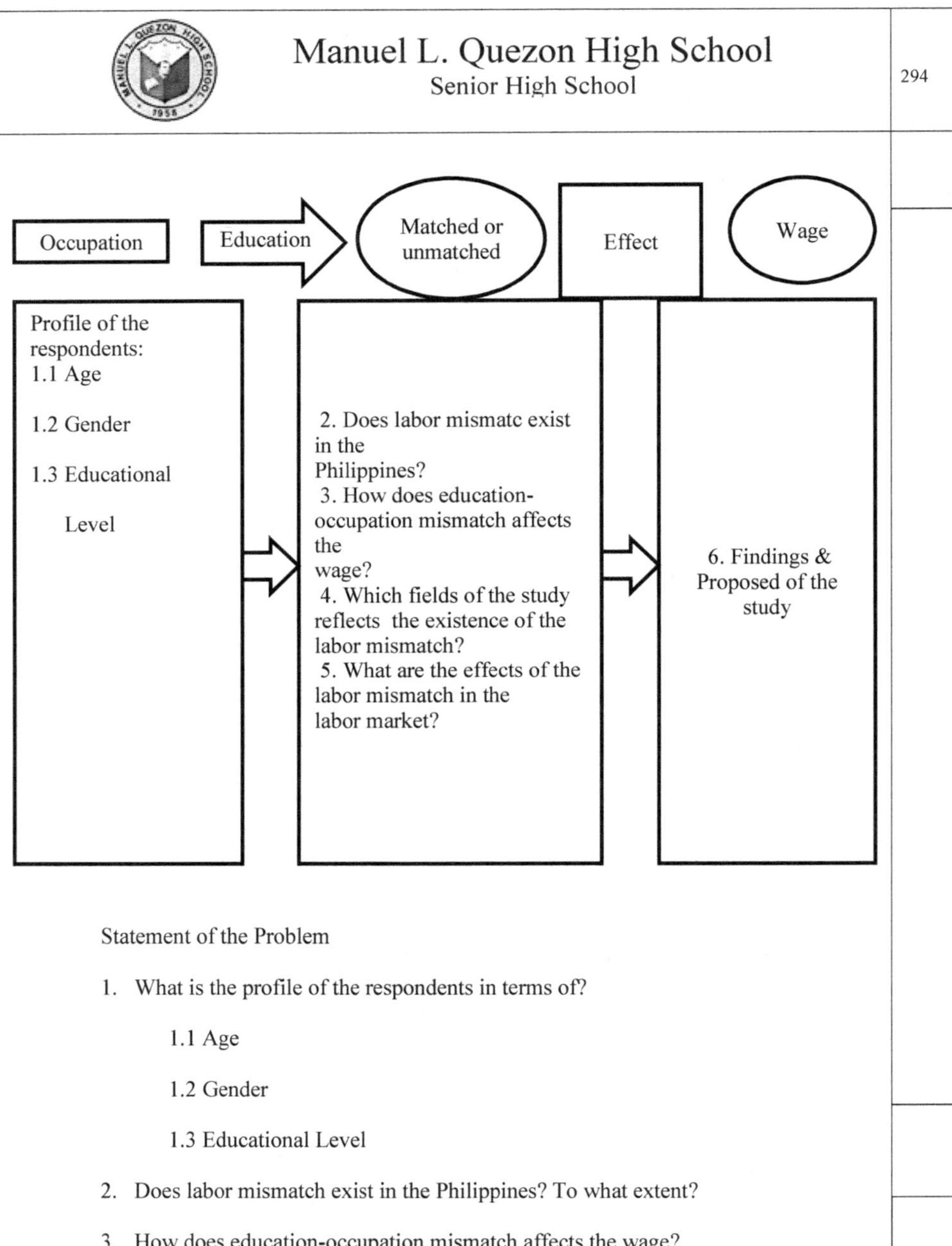

Statement of the Problem

1. What is the profile of the respondents in terms of?

    1.1 Age

    1.2 Gender

    1.3 Educational Level

2. Does labor mismatch exist in the Philippines? To what extent?

3. How does education-occupation mismatch affects the wage?

4. Which fields of the study reflects the existence of the labor mismatch in the Philippines?

5. What are the negative effects of the labor mismatch in the labor market?

6. Based on the findings, what can be the propose of this study.

7.

Significance of the Study

The Government- mismatch worsen the employment circulation of the labor market and brings a negative effects to the workers in the labor market who face the occupational downgrading in their careers as in the case of underemployment in which workers that are highly skilled work in low playing and low skilled jobs. The research can help the government in addressing these problems.

The Students- the study would be beneficial to the high school students as the study would provide information that can help them on their career choice in the field of the study that they would be taking in their course. This study can also help the graduating college students in choosing their path of careers.

The Researchers- it would be significant to the researchers for this paper will enable them to apply what they have learned in the 2 years of study and would enable them to learn and discover new findings relevant to their field of study such as Economics.

Scope and Limitation

The study will covers only the following parameters. The research analyzed the impact of education-occupation mismatch on wage in the Philippines through the use of the data from the National Statistics Office's Labor Force Survey (LFS). The researchers used the CSPro or Census and Survey Processing System which is a public domain statistical packaged provided by NSO to obtain the necessary data to be used in the study.

Definition of Terms

a. Education- it is a powerful driver of individual development and one of the strongest instruments for reducing poverty. It is improving the health, gender equality, peace and stability.

b. Occupation- it is an activity in which one engages the principal business of one's life.

c. Mismatch- to the situation where two subjects or people do not go together.

d. Matched- closely resembles or harmonizes with another.

e. Unmatched- does not closely resembles or harmonizes with another.

f. Wage- it is the base pay to the employees that they will receive this pay at a minimum, while the extra forms of pay may increase the total pay above this level.

CHAPTER II

REVIEW OF RELATED LITERATURE

1. The Impact of Education-Occupation Mismatch on Wage

Education and Income Distribution

According to Tilak (1989), he presented the following studies by the explaining of the relation between education and income distribution. According to Simon Kuznets (1955), he was predicted that the income distribution in capitalist countries would become more equal as the labor force becomes more educated. According to Knight and Sabot (1983) they observed the change in educational composition of the labor force itself has an effect on inequality. Whether it raises inequality or lowers inequality, assuming all other factors are held constant, it depends on the relative sizes of different categories, their relative mean wages and their relative wage dispersions. The process of education is affecting income distribution can be simply explained as follows: education creates a more skilled labor force. This will produce a shift from low paid, unskilled employment. This shift produces higher labor incomes, a reduction in skill differentials and an increase in the share of wages in total output. This is research study of Muysken and and Hope (2002) about The Impact of Education and Mismatch on Wages.

The Impact of Education and Mismatch on Wages

Germany, it is cited that in the study taken in the Netherlands. Muysken and Ruholl traced that personal characteristics which entails education and experience, and job characteristics which entails the skills required are the two important determinants used to explain the wage.differentials since the changes in personal characteristics explains about half of the variation of wages and job characteristics explains at least thirty percent of the variation of wages. This assumption was supported by the established similar results in the United States. In the estimation results of the study, it is figured out that variables used in personal characteristics which pertains to age, working experience, education received and number of hours worked, and job characteristics which pertains to size of the firm and level of skills required ar significant in defining the variation of wages, in fact as the job requires a higher level of skills the earning wages yields higher. The experiences attained by a worker also generate a positive impact towards defining wage. Job characteristics and experience plays an important part in determining the wage differences of the educational category of workers and the educational category of workers and the educational level is the one to define the remaining part of it.

Education and Occupation Mismatch in the Labor Market

The educational market and the labor market are the two market systems that facilitate the matching of education and occupations. Both are systems of controlling demand demand and supply, and systems of evaluation and allocation of positions and agents. As a rule, education qualifies mainly for the labor market, not for the work or occupation itself by Masuda, T. & Muta, H. 1996). The Matching of

Educational and Occupational Structures in Sweden and Finland" explains that apart from having a strong connection of education and occupation in the professional fields, individuals who possess different educational backgrounds can also have an essay way to get matched up with various occupations in a relatively elastic way by Ahola 1991.

Occupational domains are narrowing or sometimes widening in certain fields. Narrowing occupational profiles can be found in the fields where vocational/professional educational programmes have been developed to meet the needs specialized occupational tasks by Ahola 1999. Vocational schooling as an Advantage Tool in the Labor Market The study of Vocatioanl Schooling Occupational Matching and Labor Market Earnings in Israel concluded that vocational schooling is more cost effective than the general academic training in Israel. The students who came from vocational programs and seek out for work that are related to their field of study had earned more. In fact, their wages are generally higher by up to ten percent a month than those who studied academic secondary schools but found employment in occupations not related to their field by Neuman, S & Ziderman A. 1991.

According to Patrick van Eijs and Hans Heijke 1996 their study of Productivity in Matched Occupation-Education. This concludes that through the matching of the laborer's specific education skills with the occupational job characteristics which yields efficiency, the human capital of labor force is being utilized well and this paves a way to achieve the right and deserved wage for the rendered skill. Income Penalty of Mismatch but in the labor market there are existing problems that hinders the right allocation of deserved wages and this is due to the education-occupation mismatch that creates an income penalty to the workers. A study supporting this conclusion is the pioneering paper of Robst which had shown that in the date where in US college graduates who do not matched their occupation to the major course they have taken had almost 11 percent lower annual income as to be compared to the graduates who had a matched one. Also in the study done by the 2006 Survey of Labor and Income Dynamics (SLID) of Canada it is concluded in the survey results that those 58 percent workers reported who had matched their attained education closely related to their present work and those 19 percent reported who had matched their attained education somewhat related to their present work have a 35 percent higher wage given a $27 mean wage rate than those 23 percent workers reported who did not found their attained education to be related to their work given $20 mean wage rate. Reasons for having Occupations not related to the Field of Study the general personal reasons for choosing the occupation even if it is not related to the field of study are job security where in the worker had found the secureness, assurance and continuity of gainful employment to the said occupation even if it is not inclined to his taken course, professional growth in University of Santos Tomas 17 which they had achieved the sense of fulfillment and usefulness of their personal drive on the said occupation they have taken even if it is unmatched to their field of the study.

CHAPTER III

METHODOLOGY

Research Design

This study conducted according to the design of mix experimental and non-experimental design of quantitative research. In the Experimental design it tries to emphasize objective measurements and the staatistical analysis of data collected through questionnaires. While in the non-experimental design it is a descriptive type studies that used to observe, document and decribe regarding the An Analysis of the Impact of Education-Occupation Mismatch Effects on Wages of Filipino Workers years 2018.

Sampling procedure

Slovin's Formula is used to calculate the sample size (n) given the population size (N) and a margin of error (e). It is a random sampling technique formula to estimate sampling size this method will be used to get the number of respondents in this study to gather a data regarding an Analysis of the Impact of Education-Occupation Mismatch Effects on Wages of Filipino Workers years 2018.

It is computed as n=N/(1+N).

Whereas:

n= no. samples

N= total population

e= margin of errors

Instrument of the Study

The researchers used the CSPro or Census and Survey Processing System which is a public domain statistical packaged provided by NSO to obtain the necessary data to be used in the study. The survey processing system was divided into three parts which are the profile of the respondents regarding to Analysis of the Impact of Education-Occupation Mismatch Effects on Wages of Filipino Workers years 2018.

AN ANALYSIS ON HOW PH R.A 10963 (TRAIN LAW) WILL AFFECT

CONSUMERS OF SWEETENED BEVERAGES:

PERCEPTION OF ABM STUDENTS

A research paper presented to the faculty of

practical research in Manuel L. Quezon

Senior High School

Submited by:

Leila Joyce B. Demapanag

Submitted to:

Dr. Mark Vincent B. Emit

March 2018

CHAPTER I

THE PROBLEM AND ITS BACKGROUND

Background of the Study

December 19 2017, President Rodrigo Duterte signed into law the first package of the much-awaited tax reform program the central piece of the government's plan to raise the bulk of needed funds for the Duterte's administration ambitious infrastructure drive. Known as the Tax Reform for Acceleration and Inclusion law, the tax program overhauls the country's 20-year-old tax regime in a bid to make the tax system fairer and simpler. Under the TRAIN, personal income tax rates will be adjusted to shift the burden off lower-income segments toward the "ultra-rich." Meanwhile, projected revenues to be foregone from lower personal income tax will be offset by higher excise levies on petroleum and automobiles, among others. Under its P8.44-trillion 2017-2022 "Build, Build, Build" program, the government aims to jack up its spending on infrastructure alone to P1.899 trillion, equivalent to 7.45 percent of gross domestic product, by the time Duterte ends his term in 2022. However, the estimated tax take from the new tax law is less than the Department of Finance had hoped to raise , with TRAIN expected to generate $1.8 billion in revenues in its first year. Duterte's TRAIN had also encountered some resistance, with some lawmakers criticizing certain "anti-poor" provisions of the bill.

The TRAIN law, or Republic Act 10963, is expected to generate P130 billion in revenues. Seventy percent of the revenues will finance the administration's "Build, Build, Build" infrastructure program, while the remaining 30 percent will fund socioeconomic programs. Moreover, the law is expected to reduce personal income tax.

Sweetened beverages are affected of this train law. This Law means imposing higher tax on sweetened beverages products.

Conceptual Framework

(IPO)

Input	Process	Output
Profiles of the respondents 2. Number of students who are in favour of TRAIN law. 3. Number of students who are not in favor of train Law	• Survey questionnaires • Analysis of Data	1. Recommendations

Statement of the Problem

The study aims to answer the following questions:

1. What is the profile of the students?

1.1 Number of students who are in favor to Train Law

1.2 Number of students who are not in favor to Train Law

2. What are the sources of income?

3. What are the products they consume that is affected of Train Law?

4. Is there a significant difference of the scores of students who are in favor and not in favor to Train Law?

5. Based on the findings, what can be recommended for improvement?

Significance of the Study

The result of the study is significant to the following individuals:

Students- They will know the effects of Train Law to their lifestyle

Store owners-

Scope and Limitations

The study will be confined to the ABM students of Manuel Luis Quezon Senior High School. The study will cover the analysis of effects of Train Law to consumers of sweetened beverages.

Definition of Terms

The following words are defined for better understanding of the study.

Train Law- Tax Reform Acceleration and Inclusion Law

R.A 10963- the first package of the comprehensive tax reform program (CTRP) envisioned by President Duterte's administration, which seeks to correct a number of deficiencies in the tax system to make it simpler, fairer, and more efficient. It also includes mitigating measures that are designed to redistribute some of the gains to the poor

Consumer- is the one who pays something to consume goods and services produced.

Sweetened Beverages- are drinks with added sugar including: non-diet soft drinks/sodas, flavored juice drinks, sports drinks, sweetened tea, coffee drinks, energy drinks, and electrolyte replacement drinks

CHAPTER II:

REVIEW OF RELATED LITERATURE

Related Literatures

Filipinos are fond of drinking sweetened beverages which is probably the reason of high number of obesity and diabetes cases. TRAIN law taxes sugar-sweetened beverages P6 per liter, while those with high fructose corn syrup are taxed P12 per liter. Milk products, natural fruit and vegetable juices, and pre-packaged coffee products are exempted. (Coins.ph 2017) In a statement, Bantay Konsumer, Kalsada, Kuryente (BK3) said its supports the Philippine Association of Stores and Carinderia Owners (Pasco) in its campaign against the tax. According to BK3, Pasco has gathered more than 300,000 signatures to oppose the tax measure forwarded in House Bill (HB) 5636, which is part of the government's banner tax reform program known as "TRAIN."Earlier this year, the House of Representatives approved the so-called sweet tax, which imposes an excise tax of P10 per liter on drinks with local sugar and P20 per liter on those with imported sugar or sweeteners BK3 convenor Louie Montemar said that, based on the group's computation, 40 percent of the daily income of store owners comes from the sales of drinks, such as juices and flavored instant coffee in sachets. "We understand that the government needs to generate revenues to support its programs. However, the proposed excise tax could only worsen the already difficult life of low-income consumers," he added.

The convenor noted that there are other development schemes and revenue options that could be considered. One would be shifting to a public-private partnership (PPP) model, instead of getting funds from the country's budget to support its infrastructure program.

This would allow the government to "free up its resources to help the poor, instead of imposing additional burden on them," Montemar said.

He also said the government can also focus its revenue-generation program on stopping revenue leaks caused by smuggling, illicit trade, poor tax collection and corruption.

Citing a multi-industry study by the University of Asia and the Pacific (UAP), BK3 said illicit traders smuggled at least P904.6 billion worth of goods into the country over five years. The Department of Finance estimates that potential revenues from the sugar tax is about P47 billion.

"Revenue from those illegal activities could easily cover whatever revenue is generated from the SSB tax," Montemar said.

Health concerns related to the consumption of sugary drinks and obesity are also "relatively weak," he added, noting that data from the 2017 State of Food Security and Nutrition in the World by the Food and Agriculture Organization (FAO) show that undernutrition, not obesity, is the more serious problem in the Philippines.

Beverages are one of the key export sectors cited in the Philippine Export Development Plan 2015 to 2017. Notwithstanding the two-tier tax structure, the imposition of such an exorbitant tax will have a negative impact on the further development of and investment in not only the agricultural sector, but also the beverage and food processing sectors in the Philippines.

Strong opposition to the proposed taxes on sweetened beverages has already been voiced by consumer groups and experts who understand international business and economics such as the Beverage Industry Association of the Philippines, Bantay Konsyumer, Kalsada, Kuryente and the Philippine Association of Stores and Carinderia Owners, which is conducting a petition against the tax, among others.

Micro, small and medium-sized enterprises and low-income earners are poised to be hit hardest by the measure, as 40 percent of sari-sari store and carinderia earnings come from sweetened beverages, and 80 percent of sweetened-beverage consumers are low-income earners, according to surveys conducted by the Nielsen Corporation, a global marketing research firm.

Drinks with caloric and non-caloric sweeteners will be taxed P6 per liter while those using high-fructose corn syrup, a cheap sugar substitute, will be charged P12 per liter. The rates were revised from the original proposal of P10 per liter.

CHAPTER III

METHODOLOGY

Research Design

This section presents the research methodology of this study. It is a quantitative research. It is quantitative in nature because the researcher wants to analyse the Effects Of train Law to consumers of sweetened beverages: and to those consumers who are in favor and not in favor to Train Law.

Population and Sampling Procedure

The subject of this study is analysis on how PH R.A 10963
(Train Law) will affect Consumers of Sweetened Beverages. The researcher will use Stratified Random Sampling to get the population of grade 11 and grade 12 respondents

Research Instruments

The researcher will classify the respondents into two groups, first group is who are in favor to train Law and the second group is those who are not in favor to train law. The researcher uses a checklist of questionnaire in getting the relevant information for the study. It is adopted from the questionnaire used by Lauretta (2006) and Tacti (2013). The questionnaire is slightly modified to suit the purpose of the study.

Data Gathering Procedure

A letter of request signed by the researcher and noted by the adviser was submitted to the respective department heads, in to gain appropriate institutional approval to collect data and distribute questionnaires to the intended respondents.

The researcher personally distributed the questionnaires to the respondents. The respondents were specifically instructed to answer all the questions as honestly as possible or as closely as possible to their recall of their actual experience. Furthermore, the respondents were assured that their responses would be treated with strict confidentiality and would be used only for the intended purpose of the study. The researcher retrieved the accomplished questionnaires.

THE ANALYSIS OF THE CAUSE-EFFECTS OF SOCIAL MEDIA AS A

CHANNEL ON CYBER BULLYING IN RELATION TO ACADEMIC

PERFORMANCE.

A research paper presented to the faculty of

practical research in Manuel L. Quezon

Senior High School

Submitted by:

Kweenee Eliza Ducay

Submitted to:

Dr. Mark Vincent B. Emit

March 2018

CHAPTER 1

THE PROBLEM AND ITS BACKGROUND

Background of the Study

According to Gonzales, (2013) Cyberspace represents the medium of communication. It creates new ways for citizens to communicate, come together, and share information of a social nature (Internet Journal of Philosophy, 2011). Also, it develops the social, political and economic activities of people all over the word and its impact can be seen everywhere. (Gonzales, 2013).

In cyberspace, actions and reaction are essentially instant and this is why the internet is pleasing and satisfying. This also made an impact to the society. This change how people do in society, how they communicate, how people form ties and other sites to post thoughts, pictures, send emails or chat in real time. "Social" is considered in these tools that post pictures and shape news because in addition to the function they perform and created in ways that also integrate user's sharing and communication with others. (Gonzales, 2013). Internet distributed meaningful development to the lives of people especially in the aspects of communication between humans. It serves as the root that allows expressing and communicating various idea or thoughts.

Ironically, while others is enjoying using internet it also gives other people chance to misuse it and gain personal advantage by victimizing others.

There are too few places to spend time in this age of technology, therefore many young are involve in internet based social networking websites or different kind of web based applications where they are able to communicate with other people whether local or international, to search new friends, persons and also share thoughts or personal data over internet. However the continuously arising internet accessibility brought a societal problem that needs an attention and it must be addressed straightaway on cyber bullying.

Cyber bullying is a type of bullying that uses electronic media. People who cyber bully can use email, IM, text messages and images accessed from a phone or computer. (Hunter, 2012). It occurs among young people but when an adult is involved, cyber bullying may accelerate to a more serious act called as cyber-harassment or cyber-stalking, a crime that can have legal aftermath and involve jail time.

Cyber bullying or cyber harassment is a form of <u>bullying</u> or <u>harassment</u> using electronic means. It has become increasingly common, especially among teenagers Harmful bullying behavior can include posting rumors, <u>threats</u>, sexual remarks, a <u>victims' personal information,</u> or pejorative labels. Bullying or harassment can be identified by repeated behavior and intent to harm Victims may have lower self-esteem, increased <u>suicidal ideation,</u> and a variety of emotional responses, including being scared, frustrated, angry, and depressed. Cyber bullying may be more harmful than traditional bullying. Awareness in the United States has risen in the <u>2010s,</u> due in part to high-profile cases. Several US states and other countries have laws specific to cyber bullying. Some are designed to specifically target teen cyber bullying, while others use laws extending from the scope of physical harassment in cases of adult cyber harassment, these reports are usually filed beginning with local police.

The institution of Manuel L. Quezon Senior High School it is an extension of Manuel L. Quezon High School, where in the student enter Senior High School. This building of Manuel L. Quezon Senior High School was constructed within 10 years with different contracts. The Manuel L. Quezon Senior High School building consists of five (5) floors, ground floor 2nd floor within three (3) classrooms, 3rd floor, 4th floor and 5th floor with social hall and terrace. Manuel L. Quezon Senior High School has 254 total populations including all the school authorities.

Conceptual Framework

This study used I.P.O model. The I.P.O model shows the input, process and output of the research. The step to solve any problem of conducting is called process. The output is the findings of research or results.

According to Business Dictionary, which can be accessed throughhttp://www.businessdictionary.com/definition/input-process-output-diagram.html, a graphical representation of all the factors that make up a process? An input-process-output diagram includes all of the materials and information required for the process, details of the process itself, and descriptions of all products and by-products resulting from the process.

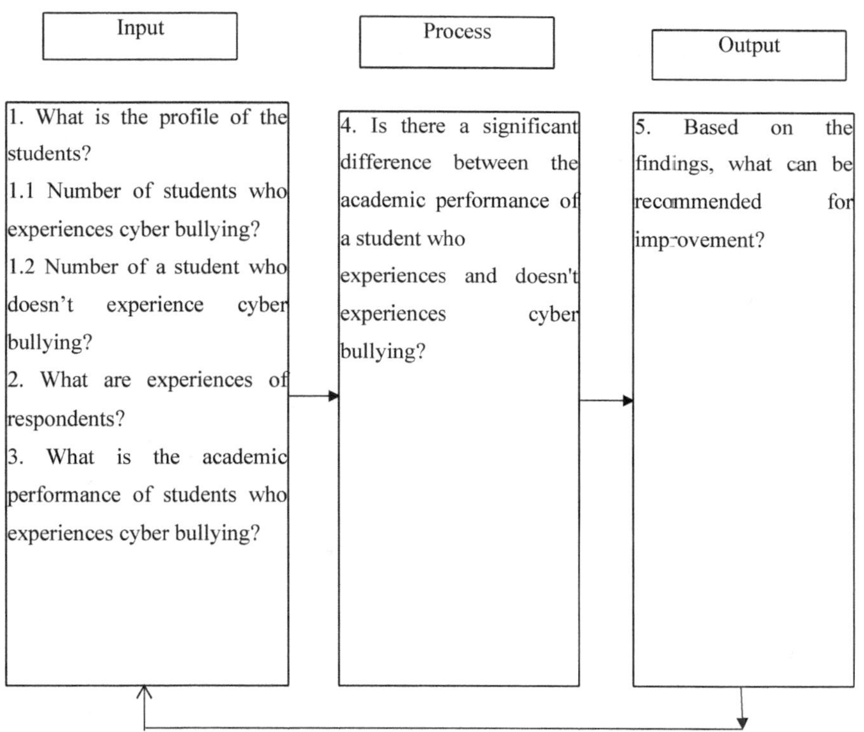

The conceptual framework shows the flow of the study. For the input, it inscribes the profile of respondents in terms of Number of students who experiences cyber bullying and Number of a student who doesn't experience cyber bullying. Also, the Number of a student who doesn't experience cyber bullying. Moreover, is the academic performance of students who experiences cyber bullying. Consequently, the process shows if there is a significant difference between the academic performance of a student who experiences and doesn't experiences cyber bullying. Hence, the output shows off the expected result from the respondents and what can be proposed.

Statement of the Problem

1. What is the profile of the students?

    1.1 Number of students who experiences cyber bullying?

    1.2 Number of a student who doesn't experience cyber bullying?

2. What are experiences of respondents?

3. What is the academic performance of students who experiences cyber bullying?

4. Is there a significant difference between the academic performance of a student who experiences and doesn't experiences cyber bullying?

5. Based on the findings, what can be recommended for improvement?

Hypothesis

    H_o: there is no significant difference between the academic performance of a student who experiences and doesn't experiences cyber bullying

Significance of the Study

Students- The students should become aware regarding cyber bullying. Teachers- This study should use by the teachers to have an effective skills on spreading knowledge about cyber bullying.

Parents- This study will help to inform and to share the information to their children about cyber bullying.

Researchers- The data that gathered from this study will use by the researchers to conduct another research that is related to this study.

Scope and limitation

This study scoped the information that gathered by the researchers that may add some knowledge to the readers regarding cause and effects of cyber bullying, the experiences, and the academic performance of the students who experiences cyber bullying. The researcher was interviewing their selected respondents inside Manuel L. Quezon Senior High School.

This study has a limitation because the students and teachers only in Manuel L. Quezon Senior High School are involved. The researchers believe that this research will know and focus on The cause and effect of social media as a channel on cyber bullying

Definition of Terminologies

Cyber bullying. Is bullying that takes place over digital devices like cell phones, computers, and tablets.

CHAPTER II

RELATED STUDY AND LITERATURE

Review of Related Literature and Studies

Presented in review of related literature and studies are the ideas, information, generalization or conclusion that were included. In this chapter helps in familiarizing data that are relevant and similar to the present study.

According to (Adele, 2017). In digital age where netizens have the freedom to express thoughts and opinions online, there are victims and instances of cyber bullying which occurs every day. (Adele, 2017). "Cyber bullying is the unfortunate by-product of the union of adolescent aggression and electronic communication and its growth is giving cause for concern" (Hinduja and Patchin, 2013).

Also, In a ratio, 1 in 3 young people have experienced cyber-bullying. Cyber bullying has a greater impact on a person either than traditional bullying. (Bauman and Newnam, 2013). Teenagers who are bullied by someone are more likely had to suffer on different problems. They are also had to experience depression and anxiety on their everyday life.

Hence, It may be hard for those who are bullied to maintain their everyday task because of the back of their minds they have doubt to do what they used to do, they are afraid to bully again so there are people who choose to commit suicide than to be criticize again and also, they are experiencing mental health disorders. (Nixon, 2014)

Moreover, Cyber bullying is caused by the eagerness of a person to damage someone's emotions through social networking sites. Also, this caused by frustration or revenge. (Fabian, 2014). "Anyone can be a cyber-bully, and such persons usually have few worries about having a face to face confrontation with their victims. (Polan, 2010). Cyber bullying needed two people or more, bullies commonly reporting mean or hurtful comments and spreading rumors online. Bullies have a fewer worries to show themselves so that they post in it any social networking sites instead of the person (Bullied) face to face. (Qing, 2010).

Consequently, Almost 80% of the U.S teenagers are non-using a social media as a form of communication. According to the study of Bauman and Newnam, there are 56.5% cases of cyber bullying reported in U.S at the year of 2016 this is higher than the 50.7% reported cases on 2015. This implies that as the time goes by, the more that teenagers engage in social media there are high expectancy of cyber bullying. Meanwhile in the Philippines, netizens experiences cyber-attack and online harassment every day.

Furthermore, Philippines is number 4 in the world looking up cyber bullying online (Adele, 2017). There are 782 cases were reported on the ACG in the year of 2016, significantly higher than the 458 incident recorded in 2015. A majority of the cases involved online libel with 498 in this case. Cyber bullying have increased by 70.74% in the year 2016. (Tupas, 2016).

Hence, Cyber bullying can be briefly defined as "sending or posting harmful or cruel text or images using the Internet or other digital communication devices" Willard, N. (2004b, p. 1). This section starts with a definition of the term and an exploration of various forms of cyber bullying. Then, findings from some empirical studies are discussed to provide background information for this study.

According to Poland, 2010The word cyber bullying did not even exist a decade ago, yet the problem has become a pervasive one today. Cyber bullies do not have to be strong or fast; they just need access to a cell phone or computer and a desire to terrorize. Anyone can be a cyber-bully, and such persons usually have few worries about having face-to-face confrontation with their victims. In fact, the anonymity of cyber bullying may cause students who normally would not bully in the tradition-sense to become a cyber-bully (Poland, 2010).

Also, In Mishna's et al (2012) study, over 30% of the students identified as involved in cyber bullying, either as victims or perpetrators; one in four of the students (25.7%) reported having been involved in cyber bullying as both a bully and a victim within a three month period. In Adams' (2010) research, approximately 20% of students admitted to having been cyber bullied.

However, many more students reported incidents that fall under its definition. Posting mean or hurtful comments and spreading rumors online was the most common complaint in their random survey of 4,400 students ages 10 to 18 in

February 2010. Not surprisingly, cyber bullying is most prevalent among middle schoolers.

Moreover, the incidence of cyber bullying increases slightly with age. Finally, teens spending much time on the Internet, reporting higher ICT expertise and owning a computer with privileged online access share an increased likelihood of online bullying behavior (Walrave & Heirman, 2011).

Hence, Cyber bullying can be devastating for victims and their families. The psychological harm inflicted by cyber bullying, just like bullying, is reflected in low self-esteem, school failure, anger, anxiety, depression, school avoidance, school violence, and suicide. It is even possible that the damage from cyber bullying would be greater than bullying because there is no escape for the victims; harmful material could be easily preserved as well as quickly and widely spread. Further, many people who would not harass others face-to-face might cyber bully peers because they believe that they could hide or it would be acceptable to engage in such behavior virtually. (Beran & Li, 2005Li, Q. 2005. Willard, 2004)

The psychological impact of cyber bullying on its victims is similar to traditional bullying. It includes low self-esteem, depression, anger, anxiety, academic difficulties, school avoidance, school violence, and suicide (Beran, T., & Li, Q., 2005)

Olweus (1991, 1993) described bullying behavior as occurring when a student is repeatedly exposed to negative actions by another person(s), creating an imbalance in power between the perpetrator and victim. However, this definition is limited to school samples and traditional bullying behaviors such as physical threats (punching, kicking and hitting), verbal (e.g., name calling) and/or psychological relational bullying (e.g., peer exclusion). More recently, Tokunaga (2010) proposed the following definition of cyber bullying *"any behavior performed through electronic or digital media by individuals or groups that repeatedly communicates hostile or aggressive messages intended to inflict harm or discomfort on others"*

StopBullying.gov reports that youth who are bullied have a higher risk of depression and anxiety. Symptoms may include:

6. increased feelings of sadness and loneliness

7. changes in sleep and eating patterns

8. loss of interest in activities

9. more health complaints

Youth who are bullied are more likely to struggle personally and at school. They may:

- miss, skip or drop out of school

- receive poor grades

- have lower self-esteem

- use alcohol and drugs

Bullying can lead to thoughts about suicide, sometimes persisting into adulthood. In one study, adults who were bullied as youth were three times more likely to have suicidal thoughts or inclinations. Youth who are bullied may retaliate through violent measures. In 12 of 15 school shooting cases in the 1990s, the shooters had a history of being bullied.

According to (Willard, 2007) the causes and effects of cyber bullying Sarah C. Edwards National American University The Cause and Effect of Cyber Bullying. Cyber bullying is the use of mobile phones, prompt messaging, e-mail, chat rooms, or social networking sites like Facebook and Twitter to annoy, impend, or threaten someone. Cyber bullying is a problem that has been aggregating rapidly these past couple of years (Willard, 2007). The following are some of the Causes and Effects of cyber bullying among students.

Also, Causes of cyber bullying Motivated by revenge: There is a predisposition for some kids who are victims of harassment to find a way to strike back. They feel correct in their movements because they, too, have been stressed and anguished. By bullying others, they feel a sense of relief and justification for what they experienced. These kids will go after the bully directly, or they will aim someone whom they recognize to be weaker or more susceptible than them.

Hence, Humans are living in the world where people bully and get bullied. According to an anonymous (2014), "Cyber bullying happens for many of the same reasons as any other type of bullying, but it may be even more appealing because it can be done anonymously". Cyber bullying is an action of using the social media technology to bully others and in main cases, it is used anonymously.

Consequently, by using cell phones or any other devices, such as computers and tablets to connect to the internet, a large number of individuals have been spending their time bullying other people. Cyber bullying may not harm somebody physically; instead it may harm them mentally.

According to another anonymous (2015), there are two kinds of people who are likely to bully; the socially active people and the socially inactive people. It is said that bullying results in an upgrade of confidence, thinking the control is on the hands of the bully as it is also the main reason of why socially active people may bully other people; it makes them feel powerful as it is also a way to maintain their popularity.

Moreover, How about the socially inactive people? Socially inactive people may bully other people as it is a chance to fit in and to prove that they are not weak and that they are compatible with their surroundings. Like the socially active people, bullying also makes socially inactive people feel powerful. Cyber bullying is a great danger to the society. It causes harm to people and results negatively for, both, the bully and the victim. It is said that cyber bullying is a serious worldwide issue and that it needs to be resolved. If they cannot do cyber bullying anonymously, they will go as far as they will face claim other people only to do cyber bullying.

Who's targeted? **How often does it happen?** Depending on the type of harassment, between 9-34% of young people say they have been targeted for cyber bullying in the past year (about 16% say they've been targeted monthly or more often):

8. 31% report being targeted by rude or mean comments

9. 13% report having rumors, true or false, spread about them

10. 14% report being targeted by threatening or aggressive comments

11. 9% report they've felt worried or threatened because someone was bothering or harassing them online

12. 4% report someone has used the Internet to threaten or embarrass them by posting or sending information for others to see

In the other hand, who is targeted? Boys and girls appear to be equally likely to be targets of harassment online. There is some indication that girls may be more likely than boys to be targeted infrequently (once or twice), but just as likely to be targeted frequently (monthly or more often).

- Older teens seem to be more likely to be involved than younger teens. In fact, a recent national survey of youth reports that the average age of a teenager involved in cyber bullying is 15 years old.

- Youth who bully others online as well as those who are bullied offline are more likely to be targeted online.

- Some youth have related or unrelated social problems.

You should also know that teens that are targeted by harassment are more likely than teens who are not harassed to report harassing others online too. Often this can be retaliation. But, just because someone sends you a mean or harassing message doesn't mean it's not harassment if you do the same thing back.

Furthermore, being upset by the experience: Most teens that are targeted are not upset by the experience. So, if you have been targeted but are not upset by it, that's OK. Data shows that youth who are bullied at school are more likely to be extremely upset by what happened than those who are bullied online.

One-third of teens who have been targeted say they felt very upset or afraid because of what happened. So, if you have been targeted and are upset by it, that's OK, too.

Teens that are upset by the experience are more likely to:

- Report that the harasser was over 18 years old.
- Be younger themselves (like 10-12 years old).
- Report aggressive or "creepy" messages, like being asked to send a picture, or being telephoned by the harasser.

Also, For kids and teens Know that it's not your fault. What people call "bullying" is sometimes an argument between two people. But if someone is repeatedly cruel to you, that's bullying and you mustn't blame yourself. No one deserves to be treated cruelly. Don't respond or retaliate. Sometimes a reaction is exactly what aggressors are looking for because they think it gives them power over you, and you don't want to empower a bully. As for retaliating, getting back at a bully turns you into one – and can turn one mean act into a chain reaction. If you can, remove yourself from the situation. If you can't, sometimes humor disarms or distracts a person from bullying.

Consequently, Save the evidence. The only good news about bullying online or on phones is that it can usually be captured, saved, and shown to someone who can help. You can save that evidence in case things escalate. Tell the person to stop. This is completely up to you – don't do it if you don't feel totally comfortable doing it, because you need to make your position completely clear that you will not stand for this treatment any more. You may need to practice beforehand with someone you trust, like a parent or good friend.

Furthermore, Reach out for help – especially if the behavior's really getting to you. You deserve backup. See if there's someone who can listen, help you process what's going on and work through it – a friend, relative or maybe an adult you trust.

Use available tech tools. Most social media apps and services allow you to block the person. Whether the harassment's in an app, texting, comments or tagged photos, do yourself a favor and block the person. You can also report the problem to the service. That probably won't end it, but you don't need the harassment in your face, and you'll be less tempted to respond. If you're getting threats of physical harm, you should call your local police (with a parent or guardian's help) and consider reporting it to school authorities. Protect your accounts. Don't share your passwords with anyone – even your closest friends, who may not be close forever – and password-protect your phone so no one can use it to impersonate you. You'll find advice at

Hence, If someone you know is being bullied, take action. Just standing by can empower an aggressor and does nothing to help. The best thing you can do is try to stop the bullying by taking a stand against it. If you can't stop it, support the person being bullied. If the person's a friend, you can listen and see how to help. Consider together whether you should report the bullying. If you're not already friends, even a kind word can help reduce the pain. At the very least, help by not passing along a mean message and not giving positive attention to the person doing the bullying.

Moreover, Additional advice for parents Know that you're lucky if your child asks for help. Most young people don't tell their parents about bullying online or offline. So if your child's losing sleep or doesn't want to go to school or seems agitated when on his or her computer or phone, ask why as calmly and open-heartedly as possible. Feel free to ask if it has anything to do with mean behavior or social issues. But even if it does, don't assume it's bullying. You won't know until you get the full story, starting with your child's perspective.

Work with your child. There are two reasons why you'll want to keep your child involved. Bullying and cyber bullying usually involve a loss of dignity or control over a social situation, and involving your child in finding solutions helps him or her regain that. The second reason is about context. Because the bullying is almost always related to school life and our kids understand the situation and context better than parents ever can, their perspective is key to getting to the bottom of the situation and working out a solution. You may need to have private conversations with others, but let your child know if you do, and report back. This is about your child's life, so your child needs to be part of the solution.

According to Fayol (2015) Respond thoughtfully, not fast. What parents don't always know is that they can make things worse for their kids if they act rashly. A lot of cyber bullying involves somebody getting marginalized (put down and excluded), which the bully thinks increases his or her power or status. If you respond publicly or if your child's peers find out about even a discreet meeting with school authorities, the marginalization can get worse, which is why any response needs to be well thought out.

Also, More than one perspective needed. Your child's account of what happened is likely completely sincere, but remember that one person's truth isn't necessarily everybody's. You'll need to get other perspectives and be open-minded about what they are. Sometimes kids let themselves get pulled into chain reactions, and often what we see online is only one side of or part of the story.

What victims say helps most is to be heard – really listened to – either by a friend or an adult who cares? That's why, if your kids come to you for help, it's so important to respond thoughtfully and involve them. Just by being heard respectfully, a child is often well on the way to healing.

Hence, The ultimate goal is restored self-respect and greater resilience in your child. This, not getting someone punished, is the best focus for resolving the problem and helping your child heal. What your child needs most is to regain a sense of dignity. Sometimes that means standing up to the bully, sometimes not. Together, you and your child can figure out how to get there.

Consequently, One positive outcome we don't often think about (or hear in the news) is resilience. We know the human race will never completely eradicate meanness or cruelty, and we also know that bullying is not, as heard in past generations, "normal" or a rite of passage. We need to keep working to eradicate it. But when it does happen and we overcome it – our resilience grows. It's not something that can be "downloaded" or taught. We grow it through exposure to challenges and figuring out how to deal with them. So sometimes it's important to give them space to do that and let them know we have their back. In the digital age where netizens are given freedom to voice their opinions online, throwing and receiving cyber-attacks has become a daily occurrence. Since it is easy for netizens to hide their faces behind their social media accounts, it has also become easier for many to respond to various issues or people with vulgar and threatening words. In the Philippines alone, several netizens experience cyber bullying and online harassment every day.

According to Nobullying.com, the Philippines is Number 4 in the world in looking up cyber bullying online, which, it says, shows that has become an issue. Camarines Sur Rep. Rolando Andaya, author of the Anti-Cyber-Bullying bill said cyber bullying can potentially affect not only school-age children but also any individual who has access to a mobile phone or the internet. He defined cyber bullying as acts of cruelty committed using the internet or any form of electronic media or technology that has the effect of stripping one's dignity or causing reasonable fear or physical or emotional harm. The lawmaker also considered repeated sending of offensive, rude and insulting message, distributing of belittling information about the victim, as a form of cyber bullying as well as posting or sending of offensive photos of the victim, whether digitally altered or not or were taken with or without consent, as long as it has the intention to humiliate and embarrass the victim.

"Cyber bullying is one of the most dangerous things that can confront a child on the Internet, because it can have a negative impact on their psyche and cause problems for the rest of their lives. The best solution in this case is to talk to your child and to use parental control software that can alert you to any suspicious changes to their social network page," he explained. - Alixandra Caole Vila (2016)

According to Sherri Gordon (2017) Bullying, no matter whether it is traditional bullying or cyberbullying, causes significant emotional and psychological distress. In fact, just like any other victim of bullying, cyberbullied kids experience anxiety, fear, depression, and low self-esteem. They also may deal with low self-esteem, experience physical symptoms, and struggle academically. But targets of cyberbullying also experience some unique consequences and negative feelings.

Also, Here are some common feelings cyberbullied teens and tweens often experience. Feel overwhelmed. Being targeted by cyberbullies is crushing especially if a lot of kids are participating in the bullying. It can feel at times like the entire world knows what it is going on. Sometimes the stress of dealing with cyberbullying can cause kids to feel like the situation is more than they can handle.

Feel vulnerable and powerless. Victims of cyberbullying often find it difficult to feel safe. Typically, this is because the <u>bullying</u> can invade their home through a computer or cell phone at any time of day. They no longer have a place where they can escape. To a victim, it feels like the bullying is everywhere. Additionally, because the <u>bullies</u> can remain anonymous, this can escalate feelings of fear. Kids who are targeted have no idea who is inflicting the pain—although some cyberbullies <u>choose people they know.</u>

Feel exposed and humiliated. Because <u>cyberbullying</u> occurs in cyberspace, online bullying feels permanent. Kids know that once something is out there, it will always be out there. When cyberbullying occurs, the nasty posts, messages or texts can be shared with multitudes of people. The sheer volume of people that know about the bullying can lead to intense feelings of humiliation.

Feel dissatisfied with who they are. Cyberbullying often attacks victims where they are most vulnerable. As a result, targets of cyberbullying often begin to doubt their worth and value. They may respond to these feelings by harming themselves in some way. For instance, if a girl is called fat, she may begin a crash diet with the belief that if she alters how she looks then the bullying will stop. Other times victims will try to change something about their appearance or attitude in order to avoid additional cyberbullying.

Feel angry and vengeful. Sometimes victims of cyberbullying will get angry about what is happening to them. As a result, they plot <u>revenge</u> and engage in retaliation. This approach is dangerous because it keeps them locked in <u>the bully-victim cycle</u>. It is always better to <u>forgive a bully</u> than it is to get even.

Feel disinterested in life. When cyberbullying is ongoing, victims often relate to the world around them differently than others. For many, life can feel hopeless and meaningless. They lose interest in things they once enjoyed and spend less time interacting with family and friends. And in some cases depression and <u>thoughts of suicide</u> can set in. If you notice a change in your child's mood, get him evaluated by a doctor as soon as possible.

Feel alone and isolated. Cyberbullying sometimes causes teens to be excluded and <u>ostracized</u> at school. This experience is particularly painful because <u>friends</u> are crucial at this age. When kids don't have friends, this can lead to more bullying. What's more, when cyberbullying occurs, most people recommend shutting off the computer or turning off the cell phone. But, for teens this often means cutting off communication with their world. Their phones and their computers are one of the most important ways they communicate with others. If that option for communication is removed, they can feel secluded and cut off from their world.

Feel disinterested in school. Cyberbullying victims often have much higher rates of absenteeism at school than non-bullied kids. They skip school to avoid facing the kids bullying them or because they are embarrassed and humiliated by the messages that were shared. Their grades suffer too because they find it difficult to concentrate or study because of the anxiety and stress the bullying causes. And in some cases, kids will either drop out of school or lose interest in continuing their education after high school.

Feel anxious and depressed. Victims of cyberbullying often succumb to anxiety, depression and other stress-related conditions. This occurs primarily because cyberbullying erodes their self-confidence and self-esteem. Additionally, the added stress of coping with cyberbullying on a regular basis erodes their feelings of happiness and contentment.

Feel ill. When kids are cyberbullied, they often experience headaches, stomachaches or other physical ailments. The stress of bullying also can cause stress-related conditions like stomach ulcers and skin conditions. Additionally, kids who are cyberbullied may experience changes in eating habits like skipping meals or binge eating. And their sleep patterns may be impacted. They may suffer from insomnia, sleep more than usual or experience nightmares.

Feel suicidal. Cyberbullying increases the risk of suicide. Kids that are constantly tormented by peers through text messages, instant messaging, social media and other outlets, often begin to feel hopeless. They may even begin to feel like the only way to escape the pain is through suicide. As a result, they may fantasize about ending their life in order to escape their tormentors. If your child is being cyberbullied, do not dismiss their feelings. Be sure you communicate daily, take steps to help end the torment and keep close tabs on changes in mood and behavior. Get your child evaluated by a health care professional if notice any personality changes at all.

According to nobullying.com (2016) Cyber bullying affects people from any age or walk of life, including children, teens and adults who all feel very distressed and alone when being bullied online. Cyber bullying can make you feel totally overwhelmed which can result in many feeling embarrassed that they are going through such a devastating time, and not knowing what support is available to them. Many children feel unable to confide in an adult because they feel ashamed and wonder whether they will be judged, told to ignore it or close their account which they might not want to do.

Cyber Bullying. That term has been used quite a bit in recent years. Although it's becoming more common, there is still some confusion on what it really means. What exactly is cyber bullying, and what are the effects of cyber bullying? This is when someone uses technology and electronic devices to do mean things, such as start rumours, post embarrassing things on social media, or send inappropriate content or text messages <u>meant to incite violence</u> or hurt feelings in some way. These bullies use any kind of device they can to attack their victims: computers, phones, tablets, chat rooms, <u>through online gaming and social media sites</u>.

When cyber bullying occurs it is often followed by negative effects. The <u>2011 Youth Risk Behavior Surveillance</u> Survey showed that 16 per cent of students in grades 9-12 were cyber bullied in the past year. Additionally, the <u>2008-2009 School Crime Supplement</u> showed 6 per cent of students in grades 6-12 had encountered some form of cyber bullying. Online bullying can lead to loss of self-esteem, and even contemplation of suicide. With access to so many tools that could potentially do harm, safety is a primary concern to teachers and parents. Due to this, the effects of cyber bullying are more important to be aware of then ever before.

The Effects of Cyber Bullying The effects of <u>cyber bullying</u> may not be noticeable at first, but the stress factor builds up over time. Many students experiencing cyber bullying <u>feel alone and scared</u>. In most instances, cyber bullying doesn't start online, but in person. The situation then escalates. The signs of cyber bullying include:

- Not wanting to go to school.

- A sharp drop in grades and performance.

- Skipping school.

- Sudden self-esteem issues.

- Complaints of illnesses.

- Acting withdrawn.

- <u>Use of alcohol or drugs</u>.

The Effects of Bullying on Children <u>Cyber bullying is a very serious matter</u>. Students have taken their own lives because they felt pressured, embarrassed and felt they had no other alternatives. With so many technology devices available, and the online world mostly unsupervised, there is a lot of room to someone to act maliciously.

What to do if you've been cyber bullied, or are worries about someone who may be the victim of bullying? The first thing that usually has a positive impact is communication. If you're a student, <u>talk to an adult and explain how you're feeling</u> and what has been happening. If you're a parent or adult, start random conversations about cyber bullying and what to do if it occurs, especially if you're recognizing symptoms. Sometimes the student may not want to say anything in <u>fear of the ramifications</u>. By starting a healthy, non-threatening dialogue, it could make the difference between a positive or negative consequence. Other things that can be done:

- Don't give out passwords for your computer, cell phone or social media profiles.

- Don't share anything personal with anyone that could potentially put it on the Internet. That includes pictures, secrets or information on others that you may have.

- Save the bullying messages or postings as proof.

- Block the person doing the cyber bullying.

- Turn off your technology. Sometimes you need to take a break and step away from being engaged all the time.

The effects of cyber bullying are very serious topics, <u>with many sad stories</u>. However, the entire outlook isn't bleak: The U.S. Department of Health and Human Services has an initiative to counteract cyber bullying. There are also many organizations that encourage healthy dialogue and offer solutions to situations that may occur. Here at <u>Nobullying.com,</u> we advocate for educating, advising and counselling individuals who are concerned with the effects of cyber bullying. Take a stand with us to fight for what's right. Someone's future could depend on it.

The Effects of Cyber Bullying: Five Steps To Take Action Today If you want to know what to do about the effects of cyber bullying, here are five steps you can take to protect yourself and your family today to prevent such atrocities:

- <u>Report EVERY incident of bullying</u>, no matter how small. This does not mean that you have to go to federal court with a minor incident, but it does mean that you should take every incident seriously and take the appropriate actions to prevent it from happening to someone else.

- Consider the source and report to network administrators, as well as authorities. When an incident occurs online, you have the right to report this to system or network administrators and let them know what happened, when, whom it involved, and other information. Local police may need to be involved depending on the severity of the case. Often the system administrator of the website on which the bullying occurred will be best able to help. They will also be able to identify the culprits of the bullying so that you can report the names to proper authorities.

- You could install <u>monitoring software</u> on your computers. This is not always the best option; as it is better to be open an honest with your children, rather than spying on them. By monitoring the behaviour and sites visited of your child while online, you can get an idea of the patterns that preceded the incident and this can be valuable information to use to tell authorities should bullying reach higher levels.

- Have a *zero tolerance* policy against cyber bullying. Explain to your children that you will neither tolerate their being bullied, nor will you tolerate their bullying of other children online. Just like in the real world, they all need to understand that <u>bullying is harassment</u> when it occurs off campus and is punishable by law.

- Get involved. Perhaps the best thing parents can do in this day and age is to get involved in what your child is doing. This is just good parenting and involves a lot more than asking what they did at school. Really probe and find out whom their friends are, what is on their mind, and why their grades have fallen. Often falling grades is the result of a problem at school. A child and you may need to take up some issues with the school counsellor in order to get to the bottom of it.

Spread the word about The Effects of Cyber Bullying Now! The effects of bullying online and offline are very hard for a teen to overcome. Bullying is not a rite of passages, and the effects of bullying online and offline can remain forever in a child's psyche. Let's prevent the effects of bullying from falling on the coming generations now. Please help us in this battle by sharing this information, and other cyber bullying information, on social media. Also we welcome you to post a comment and join the discussion below

CHAPTER III

RESEARCH METHODOLOGY

Research Design

This study conducted according to the design of mix experimental and non-experimental design of Quantitative research. In the Experimental design, it tries to emphasize objective measurements and the statistical analysis of data collected through questionnaires. While in the non-experimental design, it is a descriptive type studies that used to observe, document, and describe regarding The cause and effect of social media as a channel on cyber bullying

Sampling procedure

Slovin's Formula is used to calculate the sample size (n) given the population size (N) and a margin of error (e).It's a random sampling technique formula to estimate sampling size this method will be used to get the number of respondents in this study to gather a data regarding The cause and effect of social media as a channel on cyber bullying.

-It is computed as $n = N / (1+Ne^2)$.

Whereas:

n = no. of samples

N = total population

e = Margin of error

Instrument of the study

The researchers used survey questionnaire for their instrument to gather a data that was used for this study. The survey questionnaire was divided into two parts which are the profile of the students and the survey regarding to The cause and effect of social media as a channel on cyber bullying

. According to Dave Vannette 2015 a survey is a method of gathering information from a sample of people, traditionally with the intention of generalizing the results to a larger population. Surveys provide a critical source of data and insights for nearly everyone engaged in the information economy, from businesses and the media to government and academics.The survey is the collection of information regards to the kind, action or opinion of large group of people that define as one population or widepart of research that made of variety of styles under the questions for respondents.

Data Gathering

Data gathering procedure is a process of collecting information from the respondents surveying actually involves gathering responses from the topic of the study through a written medium. The researchers will distribute the survey questionnaires to their selected respondents for the needed answer regarding The cause and effect of social media as a channel on cyber bullying

The researchers used Stratified random sampling is a method of sampling that involves the division of a population into smaller groups known as strata. In stratified random sampling, the strata are formed based on members' shared attributes or characteristics. A random sample from each stratum is taken in a number proportional to the stratum's size when compared to the population. These subsets of the strata are then pooled to form a random sample.

Data Analysis Techniques/ Statistical Treatment

According to Ronald Fisher 2012 Analysis of variance or also known as ANOVA is a collection of statistical model used to analyze the differences among group means and their associated procedures.

The researchers will be use analysis of variance test to determine the result independent variables have on the dependent variable into the middle regression study. The researchers utilize ANOVA test results in an F-Test to generate additional data that aligns with the proposed regression model.

Formula:

$$\bar{x} = ⸮\frac{⸮\frac{\Sigma xi}{⸮}}{n}$$

Notations:

$\bar{x}$ just stands for the "sample mean"

Σ means "add up"

xi "all of the x-values"

n means "the number of items in the sample"

INFLUENCE OF HAVING KPOP IDOLS AMONG

STUDENTS IN MANUEL LUIS QUEZON S

ENIOR HIGH SCHOOL

A research paper presentedto the faculty of

practical research in Manule L. Quezon

Senior High School

Submitted by:

Merry Jane Iligan

Submitted to:

Dr. Mark Vincent B. Emit

March 2018

CHAPTER 1

THE PROBLEM AND ITS BACKGROUND

The first chapter of this study will show and discuss the statement of the problem, scope and limitation and theoretical framework. Aside from these, the researchers did some research findings to support and answer the study we are aiming to solve and help better understand the entire study.

Introduction

In the past events, the Philippines had been colonized by foreign invaders such as Spain, America and Japan that made the Filipinos learn and adopt some cultures, beliefs and values inherited from them. Now the Philippines are still experiencing the feeling of 'being colonized' by the culture of South Korea.

The popularity of Korean Wave or 'hallyu' started in late 1990's. Part of the Korean wave is their overwhelming success not just in music but as well as in South Korean dramas and movies. K-dramas and K-pop go to its extent through the East, South and Southeast Asia. As the time goes by, Korean Wave was known all over the world carried by the Internet and social media and the popularity of K-pop music videos on YouTube. The term Korean pop music does not only pertain to music but with accompaniment of movement that makes South Korea popular in Asia and neighboring countries from 1990's until present (Villano,2010).

Korean Pop Music originated from South Korea and has now become a trend in the Philippines. It is evident that their music has already been accepted by the young people.

Nowadays, it is very common to the 21st generation. It reached our country rapidly and lots of teens are fond of it. Korean fashionable clothes, gestures, dance steps, coal eyeliners and the bangs flip trademark caught the attention of vast number of teens. No doubt, Korean music became part of the daily life routine of students.

In this study, we will use the term "Kpop" to introduce the culture of Korea here in the Philippines. Kpop is a coined term not only for their popular music but all the related reasons behind the success of dominating Korea's popular works that was already introduced here in the Philippines. Examples of that are the K-drama, music videos, dance covers, Korean movies, Korean music and others.

As researchers, we are seeking answers regarding some questions about the sudden popularity of Kpop invasion. We want to distinguish what are the good and bad influences of fantasizing their idols. Does it affect the performance of the students? Does it change the way people behave? How do K-pop fans interact with others?

Because of the rising popularity of Korean culture in our country, the curiosity motivates us to conduct and perform this study.

Conceptual Framework

IPO (Input, Process, and Output) Models of teamwork that examine relationships between variables people bring with them to an interaction (inputs), the interaction among people (process, and the subjective and objective outcomes of this interaction (output). A graphical representation of all the factors that make up a process. An input-process-output diagram includes all of the materials and information required for the process, details of the process itself, and descriptions of all products and by-products resulting from the process. The researcher uses this model to easy determine and they use this to easy understand what the flow of the

INPUT	PROCESS	OUTPUT
1. What is the demographic profile of the respondents in terms of: 1.1Number of students have been influence 1.2Number of students who not been influence 2.How does a kpop idol influence the students? 2.1Good influence 2.2Bad influence 3. What is the level of influence having kpop idols in the students?	Is there any significant difference between the influence of kpop idols in the students	Based on the findings, what can be recommended for improvement?

Significance Of The Study

This study deals with the influence of having Kpop idols on one's social behavior, as well as their social life and academic performances. This study will help the following people and be benefited.

Through this study, the researchers believe that students will become aware on what is fad nowadays. Through this research, people might get some information on how will act, behave and socialize in an appropriate manner in their environment. They can also gain understanding of their fandom and how the Kpop media content affect their decisions and participation in many activities in their lives.

The outcome of this research may also help businessman. They will be able consider the taste of their consumer. Business about Korean stuff such as their favorite K-pop Idols souvenir items, concert tickets, albums are now in-demand in this generation. Filipino markets are now recognizing the presence of Kpop trends. This study may also help the broadcasting networks such as GMA 7 or ABS-CBN to create strategies targeting Kpop fans as potential audience and increase their network's ratings. "Top Philippine TV stations GMA Network and ABS-CBN are leading the way in importing Korean drama (Hicap, 2009)."

This study also encourages the parents to monitor the behavior of their children who are fond of K-pop Idols. It will enable them to guide and discipline their children to not get too attracted to what they are fond of.

Lastly, future researchers may also benefit from this research. They can take advantage of specified information and ideas for their future research.

Scope And Limitations

This study covers the influence of Korean music, dances, shows and dramas among ABM students of Pamantasan ng Lungsod ng Valenzuela. The interview will be comprised of the discussion about the influence of having Kpop idols and how it affects their social life and behavior, and also the students' academic performance. In addition to that, we will focus primarily on Kpop artists and their works such as their videos, fashion, dance choreography that really fascinates the Filipino youth. Also, this study is not only for the respondents who likes Kpop and does not attempt to generalize the Filipino teenage Kpop fans with the non- Kpop fans. This study attempts to understand the individual fandom of the Filipino by means of survey and questionnaires. There are ten respondents from selected students of ABM strand who will answer all our questions. The ages of selected students range from 15- 19 years old. Aside from interview, the researchers will conduct survey and categorize all gathered information and tally the data for the research.

The possible questions that may arise in our study is that the weakness of conducting a survey and questionnaires that may not answer truthfully by them. This may cause for the researchers to the difficulty of generalizing all ideas gathered. Nevertheless, to ensure that the survey we are going to conduct can get in-depth information through forming sensible questions that can be easily answered by using specific multiple choices in a certain question.

Definition Of Terms

This section helps you to understand the used terms or words in this study.

Fan – a group of person who adore a specific performer.

Fan – a person with an intense enthusiasm or attachment to Korean popular music, videos and artists.

Fandom – the state or attitude of being a fan.

Fantasize – to imagine doing things that are very unlikely to do.

Hallyu – Korean Wave is a rising popularity of Korean culture.

Idol – a greatly loved or admired person.

K-pop (Korean Popular Music) – is a musical genre originating in South Korea that is characterized by a wide variety of audiovisual elements.

Kpop – all about the Korean culture includes fashion trends, language, beliefs, great works and etc.

CHAPTER II

REVIEW OF RELATED LITERATURE AND STUDIES

This chapter aims to present related literature and related studies in local or foreign. This chapter is our baseline data of the problem states and provides a general picture of our research topic.

Local Literature

The "Hallyu" refers to the "wave" of popularity of South Korean entertainment and culture that starts in late 1990s. The first Korean telenovelas aired locally in 2003. The Korean culture become increasingly popular when the Korean Cultural Center in Manila organize Hallyu sa Pinas which is about the impact of the so-called "Korean Wave". Dr. Flores, a Filipino Literature professor at UP Diliman, told RAPPLER that Korean Soap Operas were quite different from the locally-produced series. The target audience of the Korean drama is the lower middle class, with aspirations to advance in their economic and social status. "The effect on the Filipino audience is that when the view urban scenes of Seoul, there is a dream, an aspiration to go to Korea." Dr. Flores explained.

A professor from UP, Florinda Mateo noted "The primary reason why Filipinos are so enamored with Korean dramas is the storytelling. It's not as much about the plot as about the way stories are told." Mateo explained that many Filipino viewers are amazed at "how fast the story could be told, how fast a plot can be develop and a kind of acting." According to Mateo, influenced of "Hallyu" in today's Filipino soap operas is in the stories now told.

"Hallyu" is not just about telenovelas. K-Pop is also becoming more and more popular among the Filipino youth. Choy who works for music events organizing company said that crowdsourcing enables the fans to feel closer to their idols in a way that Western music cannot give them. Choy said that the Korean culture is "not a fad anymore" and K-Pop is considered a musical genre on its own. The Korean wave influenced Filipino movies such as "Kimmy Dora". "Filipinos like Korean films because they are fresher, less formulated and with a degree of violence and eroticism that appeals to local audience," said Chris Martinez, the writer of Kimmy Dora.

The fans show their fandom in their own ways to express their support toward their idols. There is a basis how those idols of their own attract them. The reason behind it is the Korea's great works of showing their talents and enhancing it which hooked most of the youth in this generation.

Foreign Literature

In a foreign article, some Vietnamese were greatly affected because of Kpop fandom. In Vietnam, K-pop has become trendy, not confined to Korea but spread worldwide, especially in Asia. The so-called Korean wave has exerted its strong influences on young people, particularly teenagers, in some Asian countries, including Vietnam. It cannot be denied that in addition to a type of entertainment, K-pop functions as "a cultural bridge" helping improve the understandings of Asian cultures in general and Korean culture in particular. However, it also affects teenagers in a negative way.

First, K-pop contributes to some severe health problems in young fans. Indeed, those who spend too much time on watching music videos, searching information about K-pop idols usually suffer asthenia as a result of lacking sleep, staying up late and skipping meals. Some are addicted to K-pop so much that they lock themselves in all day, stick to computer screen or TV screen instead of going out with friends, doing extracurricular activities, playing sports, which are good for their physical and mental health.

Consequently, they may be in a debilitating condition or even have eye diseases, memory loss sooner or later. Furthermore, it is evident that teen fans tend to be depression-prone and autism-prone. The reason simply is that they would rather talk about their idols than communicate with other people or share their own troubles.

Obviously, teenagers may suffer physical, mental and psychological problems because of heavy K-pop addiction.

Secondly, K-pop is blamed for a fall in academic achievement of some teen–aged students. This is probably because some who are into K-pop are so obsessed with some girl bands or boy bands that they do not pay attention in class and keep listening music during lessons.

They also stay at home stalking their favorite idols via Internet, wasting time on reading such nonsensical stuffs about them as scandals and debut years instead of reading books, doing homework or participating in learning groups. In other words, they are being distracted from their studies. Therefore, it will come as no surprise that they have poorer performance at school.

Last but not least, K-pop may lead to lack of social contact and affect relationships between children and parents. It is clear that most K-pop addicts do not go out as much as they used to. They prefer sitting "within four corners" and enjoying their favorite SNSD's hits or Super Junior's new album without being annoyed by others, specifically their parents. Some crazy fans publicly show extreme attitude towards, even terribly insult their own parents, who work hard every day to feed them, on Facebook, Twitter, blogs or social networks just because they are scolded, grumbled or not given money to buy new albums, buy tickets to attend shows of "Oppa".

In a worse case, K-pop not only leads to conflicts between children and parents but also contributes to tragic consequences. As can be seen in newspapers, recently, it is not rare that parents kill their own child not just because they are "not as good as oppa" but mostly because they are too disappointed.

To sum up, K-pop is not that bad but its influences are causing troubles for teenagers in particular and society in general. Health problems and poor performance at school are serious consequences. However, more importantly, K-pop threatens to destroy close-knit relationships between children and parents.

The fandom in this article causes a lot of conflicts between their families and his fandom to Kpop.

Local Studies

According to Hicap (2010), the reason why Kpop culture is very popular in the Philippines is because of the attractive looks of young stars, unique moves in dancing, and their Korean fashion which Filipino youths find it as a complete package.

Most of the Filipinos are fascinated by the Korean look. Korean has a sense of fashion. Korean hairstyles became trend in the Philippines today (Kapuso Mo Jessica Soho, 2010).

The Filipino fans are hook to Korean fashion not only in Koreanovelas and Kpop music. Students imitate the hair which is very popular to the Philippines, clothing style and shoes of Korean whether it doesn't fit to them (Ayala, 2009). Every student cut his/her hair with Korean hair approach and sometimes they violate the school policy on proper haircut but this does not matter as long as they will fit in the trend. Korean hairstyle is now at the top of young Filipino hairstyle choice. What matter to them is to look like Korean and they copy the Koreans perfectly.

The migration of Koreans to the country and the increasing popularity of Kpop contributed to the entertainment industry of Philippine TV (Ayala, 2009). Dramas originated from Korea conquer the Philippine television by buying box sets of Korean drama episode from the producers and air it to the local TV network (Hicap, 2009). The two major TV network GMA and ABS-CBN hired local voice talents who dub the lines of the actors from the dramas. Some Koreanovelas that have been aired in the Philippines that got high ratings on TV network are Stairway to Heaven, Lovers in Paris, Boys over Flowers, My Girl, Romantic princess, Memories in Bali, East of Eden, Artificial Beauty, Only You, Queen Seon Deok, Jumong, The Legend, to name a few.

According to AGB Nielsen Philippines, a media research, Koreanovelas hit the local TV network rather than the local drama of Pinoy artists.as observed in the ratings of the shows. This is how Korean dramas have affected the Philippine TV, proving that more and more Filipinos are being entertained by the Korean dramas.

This is a proof that Korean dramas continue to save the Philippine TV networks by patronizing it by the audience. Indeed, Korean dramas have affected the Filipino as well as the Filipino movies has an approach of Korean taste.

Foreign Studies

According to the studies conducted in China, big social concerns over K-Pop have arisen due to teenagers falling head over heels for K-pop idol groups. Gao YueYing (2013) explained that the negative influence of K-pop in Singapore makes some teenagers either obsess over their idols online every day or splurge on K-Pop merchandise, burning holes in their parents' pockets. This year, one tragic headline from China related to K-Pop read, "13-year girl obsessed with EXO was killed by her father". A girl named Nan was a fan of EXO and was brought up by her father. Her mother is disabled, and the family gets support from the government due to their low income. The tragedy happened on November 8, 2013. The father confessed to police that he chopped up his daughter because they had a big quarrel in the morning. The incident that touched off the accident was a conversation between daughter and father. A brief version is as follows: The father angrily said, "You have been only surfing the internet every day, don't sleep at night, don't wake up in the morning, and just spend money." The daughter retorted, "Was it all about money? I will pay you off later." "You could not pay off the money from your parents, and we don't need you to pay us off." The father stopped a moment and continued, "You should not only know about worshipping stars, stars could never be better than your parents. If you keep this up, your studies will be affected. Do you get it?" However, the daughter did not listen to him and replied, "I love stars more than I love parents. They are better than you." At that moment, the father could not bear the hurt from the last sentence and chose to "make it all over." The journalist traced the story from the neighbors and the father after the accident happened. "All of the decorations in the girl's room are related to the group called 'EXO.' She collects posters, CDs, bags, clothes, everything. She is also an organizer of an EXO fan club, busy organizing activities of fans and checking what are EXO doing."

The addicted emotions of teenage fans are criticized by Chinese netizens, and the fans are quoted with a "without mind" tag for some fans' extreme behavior showing their love to idols. Many star-specific issues are also addressed in the news with headlines such as "EXO manager hit fans at airport." Wu Wei argues that such news is not fully trustworthy:

Sometimes social media has been trying to get eye-catching news without double checking. Another thing is that, as EXO is getting so popular, Chinese fans are crazy about them. It would be very dangerous if the group were surrounded by so many fans in the airport. One really big problem is the lax regulation of the Chinese local market. For example, when EXO is invited to do a concert, the Chinese organizer either distributes the tickets to certain sellers for an unreasonably high

price or swindlers cheat fans out of their money for albums and tickets. I have been to an EXO concert in Korea, and it was easy to get better and cheaper tickets on G- market, along with a better stage view and music.

In this sense, compared to K-beauty and K-cafés, K-Pop is mostly supported by fans born in the 1990s and 2000s. Chinese people, especially the ones who are not familiar with K-Pop stars, either feel difficulty in understanding them or only know about them through social media news.

CHAPTER III

METHODOLOGY

Research Design

This section presents the research methodology of this study. It is a quantitative research. It is quantitative in nature because the researcher wants to analyse the Influence of Having Kpop Idols among Students in Manuel Luis Quezon Senior High School

Population and Sampling Procedure

The subject of this study is analysis on how the kpop idols influence the students. The researcher will use Stratified Random Sampling to get the population of grade 11 and grade 12 respondents

Research Instruments

The researcher will classify the respondents by their response on how the kpop idols influence the students. The researcher uses a checklist of questionnaire in getting the relevant information for the study. It is adopted from the questionnaire used by Lauretta (2006) and Tacti (2013). The questionnaire is slightly modified to suit the purpose of the study.

Data Gathering Procedure

A letter of request signed by the researcher and noted by the adviser was submitted to the respective department heads, in to gain appropriate institutional approval to collect data and distribute questionnaires to the intended respondents.

The researcher personally distributed the questionnaires to the respondents. The respondents were specifically instructed to answer all the questions as honestly as possible or as closely as possible to their recall of their actual experience. Furthermore, the respondents were assured that their responses would be treated with strict confidentiality and would be used only for the intended purpose of the study. The researcher retrieved the accomplished questionnaires.

THE EFFECTS OF MODERNIZATION OF PUBLIC VEHICLE IN THE PHILIPPINES

A research paper presented to the faculty of

practical research in Manuel L. Quezon

Senior High School

Submitted by:

Clarise Bernadeth B. Kasilag

Submitted to:

Dr. Mark Vincent B. Emit

March 2018

Chapter I

The Problem and Its Background

Background of the Study

According to Marc Adrian (2017) The government has earmarked ₱2.2 billion for its transport modernization plan, which will be used to provide subsidy to drivers and operators who will be buying electronic jeepneys. What does this mean to the economy? Provide new job opportunities. While it cannot be denied that the modernization of public transport will gravely affect individual and small-time jeepney operators and owners, but on the other hand it will pave the way to the car manufacturing industry in the Philippines that will create more jobs.

Also, one of the long-term goals of the jeepney modernization project is to bring the vehicle manufacturing industry into the country. This is however not yet set in stone and might not push through, as it's still being negotiated by the government with vehicle manufacturers.

Hence, enhance tourism industry According to Department of Tourism, tourism in the Philippines is thriving as it saw a 19.60% increase of visitor arrivals compared to last year and a 68% increase since 2013. With the jeepney being the primary mode of transportation all over the country, it will make transportation more comfortable and easier not just for Filipinos but also for tourists. It will enhance tourist experience in the Philippines.

Aside from that it will put a new and interesting twist to the jeepney icon, which has been in the minds of the world inseparable to the Filipino psyche. This time, the jeepneys (especially in Metro Manila) will not be viewed as a smog machine that spews deadly fumes and poses as a safety hazard to people on the streets.

Moreover, it will still be uniquely the Philippines' jeepney, but with a respectable green sheen. If the newly rolled out omnibus franchising guidelines are to be considered, new jeepneys would have at least Euro 4-compliant engines but with a host of comfort and safety features.

Furthermore, Streamline public transportation Road safety and policies will be easier to roll out since the government can easily regulate PUV operators.

Moreover, Gradually solve traffic condition According to the study conducted in 2016 by Japan International Cooperation Agency (JICA), traffic in the Philippines cost ₱2.4 billion daily to the economy and by 2030 it will peak at ₱6 billion daily if left unsolved. With the government having full control of the PUV routes, it will be easier to decongest roads and plan routes that will minimize traffic conditions in highly saturated areas.

Consequently, Increase base fare The modernization of public vehicles will lead to a higher base fare, from ₱8 to ₱12. This can be an added burden to the day-to-day expenses of commuters, but could result in higher income for drivers and operators. While the other transportation options like buses and TNVS are still likely retain their current fare rates, jeepney on the other hand is most likely to increase.

The institution of Manuel L. Quezon Senior High School it is an extension of Manuel L. Quezon High School, where in the student enter Senior High School. This building of Manuel L. Quezon Senior High School was constructed within 10 years with different contracts. The Manuel L. Quezon Senior High School building consists of five (5) floors, ground floor 2nd floor within three (3) classrooms, 3rd floor, 4th floor and 5th floor with social hall and terrace. Manuel L. Quezon Senior High School has 254 total populations including all the school authorities.

Conceptual Framework

This study used I.P.O model. The I.P.O model shows the input, process and output of the research. The step to solve any problem of conducting is called process. The output is the findings of research or results.

According to Business Dictionary, which can be accessed throughhttp://www.businessdictionary.com/definition/input-process-output-diagram.html, a graphical representation of all the factors that make up a process? An input-process-output diagram includes all of the materials and information required for the process, details of the process itself, and descriptions of all products and by-products resulting from the process.

Input	Process	Output

1. What is the profile of respondents?
    1.1 age
    1.2 gender
2. what are effects of modernization of public vehicle in the Philippines?
    2.1 safety and comforts
    2.2 health and environment friendly
    2.3 better payment system
	3.is there a significant difference between the effects of modernization in the Philippines?	5. Based on the findings, what can be proposed?

The conceptual framework shows the flow of the study. In the input inscribe the profile of respondents in terms of age and gender. Also, the effects of modernization of public vehicle in the Philippines such as safety and comforts, health and environment friendly, better payment system. In the other hand, the process partakes if there is a significant difference between the effects of modernization in the

Philippines. Hence, the output shows off the expected result from the respondents and what can be proposed.

Statement of the Problem

1. What is the profile of respondents?

    1.1 age

    1.2 gender

2. what are effects of modernization of public vehicle in the Philippines?

    2.1 safety and comforts

    2.2 health and environment friendly

    2.3 better payment system

3. is there a significant difference between the effects of modernization in the Philippines?

4. Based on the findings, what can be proposed?

Hypothesis

   H_o: there is no significant difference between the effects of modernization in the Philippines.

Significance of the Study

   The researchers are truly believed that this study has significance to the following variables:

- Students- The students should have some knowledge regarding modernization of public vehicles in the Philippines.

- Government- This study will use by the government by the recommendations on improving the modernization of public vehicles in the Philippines.

- Parents- This study will help to inform and to share the information to their children about modernization of public vehicles.

- Researchers- The data that gathered from this study will use by the researchers to conduct another research that is related to this study. The information that they gathered will be applying it to them to become a better communicator in times of interacting to their selected respondents.

Scope and limitation

This study scoped the information that gathered by the researcher that may add some knowledge to the readers regarding modernization of public vehicles, the effects of modernization of public vehicle in the Philippines in terms of safety and comforts, 2 health and environment friendly, better payment system. The researchers were interview their selected respondents inside Manuel L. Quezon Senior High School.

This study has a limitation because the students and teachers only in Manuel L. Quezon Senior High School are involved. The researcher believe that this research will know and focus on modernization of public vehicles in Philippines.

Definition of Terminologies

Modernization of public vehicles. This is an initiative of the government which will put in new and safer jeepneys on the street and phase out the old and poorly maintained ones.

Safety and comforts. Modernized vehicle promise to be clean, roomy, and commuters will have access safer.

Health and environment friendly. In fact, in 2013 according to Climate Change Commissioner Heherson Alvarez, more than 500,000 diesel-fueled jeepneys, buses, trucks and other vehicles in Metro Manila are responsible for about 70% of the total soot or black carbon emissions in the Philippines.

Better payment system. Though, e-jeepneys that will soon be hitting the streets come equipped with a tap card-based fare collection system, well-maintained regular jeepneys that are not older than 15 years old will still remain on the streets.

Chapter II

Related Study and Literature

Presented in review of related literature and studies are the ideas, information, generalization or conclusion that were included. In this chapter helps in familiarizing data that are relevant and similar to the present study.

According to Cupin B. (2017) MANILA, Philippines – "It is the right time to present this, when the details aren't complete yet?" Caloocan City 2nd District Representative Edgar Erice raised this question to transportation officials at the House hearing on the public utility vehicle (PUV) modernization program on Thursday, October 19.

Also, Erice questioned why the government had already introduced the program to the public when transportation agencies had yet to come up with a timeline for its implementation, which requires the completion of route rationalization studies for Metro Manila, Cebu, and Davao City first. The PUV modernization program seeks to phase out old jeepney units in favor of newer, safer, and environment-friendly ones. "We're still doing preparations for the timeline," Land Transportation Franchising and Regulatory Board (LTFRB) Chairman Martin Delgra III told the House committee on transportation on Thursday.

This, despite President Rodrigo Duterte's pronouncements that he would "drag away" the jeepneys of owners and drivers who fail to modernize their jeepneys by the year's end. Delgra said a draft of the Metro Manila route rationalization study will be completed in November.

Responding to Erice's questions, Delgra said the early announcements were made to press the "urgency" of modernizing the Philippine jeepney, among the top modes of transportation nationwide. "What we launched was the legal framework," explained Transportation Assistant Secretary Mark de Leon.

Hence, who benefits? Kabayan Representative Harry Roque, meanwhile, warned the Department of Transportation (DOTr), LTFRB, and other agencies that the program could be put under question because the reason for modernization was "arbitrary." Roque, a lawyer, was once legal counsel for the Alliance of Concerned Transport Organizations (ACTO), one of the transport groups represented at the hearing.

Consequently, Roque helped the group oppose proposed jeepney modernization programs during the previous administration. One reason for their opposition, said Roque, was because the program, as drafted by the government, would have advantaged one particular company. The lawmaker demanded that the LTFRB and DOTr produce a list of companies that could be tapped for the modernization of PUVs. Asked if local companies would also be able to compete, transportation officials said they could "if they have the capacity."

Furthermore, Roque criticized the vague answer and insisted that executives of the companies who joined a recent PUV expo organized by the DOTr and the Department of Trade and Industry (DTI) attend the next hearing. (LOOK: New jeepneys under the PUV modernization program) De Leon clarified that the PUV modernization program does not impose a specific make for the new jeepneys, but merely introduces "standards" for the vehicles. They must be Euro 4 compliant, meaning the new generation of jeepneys would have to be friendlier to the environment. The problem? De Leon admitted that the government does not have the means to check whether engines are truly Euro 4 compliant.

Instead, the DOTr plans to require certificates of compliance. De Leon said the DOTR was not discounting the eventual possibility of buying equipment that can check for Euro 4 compliance. Transport and leftist groups have rejected the current PUV modernization plan for supposedly putting drivers and owners at a disadvantage while benefitting bigger corporations. Zenaida Maranan, president of the Federation of Jeepney Operators of the Filipinos (Fejodap), said that while operators like herself – who can manage an entire fleet of jeepneys – can handle the financing plans under the Landbank and Development Bank of the Philippines (DBP), single operators who aren't as skilled won't be able to keep up.

LTFRB board member Aileen Lizada said that it would be Landbank and not the Development Bank of the Philippines, that would be able to handle individual applications. Maranan said that Landbank had told her otherwise. The DOT: and LTFRB was also unable to give the House information on how many jeepney drivers stand to be displaced or jobless pending the route rationalization study.

Moreover, About the provinces The route rationalization study, conducted by different agencies and groups, will determine the best mode of transportation for a specific route, based on the current and projected demand. In Metro Manila, the study is being led by the University of the Philippines.

In Cebu, it's being done by the Japan International Cooperation Agency (JICA) and in Davao City, by the Asian Development Bank (ADB). De Leon said they will be coordinating with local government units (LGUs) to help them determine routes in other areas. "We realize that the public transportation sector has political concerns with regards to LGUs dictating the route. The LTFRB will still be the one issuing franchises," he said. Still, several lawmakers expressed opposition to the idea, again citing the danger of LGUs politicizing the process.

Hence, Surigao del Sur 2nd District Representative Johnny Pimentel urged transportation officials to visit far-flung areas, such as some barangays in his district, to see the road conditions for themselves. Pimentel argued that the jeepney designs that the government has put forward would be unable to handle the rough roads of some rural villages. De Leon said the PUV designs could be expanded to include 6-wheel vehicles built for rougher terrain. The LTFRB has yet to determine how many routes currently exist in Metro Manila, although Delgra estimated it "several thousands."

According to Arago D. (2017) *The* two-day national transport strike on Oct. 16-17 in protest against the so-called public utility vehicle (PUV) modernization program, which in effect will phase-out jeepneys, is a legitimate exercise of people's rights and worth public support.The public has the right to protest and oppose government policies that are detrimental not only to people's livelihood, particularly the estimated 300,000 directly affected drivers/operators nationwide, but will also enable corporations to cash in on the poor.

In June this year, the Department of Transportation (DOTr) launched the PUV modernization program, which requires operators to own at least 20 Euro-4 compliant jeepneys and to have market capitalization of at least P7 million. The DOTr said the government will contract giant multinational corporations like Toyota and Mitsubushi to locally manufacture the vehicles numbering to about 200,000 by 2020. Each vehicle will cost about P1.2-P1.6 million, to be loaned to the driver payable in seven years at 6 percent interest. The government, through a public bank, will cover the 5 percent but not more than P80,000 financing, and the driver will have to pay the rest

Also, this means that the driver will have to shell out at least P800/day from daily earnings in order to comply with such costly amortization. If earnings are not enough to cover the amortization, drivers will have to find additional resources. Public commuters are often promised better services but are getting the exact opposite at higher rates, fees or fare. An example is MRT-3 whose "efficiency" has been used to justify the fare increase and use of beep cards to ease the horrors of riding it. The public need not look far. As e-jeep operations are privatized, corporations can increase minimum fare at their behest and without public hearing, and as in the case of MRT, the government can only comment or appeal, but cannot decide.

Moreover, The PUV modernization plan is completely ignoring the reality that today, many jeepney drivers are earning only P200-P400 a day for 12-16 hours on the road. The option given them is to be in a condition of near perpetual debt while working in order to pay for a vehicle that probably after seven years will already be in a bad state. We appeal for understanding and support from those whose travel was affected by the strike and enjoin them to be in solidarity by calling for an end to corporatization and monopoly of public services. Let us protect the livelihood and jobs of those dependent on jeepney transport, and call on the Duterte administration to come up with a plan for a government-run and operated mass transport system to ease the traffic and unburden commuters.

According to Dino Mari Testa **Who will benefit from the PUV modernization program?** To be honest, every stakeholder in this government initiative will real benefits from the PUV modernization program. To break it down:

- Commuters will have access to safer, more modern public utility vehicles, as opposed to the jeeps and buses of today that are old, dirty, and cramped. Aside from upgraded vehicles, they also come with technological features such as GPS, CCTV cameras, automatic fare collection systems, and free wireless connection.

- While PUV drivers and operators may be opposing the changes violently, their sector will also see some great benefits under the PUV modernization. For starters, the "boundary system" operators usually employ—which is where drivers and their staff have to reach a certain amount every day—will be scrapped in favor of a fixed salary system.

- As regular employees, they are also entitled to benefits like SSS, Pag-IBIG, and PhilHealth. To standardize the safety of the passengers, all drivers have to undergo training programs for safer and more efficient driving.

- The environment will also score a big win with this, especially that our urban areas are places blanketed by smog. In a report by the CNN *Philippines*, the World Health Organization announced that air pollution levels in Metro Manila are beyond tolerable—and one of the two main culprits is outdated cars. The new PUVs will come with Euro 4-compliant engines. Solar and electric-powered vehicles with low to zero emission are also being considered.

Also, what will be the role of different government agencies in this scheme? Each department will have a role to play in the three-year transition period. The following duties by the different government bodies to ensure the success of the program:

- The DOTr is the overall agency in charge of the transition, making sure that everything goes according to plan. Last Monday, Transport Secretary Arthur Tugade finally signed the Omnibus Franchising Guidelines (OFG) along with other government agencies concerned, barring all delays.
- Local government units (LGU) will be helming the planning of public transportation based on existing road networks and passenger demands. Once completed, the new plans will be included in the OFG, which will serve as the overall handbook for the overhauled public transportation scheme. The LGUs are, of course, backed by the Department of Interior and Local Government (DILG).
- Once LGUs have finally submitted their route proposals, the Land Transportation Franchising and Regulatory Board (LTFRB) will start issuing new franchises based on the new routing plans. In addition, *InterAksyon* reports that the LTFRB will also be in charge of the

proposed driving academy for PUV drivers, ensuring the safety of the commuters as well as picking up proper etiquette along the way.

- In NCR, the Metropolitan Manila Development Authority (MMDA) will act as the enforcer of the modernization scheme. While the MMDA constables are already doing this, they will start to police based on the guidelines of the PUV modernization program.

- To aid PUV owners in having a smoother transition in terms of financing new vehicles, the government tapped the Department of Finance (DOF) and Department of Budget and Management (DBM) to aid them. According to *Rappler*, the said agencies will help drivers and operators have access to credit with low interests and more flexible payment.

Hence, what will be units permitted under the PUV modernization program? The InterAksyon report furthered that while there will be standards in what will be given new licenses and what features should be available on new public vehicles, "the DOTr has yet to release specific requirements for buses, vans, and jeepneys."

However, the scheme is clear that units will only be given franchise if they either have Euro 4-compliant engines or more environmentally friendly options like electric motors or solar-powered engines.

Furthermore, Will the old public vehicles like jeeps and buses be scrapped? Top Gear Philippines reported that there will be no decommissioning that will happen under the PUV modernization program. those who decide to keep their old vehicles will have to upgrade their cars to meet the standards under the program. "Among the changes the modernization program will address is to ensure that the vehicles comply with international and local emission standards. They'll also be improving the driver's view of the road and will rid vehicles of any unsafe protrusions," *Top Gear* reported.

However, **how can PUV drivers buy new vehicles?** LTFRB chairman Martin Delgra III dispelled the rumor that operators will be needing a capital of P7 billion to get a franchise. While he said that nothing is fixed about the capital, there will be guidelines for operators and drivers to create a cooperative of drivers based on the same route.

In addition, a *Manila Bulletin* article cited Delgra saying the government will open a financing program for operators to have access to loans with good terms and low-interest rates. This is in line with what the DOF and DMB pledged to make PUV modernization happen. Rambo talabong MANILA, Philippines — On Monday, June 19, the Department of Transportation (DOTr) officially launched its Public Utility Vehicle (PUV) modernization program which orders the replacement of jeepneys aged 15 years or older.

According to Land Transportation Franchising and Regulatory Board (LTFRB) Chairman Martin Delgra, they have tallied 180,000 jeepneys that need to be replaced. This sparked complaint from transport and labor groups, saying that the program is "anti-poor" given that replacing their jeepneys would cost them at least P1 million each. (READ: Transport strike: Why pick on jeepneys to fix traffic problems?)

On top of this, the LTFRB is not keen on allowing replacement only of engines and chassis, the parts of the jeepney that the LTFRB uses as the basis of the age of a vehicle. "Some groups are saying that maybe they can repair and rehabilitate [jeepneys]. They asked if they can build their own jeepneys. Unfortunately that mode that they are suggesting is not holistic rehabilitation," Delgra told reporters during the launch. With this, critics claimed that the program is financially impossible for jeepney drivers who collect 7-peso payments, one passenger at a time.

Also, Department of Finance Undersecretary Karl Kendrick Chua begs to differ. In a phone interview with Rappler, Chua said that their department already has proposals drafted to make sure that the jeepney drivers will be able to pay for the replacement for their old vehicles.

According to Chua, they are currently considering a *hulugan* loaning system where drivers will pay every day for the loan money that they will use to purchase better jeepneys. With this, drivers would not need to pay the jeepneys in full before using them. The challenge, according to Chua, is making sure that the drivers don't get buried in debt. This is where their department comes in.

Consequently, the drivers, Chua said, may pay through offices that the government will set up, and they are considering an "automated payment system" for the jeepneys like the cards containing credits used for Metro Manila trains. "Under the automated fare collection system, [the drivers] know, and Landbank will know how much the drivers are making. So it's easy to collect seeing how much the income of the drivers," Chua said.

Furthermore, through the automated fare collection system, the bank may also use data from the income of drivers to dictate how much the bank will charge. However, the loan will not be easily accessible for all. According to Chua, they will prioritize jeepney drivers who operate under government-recognized cooperatives, formed by virtue of the revised Omnibus Franchising Guidelines under the program. This is because drivers who are part of cooperatives can easily be reached if ever they are having trouble with payment. It also assures the government they are paid back, Chua said.

Moreover, Modernizing is saving Chua assured jeepney drivers that the payment will be worth every peso. He said that by modernizing, drivers will cut down fuel costs as the new vehicles can reach almost double the distance with the same amount of fuel put in old ones. Aside from efficiency, Chua said that the new vehicles are less polluting, reducing damage to the environment. Chua also raised the concern of old jeepneys needing to be off duty at least 10 days every month for maintenance work. With new jeepneys, at most, maintenance will take only 6 days per month.

In the other hand, Chua then urged opposers of the program to see that many Filipinos have long called for modernization, and commuters are part of "the poor" too. "These are ordinary commuters, students, mothers, fathers, and families. If we do not do anything, it would be more anti-poor," Chua said. Still on hold Nevertheless, the financing is only as good as the entire inter-agency effort to modernize public transport. And currently, the ball is in the hands of the DOTr as the plan to implement the phase-out of old jeepneys still has many creases to be flattened out before the financial plan can be rolled out.

Furthermore, they have yet to release the final specifications of new jeepneys that manufacturers will use to build and sell. LTFRB's Delgra also seems uncertain how they will regulate old jeepneys. He said during the launch of the program that they follow have a "3-year transition period" where they will not strictly implement the ban on old jeepneys. The period will also serve as the time for franchisers to form the cooperatives and corporations. He later clarified that the transition period is open for extension, given that there are tens of thousands of jeepneys to be replaced. When asked what they plan to do to dispose of old jeepneys, Delgra said that they are still thinking of ways so that the parts will not simply be scrapped.

According to The Manila Times (2017) The message behind a lower court decision last month—scrapping a transport group petition to stop the Department of Transportation from implementing the Omnibus Franchising Guidelines on modernizing public utility vehicles—needs no brilliant legal mind to understand. The Public Utility Vehicle Modernization Program (PUVMP) is a long-overdue revamp of the public transport system in this country. This program badly needs a push for the sake of public commuters who suffer the daily indignities of standing in long queues of waiting passengers under the heat of the sun or in the middle of a downpour, inhaling the stench of passing smoke belching buses, taxis, jeepneys, trucks and private cars, desperate for a ride to the office or school, only to get caught in hours of traffic on the road once able to catch a ride, and then go through the same ordeal on their way back home later in the day.

The good old jeepney, a legacy of Filipino ingenuity in the aftermath of World War Two, has served us well all these years, but has failed to catch up with the changing needs of the public and made itself unappealing as a means of mass public transport in this age of the Internet of Things. Most people who have the means would rather use a ride-hailing app on their mobile phones to grab a little comfort on their way to their destination.

Also, The Transportation department argued that the certificate of public convenience—practically the license to operate—issued to PUV operators is not a right but a privilege, subject to the state's police power through the DOTr and the Land Transportation Franchising and Regulatory Board. The Quezon City court decision has paved the way for lifting the moratorium on accepting new applications for certificates of public convenience, which had been in place since 2003. "This forms part of the PUVMP that seeks to provide a safer, more comfortable and environmentally sustainable mode of public transport to commuters by upgrading vehicles to meet international safety, energy efficiency and emission standards," according to the DOTr.

Hence, the modern PUV will have an automatic fare collection system, closed-circuit television cameras, GPS navigation system, dashboard cameras, Wi-Fi and speed limit devices—the trappings of technological modernity.What a sigh of relief such accoutrement could bring the Filipino commuters once the program is in full swing starting 2018.

Consequently, the guidelines also intend to bring order to the chaotic traffic situation we all find ourselves in, by giving local government units (LGUs) the authority to plan public transport routes based on current travel patterns in their respective areas. This means LGUs may also be held accountable for their own mess if the traffic schemes along their respective routes prove to be messier than things stand now, because these routes—the Local Public Transport Route Plan—will serve as a basis for the issuance of franchises by the LTFRB. Not all, however, is set in stone as the routing scheme may still be tweaked for best results.

Moreover, to jumpstart the program, the Development Bank of the Philippines is providing a P1.5-billion financing facility, to be signed today by Transportation Secretary Arthur Tugade and DBP Chairman Alberto Romulo at the new DOTr headquarters in Clark City, Pampanga. The DBP has developed the Program Assistance to Support Alternative Driving Approaches (PASADA) as a credit vehicle for transport corporations and cooperatives to acquire new PUVs. Supposedly, the seven-year loans are payable daily and carry a 6 percent annual interest rate. What about the individual borrower? It looks like the government strategy is to push the public transportation sector into a corner where the more feasible option to riding on the benefits of the PUVMP is consolidation, despite the protestations of unfair policy treatment by transport groups earlier this year.

By joining a transport cooperative, the lone PUV owner—whose vehicle might be a "colorum," lacking the backing of regulatory requirements—becomes a part of the system but abiding by its rules, which should make it easier for the government to monitor and keep in check any violation.

Furthermore, but no tide waits for any man and the PUVMP is good to go, signifying change and progress in the public transport system that has long been ignored and allowed to deteriorate by past administrations. Time is ripe for the public Filipino commuters to get their fares' worth every time they take a PUV.

According to Vic Claros Obaob (2017) Jeepney is one of the country's low-cost modes of transportation. It is tagged by the name "King of the Road." The Department of Transportation (DOTr) and the Land Transportation Franchising and Regulatory Board (LTFRB) are pursuing the Public Utility Jeepney (PUJ) Modernization Program, as a measure to lower the country's greenhouse gas emissions. In the said program is the phasing out and the setting of the mandatory 15-year age limit to public utility jeepney (PUJ) units. Public Utility Vehicle Modernization Program (PUVMP) is long overdue.

Also, "A transport system with modern and roadworthy PUVs plying the national roads prevents pollution and ensures a reliable and safe commute for the ridging public," explains former LTFRB Chairman Winston Ginez.

Here are the advantages of jeepney modernization program.

1. Safe and comfortable transport. Modernized vehicle promise to be clean, roomy, and commuters will have access safer. Modern vehicles will also be provided with

GPS navigation system and closed-circuit television (CCTV) cameras to monitor passengers and the drivers, an Automatic Fare Collection System (AFCS), speed limiters, dashboard cameras, and Wi-Fi. It will also have easier access for PWDs and senior citizen.

2. New features. The doors will be on the side of the vehicle. It's also equipped with power steering, and hand brake, and some units are air-conditioned. It also has a bigger passenger accommodation due to longer frame.

3. Drivers and Operators has benefits. Jeepney drivers will get monthly salaries and will also be given opportunities to take part in government-sponsored driving training programs, as well as the operators which involves safety measures in operating PUJs and proper etiquette when dealing with the passengers.

4. Decrease of greenhouse gas emission. Transportation department cited that jeepneys as the biggest source of carbon dioxide emission. The new vehicle is required to either powered by Euro 4 engines or electric powered engine with solar panels for roofs. On the said program, vehicles that are 15-year old will be replaced by vehicles with "low-carbon and low emission technology. Both passengers and drivers it allows less exposure to air pollution.

In the other hand, We can expect to see the modern transport system in this modern development, However, despite the advantages of the modernized vehicle has to offer, financing is also other concern. Almost all of the drivers and small business operators cannot afford to franchise this new vehicle that the government is soon going to implement the PUV modernization program.

According to Marc Adrian (2017) Whether commuters or the public transport operators like it or not, change is upon the transportation scene in the Philippines. The awful traffic in Manila coupled with its prehistoric Public Utility Vehicles (PUV) have been the cause of suffering for all commuters. Not only are these vehicles causing a lot of inconvenience to the public, but are also a threat to their health and the environment.

Also, This initiative aims to improve the quality of life of the riding public and has been in the government's to-do list for a long time now. However, it's been consistently pushed under the rug because it's bad news for the jeepney drivers and their operators despite the financial assistance that the government will extend to jeepney operators and drivers making it less of a burden.

To understand the context and coverage of this program, let's break down the real deal behind what jeepney modernization really means.

Hence, what is the jeepney modernization program? This is an initiative of the government which will put in new and safer jeepneys on the street and phase out the old and poorly maintained ones. This was initially introduced by the Land Transportation Franchising and Regulatory Board (LTFRB) in 2015. It seeks to minimize outdated (and almost lethal) jeepneys in the streets, boost passenger safety, and prevent pollution by imposing an age limit for transport vehicles that are allowed to operate.

According to this resolution by the LTFRB, public vehicle operators will not be approved for a franchise, extend their Certificate of Public Convenience (CPC), increase of number of vehicles, or substitute their vehicles if their unit is more than the minimum age requirement. The unit should not be more than fifteen (15) years old reckoned from the date of manufacture of subject vehicle. Basically, this program isn't only going to regulate jeepneys that are older than 15 years, but also the buses and other public vehicles in the streets.

There are three areas where the program will address:

1. New franchising system. Compared to the current franchising system where jeepney operators propose the routes of jeepneys, the new franchising system will be fully regulated by the government.

- The routes will be planned by the government.
- Single unit operators will no longer be eligible for a franchise.

- Initially, the minimum number of jeepneys for franchise is 20. By 2019, the minimum number will be raised to 40.

- Standardize income of jeepney driver, provide them with regular employment benefits, and abolish boundary system.

2. Improving PUVs to international standards. The government has also imposed a set of guidelines for all vehicles to meet before getting approved to operate. In order to uphold safety, comfort, and environmental soundness, all vehicles and services will comply with the national standards and international vehicle safety conventions. Depending on the type of PUV, there are various specifications that they must meet as imposed by Department of Transportation's Omnibus Guidelines.

Here is a quick rundown of the most common and impacting upgrades imposed on the future of PUVs in the Philippines:

1. Vehicles with combustion engines must have low emissions in compliance with the EURO IV emission standards or better.

2. Speed limiters

3. Closed-circuit television (CCTV) camera for selected types of PUVs

4. Dashboard camera

5. GPS

6. Person with disability (PWD) friendly

7. Comfortable seats

8. Provision of Wi-Fi access

9. For buses, standing passengers must not exceed five persons

3. Training for drivers. The modernization of the public transport will not be successful without the cooperation from the drivers manning the roads This is why the modernization program will also include training for these PUV drivers.

   The training will serve as a refresher (and a crash course) on the technicalities of driving, safe measures, and proper etiquette in dealing with passengers.

   Moreover, what are the economic implications? The government has earmarked ₱2.2 billion for its transport modernization plan, which will be used to provide subsidy to drivers and operators who will be buying electronic jeepneys. What does this mean to the economy?

1. Provide new job opportunities. While it cannot be denied that the modernization of public transport will gravely affect individual and small-time jeepney operators and owners, but on the other hand it will pave the way to the car manufacturing industry in the Philippines that will create more jobs. One of the long-term goals of the jeepney modernization project is to bring the vehicle manufacturing industry into the country. This is however not yet set in stone and might not push through, as it's still being negotiated by the government with vehicle manufacturers.

2. Enhance tourism industry. According to Department of Tourism, tourism in the Philippines is thriving as it saw a 19.60% increase of visitor arrivals compared to last year and a 68% increase since 2013. With the jeepney being the primary mode of transportation all over the country, it will make transportation more comfortable and easier not just for Filipinos but also for tourists. It will enhance tourist experience in the Philippines.

Aside from that it will put a new and interesting twist to the jeepney icon, which has been in the minds of the world inseparable to the Filipino psyche. This time, the jeepneys (especially in Metro Manila) will not be viewed as a smog machine that spews deadly fumes and poses as a safety hazard to people on the streets.

It will still be uniquely the Philippines' jeepney, but with a respectable green sheen. If the newly rolled out omnibus franchising guidelines are to be considered, new jeepneys would have at least Euro 4-compliant engines but with a host of comfort and safety features.

3. Streamline public transportation. Road safety and policies will be easier to roll out since the government can easily regulate PUV operators.

4. Gradually solve traffic condition. According to the study conducted in 2016 by Japan International Cooperation Agency (JICA), traffic in the Philippines cost ₱2.4 billion daily to the economy and by 2030 it will peak at ₱6 billion daily if left unsolved.

With the government having full control of the PUV routes, it will be easier to decongest roads and plan routes that will minimize traffic conditions in highly saturated areas.

5. Increase base fare. The modernization of public vehicles will lead to a higher base fare, from ₱8 to ₱12. This can be an added burden to the day-to-day expenses of commuters, but could result in higher income for drivers and operators. While the other transportation options like buses and TNVS are still likely retain their current fare rates, jeepney on the other hand is most likely to increase.

Furthermore, What's in store for commuters? It's a promising initiative aimed at improving the mode of transportation for commuters. Aside from the sleek new jeepneys that can take you from point A to B safely, there are a handful of benefits that the riding public will enjoy when the Jeepney Modernization Program hit the ground.

1. Safety and comfort. A safer and more comfortable transportation system is the highlight of this modernization program. The new vehicles that are showcased by the government promise to be more spacious and offer a bunch of features that uphold safety and security. The doors of some of these new jeeps will be on the side of the vehicle instead of the back, and they will have a longer frame. Some units are air-conditioned to provide a more comfortable option and these modern jeepneys are also PWD friendly.

Aside from the essentials, these e-jeeps also come with GPS navigation system, a CCTV camera, dashboard camera, and even a Wi-Fi connection. These may just be the icing on the cake, but they can make a world of difference in improving the quality of commuting for passengers.

2. Health and environment friendly. Everyone can agree that jeepneys in Metro Manila are the biggest contributors of carbon dioxide emission. In fact, in 2013 according to Climate Change Commissioner Heherson Alvarez, more than 500,000 diesel-fueled jeepneys, buses, trucks and other vehicles in Metro Manila are responsible for about 70% of the total soot or black carbon emissions in the Philippines.

   Also, This can be detrimental not just to the environment but also to the health of the public. Under the program, the proposed vehicles are powered by either Euro 4 engine or electric engine with solar panels on the roof.

3. Better payment system. Is it time to say goodbye to "paki abot po" payment system that we've all grown accustomed to with jeepneys? Not necessarily, not yet. Though, e-jeepneys that will soon be hitting the streets come equipped with a tap card-based fare collection system, well-maintained regular jeepneys that are not older than 15 years old will still remain on the streets. No more passing change from one passenger to the other, all you'll need is a loaded Beep card and you're good to go.

In the other hand, will jeepney operators and drivers lose? *The major reason why* Pinagkaisang Samahan ng mga Tsuper at Operation Nationwide (PISTON) and Stop and Go Coalition are against this modernization plan is because they see this initiative as 'anti-poor' because it would lead to the loss of livelihood program of small-time jeepney owners and operators. Though, this is true to a certain extent, jeepney drivers will not necessarily feel the brunt of this change. At least, not in a bad way. Why?

For jeepney drivers who are merely renting out their jeeps, they will be getting a standard income preset by the government. They don't have to worry about the monthly amortization of the new jeepneys. At the end of the day, the jeepney operators are mandated to provide them a regular income, not affected by how much the driver is earning per day.

The burden on the other hand will be shouldered by the operator who runs a franchise of PUV. The monthly amortization will be a huge financial challenge since each unit despite having a low APR and flexible payment term carries a huge price tag. Almost all the drivers and small business operators cannot afford to franchise the new vehicles.

Hence, The high cost of e-jeepney This is the part that has caused the outrage in light with the modernization of public transport. These modern jeepneys will cost about ₱1.2 million to ₱1.6 million, which are payable for up to seven years.

The estimate for the subsidy of these vehicles is about ₱800 per day or ₱24,000 per month. While this is basically the current boundary rates of jeepney drivers in Metro Manila, operators on the other hand will not be able to profit for a long time if this gets implemented.

Moreover, Government subsidy To help PUV operators upgrade to newer jeepneys, the Department of Transportation (DOTr) in September signed a memorandum of understanding (MOU) with the Development Bank of the Philippines (DBP) for a ₱1.5-billion loan facility for PUV cooperatives. The DBP will provide loans to cooperatives to finance the acquisition of new jeepneys. The DOTr also signed an MOU with the Land Bank of the Philippines last April for a ₱1-billion financing scheme for individual jeepney operators.

The government will be subsidizing ₱80,000 per vehicle purchased by operators or drivers. However, that amount is only about 5% of the total price of these new PUVs and could hardly bring down the monthly repayment, which is the root cause of the outrage from certain transport groups.

Hence, Philippines transport scene vs the world It's worth noting that the Philippines has long been left out when it comes to modernization of mass transport, compared to its neighboring countries. As neighboring countries like Malaysia and Singapore enjoy the convenience of a seamless and a more centralized mode of transport, the Philippines on the other hand is still struggling to even implement an accurate amount of fare system (drivers will have to manually and mentally calculate the fare from point A to B). It cannot be denied that it's high time for us to actually do something about it, not just for the benefit of the commuters, but also for the environment and the economy.

For neighboring countries, public transport is run by private but Government Linked Companies, making it easier to streamline upgrades and improvements. Meanwhile, our land transport system is ran by private groups and even individuals, and unsurprisingly, it's outdated as these groups can't be bothered to upkeep their vehicles because of the cost.

Furthermore, While the modernization of public transport is indeed a welcomed initiative for the majority of the commuters, it is far from perfect. There are definitely rooms for improvement in the areas of job opportunities for those who may get displaced, and also inclusivity to the transport groups so it will not be as financially burdening for them. For the jeepney modernization program to be successful, both parties (the government and the transport groups) must come up with a win-win solution as they hold another round of dialogue in the coming weeks.

Chapter III

Research Methodology

Research Design

This study conducted according to the design of experimental design of Quantitative research. In the Experimental design, it tries to emphasize objective measurements and the statistical analysis of data collected through questionnaires regarding modernization of public vehicles in the Philippines.

Sampling procedure

Slovin's Formula is used to calculate the sample size (n) given the population size (N) and a margin of error (e).It's a random sampling technique formula to estimate sampling size this method will be used to get the number of respondents in this study to gather a data regarding an analysis of English communication skills at home in relation to the academic performance of the students for recommendation.

-It is computed as $n = N / (1+Ne^2)$.

Whereas:

n = no. of samples

N = total population

e = Margin of error

Instrument of the study

The researchers used survey questionnaire for their instrument to gather a data that was used for this study. The questionnaire is only one part. It determines the questions regarding modernization of public vehicles in the Philippines.

According to Dave Vannette 2015 a survey is a method of gathering information from a sample of people, traditionally with the intention of generalizing the results to a larger population. Surveys provide a critical source of data and insights for nearly everyone engaged in the information economy, from businesses and the media to government and academics.

Data Gathering

Data gathering procedure is a process of collecting information from the respondents surveying actually involves gathering responses from the topic of the study through a written medium. The researchers will distribute the survey questionnaires to their selected respondents for the needed answer regarding modernization of public vehicles in the Philippines. The researchers used Stratified random sampling is a method of sampling that involves the division of a population into smaller groups known as strata. In stratified random sampling, the strata are formed based on members' shared attributes or characteristics. A random sample from each stratum is taken in a number proportional to the stratum's size when compared to the population. These subsets of the strata are then pooled to form a random sample.

Data Analysis Techniques/ Statistical Treatment

According to Ronald Fisher 2012 Analysis of variance or also known as ANOVA is a collection of statistical model used to analyze the differences among group means and their associated procedures.

The researchers will be use analysis of variance test to determine the result independent variables have on the dependent variable into the middle regression study. The researchers utilize ANOVA test results in an F-Test to generate additional data that aligns with the proposed regression model.

Formula:

$$\bar{x} = \frac{\Sigma \, xi)}{n}$$

Notations:

$\bar{x}$ just stands for the "sample mean"

Σ means "add up"

xi "all of the x-values"

n means "the number of items in the sample"